LENIN: A POLITICAL LIFE

By the same author

THE BOLSHEVIK PARTY IN REVOLUTION
A Study in Organisational Change

LENIN: A POLITICAL LIFE

Volume 1
The Strengths of Contradiction

ROBERT SERVICE

M
MACMILLAN

First published 1985

Published by
THE MACMILLAN PRESS LTD
Houndmills, Basingstoke, Hampshire RG21 2XS
and London
Companies and representatives
throughout the world

Typeset by
Wessex Typesetters Ltd
Frome, Somerset

Printed in Hong Kong

British Library Cataloguing in Publication Data
Service, Robert, *1947–*
Lenin: a political life.
Vol. 1: The strengths of contradiction
1. Lenin, V. I.   II. Heads of state—Soviet
Union—Biography   III. Revolutionists—
Soviet Union—Biography
I. Title
947.084'1'0924   DK254.L4
ISBN 0-333-29390-8

To Adele and in Memory of Charles

Contents

Notes and Acknowledgements

The importance of studying the USSR is obvious; and an understanding of today's Soviet Union is hopelessly defective without acquaintance with the country's history. The October Revolution is still only decades old. Lenin was its major figure. These three volumes describe and analyse his political life.

The technical motives behind the project can be briefly summarised. Valuable investigations into portions of Lenin's career have been published; but no comprehensive examination has recently been attempted. This trilogy is aimed at filling the gap. Among its main purposes will be to demonstrate how only a synoptic depiction of Lenin can disclose the complex interplay of ideas, activity and environment in his life. In addition, it is now many years since the completion of the enormous fifth edition of his collected works in 1965. Previous rounded accounts were based largely or wholly on less extensive materials. A further stimulus has been the recent increase in monographs on Russian social, economic and institutional history. They enable us to see Lenin more precisely in context than ever before. Studies on Russian intellectual history have lately not appeared in quite the same quantity; and, in order to avoid looking at Lenin's contemporaries solely from his adopted viewpoint, these volumes include an assessment of their works as well as his. Of course, not only historians but also economists, sociologists and political theorists are interested in Lenin. I have therefore tried to answer the questions which they too ask about his life; and it is hoped to show that the riddles can be dealt with only with due cognizance of the contemporary conditions and pressures of Lenin's career.

The three volumes deal with the three great phases in Lenin's career. The first phase saw his rise to the party's heights by 1903 and his ensuing decline in influence until 1910. The second saw his re-ascent, despite recurrent back-slips, and his leadership of the Bolsheviks in the October Revolution of 1917; the third saw his struggle to keep his party at the summit of power until his death in 1924. Each volume is similarly organised. Chapters are divided into five sections apiece so as to highlight the connections between ideas, action and environment. A strictly chronological approach is taken. Discussions of Lenin's thoughts or operations in a specific area are not confined to any one part of any volume.

I have incurred many debts of gratitude in writing the first volume. The typescript was read and constructively criticised by Bob Davies, Carter Elwood, Israel Getzler, John Keep, Genia Lampert, Mary MacAuley, David McLellan and Vittorio Strada. The clearest sign of my thanks, I hope, will consist in the contrast between the typescript and the pages which follow. John Biggart, Julian Cooper, Neil Harding, Geoffrey Swain and Stephen Wheatcroft kindly clarified significant details for me. At Keele, Genia Lampert has provided much guidance; I greatly miss our daily conversations now that he has retired. Useful advice on particular matters was given by Jonathan Dancy, Peter Lawrence, Shireen Lawrence and Arfon Rees; and Arfon read and improved the final draft. Outside Keele, I have benefited from discussions about Lenin with Francesco Benvenuti, Anna di Biagio, the late Charles Duval, Oscar Gabutto and Maria-Teresa Torrassa. Bernard Finnemore at the Keele library and Jenny Brine at the CREES library in Birmingham obtained books that would have been unavailable to me; and David Sherwood at the Keele Computer Centre most expertly and generously facilitated the type-script's transfer to magnetic tape. My thanks are owed also to Douglas Gregor, who has fired the enthusiasm of so many like myself for the study of foreign countries. My family's support has been constant. Emma, Owain, Hugo and Francesca have offered a sense of propor-tion to a rather humourless subject by stressing repeatedly that even Lenin often fell off his bike. Lastly, my wife Adele has discussed and greatly improved the contents of this volume over several years. Such a remark is conventional in a list of acknowledgements: but in this instance anything said would inevitably understate reality.

It would be impossible to finish such a study without becoming aware of the limitations upon achievement. The sources, though voluminous, are also patchy; and Lenin himself operated at so many levels of politics that the task of description and analysis is most daunting. What is offered, despite its size, is only a sketch. It involves tentative projections and severe compressions. It is written, further-more, for the non-specialist as well as for the professional academic. I have used a simplified method of transliteration (except for names of authors and their works in the endnotes, where the SEER model is employed). A few exceptions recur; Witte and Zinoviev, for example, keep their conventional forms. The translations are mine. The prologue gives signposts to all three volumes. A personal standpoint is presented. Lenin was an inveterate controversialist, and several commentaries on him have caught the contagion of his highly combative style. More heat than light is frequently the result. An indication of contrary interpretations is given in the endnotes. Obviously the trilogy is intended to convince. But its parallel objective is to furnish others with the necessary data to respond to the fundamental question: what is the significance of Lenin's political life both for his times and for ours?

Keele   R.J.S.
October 1983

Prologue: The Enigma Of Lenin

Vladimir-Ilich Lenin died on 21 January 1924. The state funeral followed on a cold winter's day in Moscow, and his corpse was embalmed and laid out in a mausoleum built outside the Kremlin's walls. His rise to international fame had been meteoric. Less than seven years had elapsed since his Bolshevik party had seized power through the October Revolution. He had not been a nonentity before 1917; but his celebrity had grown inside the confines of Russia's clandestine political groups. His emergence as premier of the Soviet government changed his fortunes almost overnight. He moved to the centre of the stage. He stood forth in the general estimation as the embodiment of the Revolution. His reputation rested upon his leading role in the Bolshevik attempt to found a socialist society and extend its example to the four corners of the earth. The endeavour was fraught with problems of gigantic magnitude. The Bolsheviks were overoptimistic in their general ideas. And, in their practical assessments, they also overestimated the likelihood of imminent revolution in Europe and North America. They underrated Russian economic backwardness. They resorted too easily and too massively to violence in implementing their political programme. Nonetheless the October Revolution is the crucial event in our modern times. It transformed Russia and led to a re-shaping of politics across the European continent; its repercussions are still being registered around the globe today. Lenin helped to inaugurate a new political order. Decades after his death, it remains a matter of consequence to elucidate the meaning of his momentous life.

The spotlight was turned upon him after the October seizure of power; and a mass of information, old and new, became available. The first biography of Lenin came out in 1918.[1] His image was festooned on flags, posters and the sides of trains. A film was taken of him. Poems were addressed to him, songs sung about him. His career before 1917 was depicted in hundreds of memoirs. Streets and factories were

1

re-named after him. The Bolshevik party printed archives revealing much about his earlier activity. He himself remained a prolific writer. He continued to compose articles and pamphlets. His position in party and government involved him in the drafting of decrees, instructions and official correspondence. His speeches were regularly reported. The first edition of his collected works was begun in 1920.[2]

The output of material, already gargantuan, was augmented after 1924 as scholars in the USSR added to the chronicle of his career. Documentation appeared in profusion. A cult arose around Lenin, introduced and sustained by the Bolshevik leadership. His works were deployed to legitimate current policy; every change of direction was claimed to have preserved the link with the master's teachings. Factions in the party flung quotations at each other from his books. Political competition among the surviving leaders grew fierce. Trotski, Zinoviev, Bukharin and Stalin made their bids to try on Lenin's mantle. Among the by-products of their struggles was an increase in the amount of data relating to Lenin. The accumulation was interrupted in the late 1930s. Iosif Stalin, who by then had crushed his rivals in the leadership, saw the cult of his dead predecessor as a restriction upon opportunities to consolidate a cult of his own. Orders were issued in 1938 which effectively terminated research on Lenin.[3] Yet Stalin encountered problems. He could not prudently discourage veneration of Lenin while his own popular support was insecure. The Soviet state faced perpetual crisis in the 1940s. With a view towards winning the population's loyalty it was sensible for Stalin to associate himself with those symbols which seemed conducive to national cohesion under his own command. Lenin was such a symbol. A new and enlarged edition of his collected works was embarked upon in 1941.[4] Additional publications appeared at the end of the Second World War.[5]

Yet the fanfares of adulation for Stalin became louder in the same period; and Leninography therefore came into its own only after Stalin's death in 1953. The central party leadership under Nikita Khrushchev made reforms in politics and the economy. Stalin was posthumously denounced. He was indicted for the mass killings that had taken place in the 1930s. Khrushchev, in making his charges, found it convenient to assert and underline the continuities between Lenin's policies and his own. Research on Lenin became a state priority. An upsurge of documentation was heralded; and it culminated in the vast fifth edition of his collected works (which runs to fifty-five volumes).[6] New production has still not ceased. Unpublished articles by Lenin continue to be found and printed.[7] The principal repositories are in the Soviet Union; but in Western Europe too there are holdings of Leniniana which have contributed to the record.[8] Dozens of memoirs are newly published in the USSR every year. Khrushchev fell from power in 1964. But the Politburo since then, though effecting several alterations in political and economic policy, has shown no sign of dampening official interest in Lenin studies. If the scholarly achievement in the 1920s was to provide data upon almost every month of Lenin's career, in the 1970s the evidence became so densely-packed as to merit the preparation of a daily chronicle of his life from the cradle to his final resting-place.[9]

Yet a paradox presents itself. The mountain of documents, imposing though it is, has a vertiginous effect which must be resisted. The sources tell us a great deal about Lenin: but much also is still shrouded in mystery and contentiousness. The embalmed face staring up from its glass case in the Kremlin mausoleum is fittingly expressionless. Lenin in many ways remains an enigma.

The reasons are various. It should not pass unremarked that the documentary record is not devoid of limitations. Lenin's own attitude caused difficulties. He was reticent about autobiographical details. He commented little about his family, about his reasons for becoming a revolutionary and about the calculations in his mind at decisive political conjunctures. His friends compounded the problem. His wife Nadezhda Krupskaya wrote his biography in 1927. But her story was pressed through a mesh of personal and political considerations. She left much unsaid, and her own script was in any case subjected to revision by the party authorities.[10] Documents too were withheld from publication in the same period.[11] All writings which enjoyed official sanction underwent this rigorous checking. In the 1930s the situation was aggravated. Stalin's political triumph had the direst effects upon historical work. Documents were tampered with before publication. Stalin stopped at nothing to portray himself as 'the Lenin of today'.[12] Since the mid-1950s there has been drastic improvement. But the regulation is still enforced that material may be printed in the Soviet Union only if satisfying the requirement that the contents do not appear to undermine the Politburo's current policies and general standing. The fifth edition of Lenin's collected works is entitled 'the complete collection'. It is really an expanded selection; it does not include all his speeches and memoranda.[13] Lenin's career, so copiously recorded, still eludes total scrutiny.

Not that he would be an uncontentious figure even if access were

granted to virtually every fragment of information desirable. Inter-
pretative bias has always attended studies of Lenin. It has not been
peculiar to his admirers. Detractors too showed prejudice and
selectivity in their accounts even in the 1920s.[14]

Impartiality is an impossibility in historical scholarship. But even an
approximation to balanced treatment was hampered in Lenin's case by
the very fact that he was perennially regarded as the incarnation of an
episode so transcendentally contentious as the October Revolution. In
death, Lenin still compelled people to come off the political fence.
Acerbic clashes in interpretation were inevitable. Again, the 1930s
were a dark age for historians. Out-and-out falsification became
normal practice; lies were retailed in party textbooks.[15] Meanwhile,
investigative work on Lenin dwindled abroad. Stalin's self-
identification with Lenin, moreover, was not wholly unwelcome to the
Soviet government's external enemies. It was used by several commentators to propagate the notion that the entire epoch of Russian history
after 1917 had been filled with unrelieved, inexorable horror.[16] The
renaissance in Lenin studies was long in coming. Serious analysis was
obstructed in the USSR until its government, in the mid-1950s,
decided to knock Stalin from his pedestal. A large-scale biography
appeared in 1963.[17] Abroad the revivification began earlier; but it was
not until the 1960s that Lenin attracted examination by more than a
handful of scholars.[18] The atmosphere of international relations was a
stimulus. The adoption by the USA and the USSR of agreements on
peaceful co-existence created a propitious climate to enquire whether
the policies of Lenin and Stalin had truly been the same.

The newer accounts were no more 'neutral' than those of the 1920s.
But they broke with the work of the 1930s. They provided
empirically-grounded, analytical research. Disputes persist and will
always persist. But the debate on Lenin has already yielded a harvest of
indispensable historical monographs.

Lenin himself would probably, nevertheless, have found it hard to
recognise himself in his modern official biography. He is presented as
some kind of immaculate national saint; his iconolatry at times bears
comparison with Christ's.[19] He is envisaged as the man of totally
altruistic vision. The portrait is multifaceted. He is economist, activist,
political strategist, party chief, social theorist, philosopher, orator,
governmental premier, military planner and international statesman.
He is the complete politician. Lenin is depicted as the single authentic
leading successor to Karl Marx and Friedrich Engels; his Marxist
'orthodoxy' is held to be unchallengeable, his deepening of Marxism's

understanding of the world in the twentieth century is unrivalled. His originality is asserted in many areas of thought. His practical policies, in addition, are said to have derived entirely from a scientific analysis of the complexity of political and economic circumstances. He is described as the epitome of candour. It is also claimed that he was consistent in both basic ideas and immediate schemes; his career is portrayed as having constituted a coherent whole. The official biography implies that he was infallible. It allows that he was not always able to convince the party of the correctness of his views; but it contends that he could usually obtain acquiescence from those trained by him to act as his adjutants and followers. The Bolsheviks, despite temporary vacillations, offered him allegiance. Without Lenin, there could have been no socialist government in Russia in 1917. He was the demiurge of twentieth-century world history.

This beatification of Lenin is rejected by almost all writers outside the USSR and those other states which profess Marxism–Leninism. Important as he was, he was not superhuman. The most illuminating products of Soviet scholarship are the monographs on aspects of Lenin's career, especially his writings on the Russian agrarian economy and his running of the post-1917 governmental machine.[20] The official biography is not without value. But it is commendable more for its stated intentions than its accomplishments: it does at least aim to provide a composite portrait of Lenin and to prevent his thought from being dissociated from his activity.

By contrast, studies in Western Europe and North America have recently given us Lenin in fragments. Specialised investigations have been common. Some writers treat 'ideology' as a blind alley, looking upon Lenin as an opportunistic megalomaniac who used doctrine as a device to disguise self-centred purposes. He is said to have had a compulsive inner drive towards government and power.[21] Others have taken his ideas more seriously. But many of these question his credentials as a Marxist; instead it is proposed that Lenin belonged to a specifically Russian intellectual tradition and bore a merely superficial resemblance to the socialists of Western Europe.[22] This does not exhaust the list of interpretations. Still other writers argue that he really was what he claimed, a Marxist. They trace his lineage exclusively from Marx and Engels, asserting the originality of his political strategy as well as the accuracy of his economics. Yet they differ from Lenin's official defenders in the Soviet Union. They express doubts about his theoretical consistency; it is wondered in particular whether his policies in government matched his pre-revolutionary promises. They also enquire into the connections between the several areas of his thought. It has been suggested that economic preoccupations were the driving force of his politics; it has also been affirmed, even in sympathetic commentaries, that his philosophical disquisitions were an aberration from the remainder of his work. Thus he is treated as a theorist of the highest order, but not the omniscient genius of Soviet myth.[23]

Fewer disagreements have arisen over Lenin's activity as a practical leader. Nowadays writers incline to argue that his impact before 1917 was exaggerated by previous generations of scholarship. It has been asserted that his organisational position in the party up to and during the First World War was often extremely weak; and that obedience to his will was the exception rather than the rule.[24] His influence is recognised to have risen sharply from 1917. Even so, attempts have been made to demonstrate that definite limits circumscribed his authority as government premier and party chief after the October Revolution.[25] He was not dictator. The sharpest divergences have centred upon the reasons for his impact. His character and motivations remain controversial. While some accounts depict him simply as a very aggressive and talented leader, others more sceptically state that he was also thoroughly devious and obsessively quarrelsome. Arguments about his sincerity continue. By and large, those historians who regard him as a genuine Marxist believe that his organisational manoeuvres were nothing other than the logically necessary result of judgements already formulated by him in the domain of 'theory'.[26] But this belief is challenged. The most extreme contrary opinion holds that Lenin's chronic litigiousness indicates that he was a man without principle; and that his frequent shifts in policy are evidence of an inconsistency born of blatant political opportunism.[27]

This trilogy's aims are various. It is planned to investigate the recently-accessible sources. There is also a need to test current interpretations and to suggest alternatives where appropriate. And above all it is intended to offer a synoptic picture; and to highlight the intricate connections between Lenin's ideas, his activity and his environment.

The case against recognition of him as a Marxist is broadly unconvincing; the ideas of Marx and Engels pervaded his thinking and were no mere varnish. But Marxism was not the only doctrine to influence him. He was also affected by other schools of thought; in particular, he derived many notions from earlier Russian revolutionaries. This is no new contention. But what is less widely appreciated is that Lenin's condition was not unusual among his country's Marxists. Indeed it was the typical phenomenon; and it therefore falls to us to examine which portions of the Russian political heritage were picked up by which Marxist. The roots of Lenin's thought are not easily laid bare and disentangled. Complications abound. The excavation has to start from the recognition that Marxism and Russian revolutionary traditions were not alternatives which completely excluded each other. Russian nineteenth-century social thought drew heavily upon the work of writers in the rest of Europe; and Russian writers in turn contributed to European intellectual achievements. Numerous basic ideas, furthermore, were held in common by non-Marxist Russian revolutionaries and Marxists at home and abroad. And Marx in any case never formulated all his doctrines in a definitive manner. The result is that the nature of Marx's Marxism is problematical; and, not surprisingly, his followers have proceeded to offer a variety of distillations of his thinking. Lenin's Marxism had its specific flavour. It belonged to a particular trend within the worldwide Marxist movement. His Marxist ideas were largely authentic. But his was not the only twentieth-century version with fair claims of descent; and, furthermore, its lineage was not unchallengeable in several important aspects.

Adaptations of Marxism to Russian circumstances were already being made when the young Lenin entered political life. A further question presents itself. How close did he keep to the tenets expounded by the founding fathers of Russian Marxism? The preliminary answer is easy. In some ways he conformed, in others he rebelled.

But again the problem as posed is too restrictive. It starts from the premise that there was no controversy about the definition of Russian Marxism's foundations. It also presupposes that, by the turn of the century, guidelines had been laid down to deal with all conceivable future situations. In reality things were different. There was interminable dispute among Russian Marxists about the character of their enterprise; and they continually found themselves plunged into circumstances unanticipated in their previous discussions. Lenin's contribution to their debates was weighty. His individual ideas, with the exception of his socio-economic investigations, have little claim to originality. But he was not a plagiarist; he took and re-cast the work of other theorists, and produced a scheme of analysis and action distinctively his own. The result was a dazzling mixture. He could be extraordinarily perspicacious and incisive; he also committed extraordinary errors of judgement. He was right from 1907 predicting the unreliability of the liberals in the fight against the Russian monarchy. But he was excessively optimistic in 1917 about the future reaction of workers to Bolshevik policies in government. His mixed record is not limited to tactical planning. It is repeated along the range of his pronouncements on politics, economics and philosophy. Books like *What Is To Be Done?* and *State and Revolution* make many plausible arguments about the political problems posed by the capitalist order. But their cogency is intermittent. They make many contestable assertions about the ways to achieve socialism.

This leads to the question of Lenin's consistency. His ideas changed in the passage of his career; the alterations were often a natural evolution, but not always. He made about-turns. He did this both in his theory and in his practice. Before the October Revolution he held forth the prospect of comprehensive civic freedoms being granted to the mass of the country's people. When in power, however, he drastically curtailed these freedoms.

Yet his ideas were not amoeba-like, infinitely re-shapeable. His attachment to the ultimate objectives of communism did not falter. Furthermore, he co-ordinated the various regions of his intellectual activity. His political theory, sociology, economics and philosophy bore close affinities to each other; and it is very far from being true that any single region, be it politics or economics, held sway over all the rest for year after year. He also adhered to several basic tenets. In philosophy, he believed in the individual's capacity to ascertain exact truths about the world. In economics, he held that each stage in a society's development obeys inherent laws. In politics, he trusted in the virtues of the revolutionary vanguard; he sought also to found his programme upon an alliance between the workers and the peasantry; and he maintained that socialists should strive to effect a radical reconstruction of the pre-socialist state. These tenets guided him in most situations. But the guidance was of a general kind, leaving him much latitude for the delineation of his intellectual response to particular problems and events. He did not endeavour to codify his thought. Nonetheless the categories of his deliberations were remarkably constant. They came in antithetical pairs. His mind was pulled between central command and popular initiative; between political will and economic determinism; between massive coercion and mass persuasion; between the intuitive gamble and informed calculation. Tension and change were a touchstone of his thinking.

The interplay of tenets and categories was a patterned process for most of his career. But disruptions occurred. They took place most often when he encountered stiff active opposition. His typical reaction at such times was to choose measures of command and coercion: there was not much sign of persuasion in his economic ideas in 1920. Even when his thought maintained its pattern, moreover, it was sometimes only by means of logical contradictions. In addition, his candour (which could frequently be most audacious) was not absolute. He was not averse to fudging issues; and on occasion he evaded discussion altogether. His comments on terror in 1917 are a chilling example. Lenin, it must not be forgotten, was also a practical leader. His theoretical writings were always conditioned by organisational and institutional pressures. And, by his own admission, he regularly over-stated and distorted in order to win discussions.

Yet the dimensions of his personal influence, like everything else about him, are not open to easy assessment. It is becoming accepted that his organisational position in the party before 1917 was often fragile; it can now also be shown that he suffered numerous defeats on matters of political and economic policy in the same period. Such work makes it possible to say whether or not Lenin dominated the Bolsheviks in the pre-revolutionary years. He plainly did not. But again the problem is framed too crudely. Lenin, despite all his reverses, was a durable element in the Bolshevik leadership. Lacking omnipotence, he yet wielded a pre-eminent influence. As a politician he was affected by the constraints of the political environment in which he operated. Both the Bolshevik party and the Soviet government were living organisms. The measurement of his significance must be made in the light of the material, organisational and ideological impediments he confronted. Similar discrimination is required for the examination of Lenin's impact upon Russian society at large. It is not enough only to note that his popularity increased after 1917; it must also be shown what kind of image he possessed. What he was believed by people to represent was in many ways as important as what he himself claimed to stand for. Lenin was recipient as well as creator of his reputation. It was far from being true that every worker, peasant, manager or even party member had a clear understanding of the Bolshevik party's goals.

Nonetheless it would of course be absurd, with so remarkable a leader, to extrude his personality's intrinsic nature from the analysis. Lenin's psychology mattered. One-sided treatments of the question, in whatever form they are offered, are inappropriate. On the one hand it is difficult to imagine how he would have survived so many uphill struggles unless he had possessed that indomitable will, confidence and sense of duty and purpose. His militant nature helped him. He was also a talented organiser and administrator. And he had at his disposal a panoply of political skills. On the other hand he was quarrelsome. His irritations were not irrational: he truly believed that what appeared to others as minor grounds for dispute in fact constituted life-or-death issues for the Revolution. Yet his failures to compromise not infrequently did his own cause damage. Often before 1917 the party was bedevilled by intramural wrangles that diminished its involvement in the movement to overthrow the imperial government. Lenin was the major culprit. It was far from unusual for him to act as if his recommendations alone were the logical product of Bolshevik principles. This behaviour was unjustifiable; and his ruthlessness in pursuing his case had deleterious effects upon the party. But he was not invariably disputatious. His performance in governmental office demonstrates his immense capacity to get colleagues to mollify their discords and co-operate with each other.

A socialist government could have been set up in Russia in 1917 without Lenin's participation. But it would have been a different affair. Both positive and negative phenomena of the October Revolution were his decisive contribution.

In early 1918 he pulled Russia out of the First World War through a separate peace with Germany. In 1921 he secured the implementation of a New Economic Policy and halted the depredation of the grain of the peasants, who constituted the overwhelming majority of the population. But he was responsible too for the intensification of the Red terror in 1918–19. Throughout his years in power, furthermore, he spurned chances of close collaboration with various Russian political groupings which were not Bolshevik but yet were socialist. Many such phenomena are ascribable to his impact. They constitute an intrinsic historical web which makes it unwise to propose an unconditional verdict upon the link between Lenin, in his ideas and his activity, and Stalinism. Lenin's ideas and Stalin's were similar in many ways. But they were not identical. Lenin was no stranger to the use of administrative sanctions to suppress intra-party opposition; but he would hardly have organised the bloody political purges of the 1930s. Yet Lenin also established procedures which were greatly to assist Stalin's manipulation of the controls of power. Lenin did not create Stalin. But he cast down many barriers that would have otherwise made Stalin's policies more difficult to implement. Lenin's ideas and methods must never be idealised. It is extremely ill-considered to treat them as an acceptable strategy for radical social change in the world of the late twentieth century.

1   Cross-Currents

Early formative influences are not entirely comprehensible even by the person who has experienced them. These are general problems for the observer. They are particularly formidable when the subject of enquiry is dead. Lenin's case is among the most difficult; he died so long ago that none of his acquaintances is alive either. He also had that important defect as an autobiographer that he disliked writing about himself. The memoirs by his friends and enemies are thin gruel. And the information on his background, never very generously served, is at its meagrest for the years of his childhood and adolescence.

But let us begin with a few incontrovertible facts. He was born on 10 April 1870. He was christened as Vladimir Ilich Ulyanov; it was only many years later that he adopted his more illustrious pseudonym. His birthplace was Simbirsk, a town on the river Volga in the east of European Russia. He was the second son of Ilya Nikolaevich and Mariya Aleksandrovna Ulyanov. In 1869, a year before Vladimir's birth, Ilya had been appointed as schools inspector for the province of Simbirsk. It was the summit of a meritorious career. It meant, too, that he entered the social estate of the gentry. Ilya's material conditions as a young boy are not totally clarified; but they are unlikely to have been very prosperous. He was brought up in Astrakhan (which is situated in Russia's far south, where the Volga flows into the Caspian Sea). His father, Nikolai Ulyanov, was a tailor. Nikolai's ethnic background is undetermined. It is uncertain whether he was Russian or Kalmyk or Tartar; and the truth is unlikely to emerge so long as the Soviet authorities are embarrassed about data thought to detract from the 'Russianness' of Lenin. In any case, Nikolai married an illiterate Kalmyk girl called Anna Alekseevna Smirnova. He was in his seventies when he died. Unremitting toil had enabled him to acquire some capital and to change his status from serf's to townsman's. But Ilya Ulyanov was a lad at the time of his father's death. He would have suffered immediate destitution had it not been for his elder brother's undertaking to finance his education. Ilya was a brilliant pupil. In 1850

11

he left the Astrakhan secondary school after being awarded its silver medallion for scholarly excellence.[1]

Contemporary fiscal regulations were an impediment to youths of non-gentry stock wanting to proceed to university. Months of negotiation passed. But eventually, with his headmaster's intervention, the way was cleared and Ilya began his degree course in mathematics in the nearby city of Kazan.[2] He was an outstanding student and graduated with distinction in 1859. He obtained a job as senior master of maths and physics in the secondary school in Penza. Ilya had his father's qualities of perseverance. He made a name for himself locally not only as a fine teacher but also as director of Penza's meteorological centre. He gained acceptance among the town's professional classes. In the summer of 1863 he paid court to and wedded Mariya Aleksandrovna Blank.[3]

Mariya Aleksandrovna's background is no less uncertain than her husband's. Her father was Aleksandr Dmitrievich Blank, a doctor by occupation. Blank was possibly a Russified German; suggestions have also been made that he was Jewish. The sources leave the question unresolved. We know more about his wife, Anna Ivanovna Grosschöpf. Her father was a German merchant from Lübeck who had married a Swedish girl. The merchant Johann Grosschöpf was Lenin's wealthiest ancestor. Emigrating to St. Petersburg in 1790, he had achieved a commercial success which allowed him the pleasures of a fashionable town-house and a well-endowed personal library. His sons made notable careers for themselves. Two rose high in the civil administration, a third took a commission in the army. Anna Grosschöpf inherited a considerable fortune; and, when she died, her money and possessions passed to her husband. Not long afterwards, Dr Blank retired from medical practice. He purchased the land and the serfs of Kokushkino village in the province of Kazan. Thus Dr Blank, now the landlord of an estate, moved into the ranks of the gentry.[4] His daughter Mariya Aleksandrovna, in marrying Ilya Ulyanov, was evidently not worried about the enhancement of her social status. At all events, Russia was not quite as rigid a society as previously; and perhaps Mariya's family's immigrant past rendered it still less hidebound than Russian families of similar social position.

The marriage was a miniaturised image of the Russian empire of that epoch. The genealogy of Ilya and Mariya was a turbulent mixture of class, nationality and material conditions; it comprehended noble and serf, European and Asian, commercialist and pauper.[5]

Next to nothing is known about the impact of this variegated set of circumstances upon the marital life of the couple. Some commentaries on Lenin have bordered upon being racist. Cultural differences among the empire's ethnic groups undeniably existed; but it is a long step from this consideration to the hypothesis, often not stated expressly, that the possession of non-Russian grandparents deeply affected Lenin's world-view. There were many fierce Russians who had no Kalmyk connections (and many Kalmyks who were not fierce); and innumerable Russians were industrious without having a vestige of German, Swedish or Jewish ancestry. What is more, it has yet to be demonstrated that either Ilya's humble origins or Mariya's prosperity predetermined particular attitudes. Our comprehension of Russian social psychology in general is primitive; and the specific evidence about the Ulyanov family is of minimal assistance.[6] Only a negative point can be made with confidence. This is that nobody has recorded sensitivity about their national and social background on the part of Ilya and Mariya.[7] Nor does Vladimir appear to have been bothered about it. No source shows that he was distressed by his family's past, or even that he either knew or thought much about it. What is striking about Ilya and Mariya, in any case, is their purposefulness. They do not seem to have been the kind to fret about times past; they thought rather about the future. Their marriage was imbued with a sense that improvement would gradually come about in the Russian empire through the efforts of persons like themselves. They did nothing to undermine the tsarist political order.[8]

It is only when we look at Vladimir's childhood itself that the quality of evidence improves. Mariya bore six children. The first arrived in 1864 and was named Anna; the second was Aleksandr, born in 1866. Then came Vladimir, to be followed in 1871 by Olga. Dmitri was born in 1874 and the youngest of all, Mariya, arrived in 1878. It was not a large family by the standards of the day. The children tended to play together in pairs. Young Vladimir romped around with sister Olga. The household was happy. The Ulyanov children never lacked attention from their mother. They also kept dutifully busy. Sloth was the cardinal sin. An emphasis on hard work was not unusual among families occupying a middling rung upon the Russian social ladder; but Ilya Ulyanov was possibly exceptional in his extreme concern about his progeny's studies. A daily hour was set aside for silent reading. Trouble befell any infant who infringed the rules; the punishment was an uncomfortable period of sitting in 'the black chair' while the others got on with their books.[9] Mariya Aleksandrovna managed the home admirably. Like other middle-class families, the Ulyanovs employed a

peasant woman, Varvara Sarabatova, to help with the children and to
do the housework. The orderliness may well have been rather beyond
the ordinary. The domestic arrangements certainly impressed outsiders. Friends of the children noted how Mariya Aleksandrovna
insisted upon having a spotless white cloth on the table at tea-time;
they also remarked on the unusual degree of courtesy shown to the
parents by their offspring.[10] Ilya and Mariya Ulyanov were worthy
people, even if rather austere, and plainly deserved the esteem in
which they were held by their neighbours.[11]

Ilya was ambitious too. In 1863 he had obtained a teaching post in
Nizhni Novgorod. The rise in salary was useful. The couple would not
have to move far: Nizhni too was a Volga city. And they savoured the
prospect of its theatres, concert-halls and libraries. Ilya had an interest
in pedagogical theory. In Nizhni he would be able to attend debating
societies and conferences; he would be conveniently situated to visit
Moscow regularly.

In 1869 he earned further promotion, and the family readied itself
for the move to Simbirsk. It was not a transfer which the children in
retrospect were to feel enthusiastic about; Aleksandr would allegedly
express blunt disappointment: 'No books, no people.'[12] But this was
the reaction of a developing intellectual. Simbirsk was undoubtedly a
'nest' of the most conservative elements of the Russian nobility. But it
was more than that too. It lacked the refinements of larger cities, yet it
bustled with riparian trade up and down the Volga. Peasants crowded
into its suburbs seeking employment as dockers. A national market in
grain and industrial goods was growing vigorously, and Simbirsk was a
place of commercial importance. Russia's era of economic and social
modernisation was at hand. The role to be played in this transformation by men like Ilya Ulyanov was crucial. They were society's
enlighteners. Ilya's job in the Simbirsk schools inspectorate involved
him in the establishment of teaching premises in the Russian countryside. Educational policy was scarcely egalitarian, but popular access
to schooling was undeniably becoming less restricted.[13] It is easy to
imagine Ilya's excited belief that training in reading and writing was no
longer to be the privilege of the rich (and of the minority of the poor,
like himself, who had enjoyed extraordinary luck). Ilya Ulyanov
worked tirelessly. He was adept at finding ways round bureaucratic
obstacles; he had a keen eye for talent among local teachers; and he
accelerated progress by organising private fund-raising ventures.

Ilya and Mariya raised their children with the manners and
comportment typical of the Russian gentry of their day. Their children

continued to speak like nobles throughout their lives.[14] Perverse delight is occasionally shown by Lenin's critics that he should have come from such a family. But this attitude is misleading. Not all members of the gentry were reactionary; and men like Ilya, who had acquired their status by effort and merit rather than genetic accident, were often to be found among those who welcomed change in their country. Vladimir would eventually nurse objections to his father's liberal politics. And yet it is not unreasonable to propose that he received his own trait of optimistic determination from this middle-class domestic ambience; and that the rapid evolution of Simbirsk, taking shape before his eyes as he grew up, fortified his conviction that old Russia was dying and being replaced by a Russia that belonged to the modern world.

RUSSIA AFTER 'THE GREAT REFORM'

The first crisis struck the Ulyanovs in 1884. Ilya was informed by the Ministry of Education in St. Petersburg that he would be asked to retire prematurely within a year.[15] This was a heavy blow. He had dedicated his life to popular education; he had worked for fifteen years in projects of school construction, had created nearly five hundred new schools, and yet was only fifty-three years of age.

Ilya's personal misfortune was a symptom of the imperial government's shift away from the reforms of the 1860s. Russia's transformation caused intense strains in state and society. It occurred in a cycle of surges of governmental encouragement followed by back-tows of governmental obstruction; and each forward surge was subjected to its own constant and powerful cross-currents. The first major attempt at reform came with the Emancipation Edict of 1861. The empire, ruled by an absolute monarchy, had a predominantly agrarian economy and a rural labour-force consisting mainly of serfs. The humiliating end to the Crimean War in 1855 had induced disquiet about fundamental inadequacies in the administration, the economy and the army. The emperor Aleksandr II, succeeding to the throne in 1858, decided upon a course of change. His Edict released millions of serfs from personal bondage to the landed gentry. He followed this with a series of re-organisations in governmental, military and educational institutions. The monarchy also made concessions to principles of social representation. A jury system was introduced to law courts; elective procedures were laid down for the formation of new provincial councils (or *zemstva*) with a limited administrative authority. By 1880 Aleksandr II and his minister M. T. Loris-Melikov were contemplating giving permission for the establishment of a national elective assembly with consultative powers. The beginnings of a constitutional monarchy seemed near.[16]

The new social and political dispensations did not result from a preconceived plan. Even less prior judgement was applied to the economy. Nonetheless output increased impressively. Agricultural production rose. The peasantry, to meet the redemption payments for land received through the Emancipation Edict, cultivated more grain for sale. Monetary exchange was replacing bartering; and the growth in the purchasing power of a minority of peasants gave a boost to domestic industrial activity. Sales of agriculture-linked goods to the countryside became larger.[17]

Industrial production rose in general. Many rural inhabitants went off in search of urban employment. Factories welcomed the influx of cheap labour. Russia's industries had grown apace in the early eighteenth century under the emperor Peter the Great. Her coalmines and iron foundries had been at the forefront of European production methods; and her textile works had augmented their output immensely. Yet her advance thereafter lost impetus. Britain, the USA and other countries widened the gap in economic capacity between Russia and themselves in the nineteenth century. Various advisers to the throne, especially in the Ministry of Finances, watched the situation with concern. From the 1870s the government sponsored an accelerated programme of industrial growth. New railways were built across the country; new mineshafts were sunk in the Donbass; new factories were established in St. Petersburg. State intervention and subsidies gave additional fuel to the drive. The Russian industrial middle class grew in size. In fact the passion for industrialisation outstripped the country's financial resources; and Sergei Witte, Minister of Finances in the 1890s, looked abroad for investment capital. Loans were raised in Western Europe. Foreign enterprises were officially encouraged to set up branches in Russia. The metamorphosis of the country's economy had become a priority.[18]

These signs of progress, however, had menacing aspects. The social costs were enormous. The Edict of 1861 left the peasantry discontented; it offered them, on average, four per cent less land to sow than before; and the gentry, keeping areas of arable soil in its possession, succeeded also in holding on to many local woods and pastures. Redemption payments further embittered the peasants. At the same time a population explosion occurred in the Russian countryside. Disease did little to slow down the birth rate. Each village had its group of ill-fed, poverty-stricken families.[19]

Peasant disturbances took place in the early 1860s and at the end of the 1870s. Government officials were acutely aware that a popular revolt led by Emelyan Pugachev in the previous century had nearly overthrown Catherine the Great. As yet few believed such an upheaval was imminent. Yet the government's position was unenviable. The landowning gentry, a bulwark of tsarism in the past, played a diminishing role in the Russian agricultural economy (except in the latifundia of the South). Bankruptcies were common. Meanwhile the urban bourgeoisie had not yet matured into a robust social class in its own right. It depended heavily upon the governmental contracts. Russian capitalism was still at an early stage; and the state's troubles were aggravated by the unsympathetic attitude to the autocracy taken by so many members of the 'free professions'. But the group that potentially constituted the direst threat was the urban working class. True, there were less than two million factory workers in the empire out of a population of 125 000 000.[20] Strikes had been rare in the pre-Emancipation epoch. But in the decade before 1895 they were taking place at an annual rate of thirty three. This was not many by international standards. Yet 'the labour question' had arrived in Russia. Workers in the factories, the mines and construction sites endured degrading conditions. Wages were barely above subsistence level. Trade unions were illegal. Employers could announce mass lay-offs in periods of low profit; managers and foremen could line their pockets by means of regulations allowing them to fine labourers for indiscipline. The government enacted safety norms, but enforcement was slack. Housing and other social amenities were fearfully inadequate. In instances of labour unrest, employers could call upon the state to supply mounted Cossacks to break the picket lines.[21]

It was not extraordinary in Europe for capitalism's birth and development to create hardship and tumult. But Russia's experience was particularly arduous. The breakneck speed of industrialisation hugely intensified the material deprivations and the sense of spiritual loss; and the fact that the government was so visibly insisting on rapid economic growth was bound to make its own position doubly precarious.

Direct political opposition was suppressed. Covert criticism of the government was still made in public, but mainly in novels and artistic journals. Dostoevski, Tolstoi and several other authors were promi-

nent social commentators. The feeling was widespread that contemporary state and society were deeply flawed and in need of radical
alteration; and it was no coincidence that not a few Russian writers,
living in an epoch of such unpredictability, should have formulated
notably extreme ideas. This grasping at visions of totality affected
others too. Many political thinkers refused to content themselves with
moderate proposals. Clandestine anti-governmental groups began to
be formed in the 1860s; their adherents were mostly what later became
known as *narodniki* (or populists). Most of these were agrarian
socialists, although some of them inclined rather to anarchism. They
were horrified by the pauperisation of hundreds of thousands of
peasant households. They dreaded the inception of capitalism. They
had faith in peasant virtues. It was their assumption that the village
commune, if protected, could supply a miniature model of a socialist
society. The commune was looked upon as an essentially egalitarian
institution. The authorities exploited it as a rural self-taxation system
whereas the narodniki hoped to extend its customs of village-wide
deliberations and collective welfare to the country as a whole. Russia
could thereby immediately 'leap over' the capitalist economic stage.
She need never experience the human devastation that had been
endured in Western Europe. And this above all necessitated the
overthrow of the monarchy.[22]

The practical progress to this goal, however, was slow. The police
invariably broke up the early underground groups; and the peasantry
as a whole was not much affected by narodnik propaganda. Workers
proved more responsive. The great textile strike in St. Petersburg in
1870 encouraged the populists. By 1874 the first soundly-based
clandestine party had been created. Its designation was Land And
Freedom. It did in fact manage to attract peasant members, especially
in the Volga area. But it made progress mainly in the towns.
Working-class strikes were already beginning to show traces of
political motivation; and the Union Of Workers Of Southern Russia,
formed with help from narodniki, was unambiguously revolutionary in
aims. Relations between intellectuals and workers were somewhat
tense. Nevertheless activity continued. Leaders of Land And Freedom
joined in a mass demonstration against the monarchy on Kazan Square
in the capital in 1876. But the difficulties for Land And Freedom were
not confined to attracting popular support. They were also of an
internal nature. A perennial issue of controversy among populists had
been how to overthrow the regime; many leaders regarded the
assassination of state officials as a means of casting the authorities into

disarray and enabling the populists to seize power with popular backing. Matters came to a head at a secret congress of Land And Freedom in 1879. The party split shortly afterwards. The terrorist faction set up People's Freedom while those who favoured a strategy of long-term preparatory propaganda created Black Repartition.[23]

In 1881, People's Freedom organised a successful bid to assassinate Aleksandr II himself. Yet no revolution ensued. On the contrary Aleksandr III, heir to the throne, dispelled all expectations of further reforms too. His police crushed both People's Freedom and Black Repartition; and he made plain his distaste for liberals as much as for socialists.

Thenceforward economic modernisation was to be accompanied by increased political repressiveness. It would be astonishing if some inkling of this latest back-tow in government policy was not conveyed by Ilya Ulyanov to his children. Educational measures became more and more obscurantist. Ilya's job was laden with additional administrative difficulties; it is easy to believe that Vladimir thereby gained some acquaintance with the stultifying nature of Russian bureaucratic practices. Such knowledge would have come to him through literature even if his father had avoided the subject. Ilya took his children's civic education most seriously. He read and discussed the major Russian literary classics with them; and Vladimir, for one, developed an early passion for the novels of Ivan Turgenev.[24] The intellectual forcefulness of contemporary Russian letters became known to him. Its precise impact remains, unfortunately, a matter of guesswork. Yet it is entirely credible that Turgenev's cautious liberal outlook, with its keen sense of the uncertainties of the path of change pursued by his country in the latter half of the nineteenth century, imparted the attitude that Russia's transformation was unlikely to be a peaceful, straightforward affair. The brusque anti-liberalism of the new emperor can only have strengthened such an opinion. Seldom had the tsarist political order been so unpopular among those progressive strata of the Russian gentry to which Ilya Ulyanov belonged.

BOYHOOD AND BEREAVEMENT

The family until then had been free of stress (even though Ilya's frequent weeks away from home on official work cannot have made life easy for Mariya). Vladimir Ilich had been a boisterous baby. He was slow to learn to walk, but he was agile enough at crawling to satisfy his primordial passion to wreck the toys his parents set before him. He tugged at furniture and was noisier than any of his brothers and sisters. There was a charm to his mischief. He was seldom ill, being very robust and active. He was teased because of his shortish legs; his trunk was bulky and his head, like his father's, was disproportionately large. Ulyanov family discipline never quite tamed him. He liked to boss his younger sister Olga around, and was always eager to rival Aleksandr, his elder by four years and the favourite of the whole family.[25] Huge, imposing structures of analysis have been erected on this narrow factual ground. It has been suggested that Vladimir's destructive, active and competitive traits of behaviour give an identikit profile of the future revolutionary leader.[26] This is far-fetched. The youngster Vladimir Ulyanov is unmistakably perceptible in Lenin the man. But too much should not be deduced from this; we must also bear in mind that Vladimir as a baby was acting like most other babies.

Schooldays started for Vladimir when he was nine years old. His mother had already been to work on him. She taught her children their letters and numbers; she helped them with French and German grammar. As a proficient pianist, she tried to get Vladimir interested in learning the instrument; but it seems that he dropped practising before his adolescence. She steered clear of religious education, perhaps because she herself was agnostic. Ilya Ulyanov, however, was a regular attender of Orthodox church services and took the children along.[27]

Both boys and girls were showered with plaudits at school; they passed examinations like graceful swans moving over a tranquil lake. Vladimir lived up to expectations. Night after night he ran home to his parents to say that he had obtained full marks for his day's work. Indeed the ease of Vladimir's success bothered his father. Ilya worried lest his son should not acquire the ability to work hard. Vladimir (or Volodya, as he was affectionately called) shook off this langorous reputation. It became difficult to tear him away from his books in term-time. He was an exemplary pupil. Later, once he had become famous, his classmates were encouraged to write accounts of his behaviour: they could dredge up few instances of cheekiness or disobedience.[28] At home it was a different picture. He was the family's daredevil. He terrified his parents with antics like diving into the river Volga and swimming through the dangerous currents. Twice he had to be rescued by passers-by. The rough-and-tumble of games delighted him, and he would continue to love outdoor pursuits in later life. His playmates came from his own social grouping. In the Russian empire of the last century it would have been unthinkable for middle-class town-dwellers like the Ulyanovs to let their infants run loose with children of the working class (many of whom would in any case be out on the streets earning their living before they were teenagers). It was impossible to play around the riverside and not notice the poverty; and Volodya's father, as a liberal, was committed to its eventual eradication. Yet politics hardly impinged upon the lives of the Ulyanov children. Volodya would recall these carefree days with nostalgia: 'We did not know hunger or cold; we were surrounded by all kinds of cultural opportunities and stimuli, books, music and distractions.'[29]

Vladimir Ilich Ulyanov was a disciplined pupil and a playful risk-taker. This contrast was to be a distinct advantage for him in his career as a revolutionary; those playing him at chess saw how he enjoyed the pleasures of calculation and gamble simultaneously. His father taught him the game, and took it in good spirit when his son started to beat him regularly. Volodya was conventional but strict about rules. His brother Dmitri complained that Volodya would insist upon the regulation that noone should take back a move once his fingers had released a piece. Not that Volodya relished easy victories. Like other able players, he preferred to compete without a rook or a knight if the opposition was obviously too weak; such contests gave him the thrill of trying to 'extricate himself'.[30] His punctiliousness contrasted with the easy-going ways of elder brother Aleksandr. The Ulyanov children recorded Volodya's keenness to emulate him. But it seems that his effectiveness in controlling his outbursts of bad temper remained small.[31]

In 1881 his father returned from work with the news that terrorists had assassinated Aleksandr II. Ilya Ulyanov was outraged. He attended the service of mourning in Simbirsk Cathedral in his civil servant's uniform; perhaps he already suspected that the emperor's death would usher in an age of reactionary legislation. The revolutionary contagion was spreading everwhere. A teacher at the local secondary school had been sacked because of his political activities. Ilya's son Aleksandr was showing an interest in Nikolai Chernyshevski and other revolutionary writers, and this before he had even left school. Ilya Ulyanov became more concerned about the future. Three years later, in 1884, there came confirmation of his presentiments in the form of the notice of his compulsory retirement. Eventually his appeal against the decision succeeded. He still worked hard. But he started to suffer from insomnia in 1885. On 12 January 1886 he was brought home early from work. Next day he had difficulty in eating and lay down on a sofa in his study. In the late afternoon his wife Mariya went to him. He was shuddering painfully. She ran to fetch Volodya (since Aleksandr was away in St. Petersburg). Nothing could be done to help. He had suffered a severe haemorrhage in the brain; his doctors were unsure of the cause but the symptoms suggest the same disease as would kill Volodya too: cerebral arteriosclerosis. Volodya acted as the man of the family; it speaks volumes about the family's commitment to education that Aleksandr was not summoned back for his own father's funeral. Volodya, the sixteen-years-old second son, took his place among the pall-bearers at the Cathedral.[32]

Volodya grew up fast. Bereavement and responsibility were a burden that deprived him of enjoyments of late adolescence taken for granted by most lads of his social class. He threw himself into his school-work. He had no weak subjects, being noted for his prowess in Latin, Greek, history, geography and Russian literature.

His headmaster F. M. Kerenski (who was father of the future premier of the Provisional Government in 1917) made a sole point of criticism: his 'excessive reserve' and 'unsociable attitude' to other pupils.[33] Kerenski was well-disposed towards the Ulyanovs. Presumably his judgement was made in full knowledge of the family's misfortune. Volodya's introspectiveness can only have been increased by the loss of his father. Mariya Aleksandrovna was eager to take the children off for a holiday at her father's estate in Kokushkino village. Aleksandr joined them. He brought his books with him, and every day spent hours studying political literature and conducting biological experiments.[34] The younger children played around the country house with their cousins. It seemed as if Mariya Aleksandrovna's aims were steadily reaching fulfilment. The Ulyanovs were together again as a family and were coping with the trauma of losing their father. The emotional strain was undeniably severe. Yet we have to be cautious in interpreting its long-term effects. Medical science has made enormous progress since the nineteenth century, and many diseases such as tuberculosis and typhoid are no longer so widely encountered in advanced industrial societies. Premature death was a much more common phenomenon in nineteenth-century Russia. Vladimir's experience, profoundly painful as it was, was not abnormal in those times. And accounts that adduce his father's death to explain his subsequent career fail entirely to show why there was only one Lenin.

THE TRIAL OF ALEKSANDR

Mariya Aleksandrovna and the family were weathering the bereavement when another crisis arose. Aleksandr (or Sasha, as the family called him) had secretly involved himself in political activity. Biology lecturers at Petersburg University knew him only as an undergraduate of academic promise. But his mother noticed his disaffection from the ruling establishment. She may also have caught sight of his reading material in summer 1886; he was even starting to make translations of Karl Marx. In November 1886 he attended a demonstration commemorating the death of the oppositionist writer Dobrolyubov.[35] It was broken up by troops.

Sasha had reached his point of decision. In January 1887 he managed to contact activists intent upon resurrecting the People's Freedom organisation; he was convinced that terrorism alone would induce the authorities to effect constitutional changes and introduce democratic forms of government. His group intended to assassinate Aleksandr III. They arranged to produce proclamations, on a primitive hectograph-machine, to be issued on the emperor's death; and they used their scientific expertise on the manufacture of a bomb. Sasha impressed the others by the unshakability of his intentions. But this was not enough to kill a tsar. In March, the group was penetrated by police and arrested. Sasha demanded that the other conspirators should allow a greater share of guilt to fall upon him than was in accord with the facts. He had always perceived the personal dangers of the conspiracy. He had seen the political problems too. Like many terrorists after 1881, he did not delude himself with the expectation that assassination would spark off a peasant revolt. But despair was not in his nature. Even his incarceration was to be turned to account; his trial would give the chance to explain his reasoned hatred of the Russian autocracy to the world. His only regret was the anguish caused to his mother. Upon hearing of the arrest, she hurried off to Petersburg and secured permission to see her son in Shlisselburg prison. Nonetheless Sasha stuck to his plan to admit guilt in court.[36]

Nobody was more grief-stricken than Sasha's brother Volodya. It was still noted that Volodya, in his teens as in his younger years, founded his ambitions upon Sasha's record. Yet Sasha and Volodya had not been close. Sasha was disturbed by his brother's sarcasm; and annoyance changed to hostility when Sasha heard Volodya being uncivil to their mother after the death of their father. Sasha's description of his brother was curt: 'Indubitably a very gifted person, but we don't get along.'[37] The remembrance of these past dissensions must have exacerbated Volodya's sadness.

The trial of Aleksandr Ulyanov and his fellow conspirators began in April 1887. The prosecutor did not confine himself to the practical details of the plot but accused the defendants of intending to impose their idiosyncratic opinions upon society by means of violence. Aleksandr repudiated the charge. Despite interruptions by the judge, he argued that it was the state authorities who were depriving the people of democratic freedoms and committing the original acts of coercion. He spoke about the Russian intelligentsia. Not even scientific research was safe from political interference. Even more fiercely he denounced the social structure of the Russian empire as the cause of the immiseration of the mass of the population. There could be no alleviation while the absolute monarchy remained. Revolution was the only solution. The court was left little choice by Aleksandr's self-inculpation: he was duly condemned to death by hanging. His conduct during the proceedings scandalised a society not yet ready to abandon faith in the monarchy. But he became a martyr in the minds of those who sought revolution in Russia. His conduct conformed to the political rebel's code. At dawn on 8 May, nonetheless, Aleksandr Ulyanov was executed together with four fellow activists in the courtyard of Shlisselburg prison.[38]

Mariya Aleksandrovna was overwhelmed by misfortunes. She was ostracised by her Simbirsk acquaintances. She faced problems at every turn. She could not yet even count upon her late husband's pension being regularly forwarded.

By chance, Volodya was meant to set his final school examinations around the time of the hanging. His mother insisted upon his attendance. He took his place in the exam hall on the day of Sasha's execution; and he continued to do so for the remainder of a week dominated nationally by discussion of the terrorist affair.[39] Astonishingly, Volodya's academic performance was undimmed by the terrible circumstances. Like his brother, he won the school's gold medal for scholarly excellence. The iron self-control disguised his remorse. Grimness and taciturnity replaced brashness; outsiders began to remark that he had ceased to joke, even to smile. Only with the younger Ulyanov children was he able to revive his rumbustious self.[40] At the age of seventeen, with his father and elder brother in their graves, he was the male head of the family; and contemporary photographs of him suggest a person of almost middle-aged solemnity. But his depression of spirit was not permanent. His acquaintances in the years ahead often commented upon his raucous laughter.[41] In fact such accounts as we have of his demeanour in his late adolescence indicate that, once recovered from the initial shock, his personality was already shaped for the rest of his life. His temperament was an aggregation of choleric explosiveness and patient self-restraint; he was intellectually self-confident; he was indomitably purposeful in pursuit of his ends. He could not easily tolerate anyone's sovereignty over him. He was never more combative and ruthless than when he felt checked in the course of doing his duty. Though modest in personal relationships, he set a high value on his potential contribution to the cause of radical change in Russia.

He told nobody the date of his conversion to revolutionary ideals; but his brother's execution was almost certainly the spur. It did not take much to turn sensitive young people into political fighters against the Russian autocracy. We can only guess whether Volodya would have joined the revolutionaries in any case; all we know for certain is that he had experienced greater propulsion towards revolt than most. His executed brother had been a revolutionary. And the shunning of his mother by the family's neighbours may well have persuaded Volodya that Russian liberals were unreliable allies in the struggle for change. His shift towards activism was affected by his reading. Turgenev's novels no longer satisfied.[42] Volodya worked through Sasha's bookcase and discovered the revolutionary writings of the narodnik Chernyshevski. His explorations were probably in part a quest for his brother. He was consumed by the desire to make sense of Sasha's life and ideas; and, like Sasha, he found Chernyshevski's moral and political summons to revolution irresistible. While on holiday at Kokushkino in summer 1887, he began to re-plan his life. He no longer thought of studying Latin when he left for the university in the autumn. Instead he would take Law.[43] This was a choice widely favoured by sons of the gentry.[44] At a time of rising graduate unemployment, it offered the best chance of entrance to the civil service or the legal profession itself. Yet his calculations may well have been more political than careerist. Barristers were a profession which included many who wanted to see the autocracy dismantled.[45] By joining them, Vladimir Ulyanov would be able to play his part by taking up the defence of the downtrodden and oppressed in courts of law.

RUSSIAN AGRARIAN SOCIALISM

The intellectual world of discourse that had been inhabited by Aleksandr Ulyanov was complex, and its elements were in a condition of constant flux; and Vladimir, in seeking to understand it, was initiating an interest that engaged him intermittently over the next two decades of his life.

Russian populism was not only an active political movement: it was also a compendium of serious cultural thought. Numerous narodniki looked to the European socialist movement. They drew copiously from the considerations and experience of political rebels in the West; their works abounded in references to Proudhon, Owen, Saint-Simon and Blanqui.[46] They did not receive the European influences uncritically. They adapted them to their own perceptions of Russian conditions and also to their own psychological inclinations. Russian and Western revolutionaries, indeed, exchanged ideas. M. A. Bakunin, in the middle years of the century, emerged as a political theorist and leader of continental distinction.[47] The European contacts of the narodniki did not blind them to the contrasts of Russian society with the societies of Britain, Germany and France. Russia's economy was still largely agrarian and technically backward. The Russian populists were in any case influenced also by earlier intellectual traditions of thought in their own country which, though inimical to socialism, held the peasant commune in high esteem.[48] In addition, they conducted economic research.[49] And, by the 1880s, it was difficult to deny that capitalism had made deep inroads into the country's industrial and agricultural economy. An immediate, direct transition to a socialist society seemed less practicable as year succeeded year. Russian agrarian socialists appeared increasingly defensive when they wrote about the contemporary transformation of Russian social life.

What could a young narodnik do in the face of this? The first generation of fighters were dying; M. A. Bakunin and A. I. Zhelyabov were in their graves, and N. G. Chernyshevski was to die in 1889. The luminaries of Russian agrarian socialism in the late 1880s and early 1890s were N. K. Mikhailovski, V. P. Vorontsov and N. F. Danielson. Mikhailovski had once concurred that violent revolution would lead to fundamental political improvement. But now he appeared haunted by fears of a general bloodbath; and he drew steadily closer to the reformist ideas being spread in particular by Vorontsov.[50]

Such a perspective was unattractive to many underground groups, and Aleksandr and Vladimir Ulyanov were not alone in deeming that the surviving patriarchs of agrarian socialism had betrayed the cause. Mikhailovski, Vorontsov and S. N. Yuzhakov implied the need for a policy of 'small deeds'. They advised their followers to seek employment in the zemstva and in the state's welfare and education institutions. A war of propaganda should be waged from within the bureaucracy. Mikhailovski leant on Vorontsov's economic arguments (which in turn were amplified and refined in 1893 by Danielson). Vorontsov endorsed Russia's need for industrialisation. Chernyshevski and several other early narodniki had accepted this as a necessity; but, with Vorontsov, such an acceptance had turned itself into a matter of emphasis too. Vorontsov and Danielson rejected capitalism. Their motivation was as much practical as moral. They proposed an 'underconsumptionist' argument, holding that capitalism could be sustained only if entrepreneurs were in a position to sell products on a mass market; and that this was unrealisable in Russia since economic expansion was being financed through a level of taxation which reduced millions of peasants poverty. They argued also that capitalism could develop only in countries whose industrialists could export their manufactures. Russia's industrial growth, they declared, would be hobbled by the absence of a suitable foreign market now that the globe had been divided up by Great Britain and the other imperial powers. It followed that, if the Russian state desired industrialisation, it would succeed only if it fostered the people's material well-being. Indeed Vorontsov wanted an alliance between tsar and peasantry. The heights of the industrial economy should be nationalised; capitalists should be expropriated. Peasant communes should be invited to tender for contracts from the state and to found their own small-scale industrial associations. Economic policy should be geared to the consumer demands of the mass of the population.[51]

The attempt was made to consolidate this position through an all-out assault upon Marxism. Mikhailovski denounced what he regarded as the absence of any ethical concern in Marx's writings. Both he and P. I. Lavrov urged that all true revolutionaries should seek moral self-perfection; and amoral doctrines, they asserted, were inappropriate to a political movement bent upon the construction of a better world for all mankind.[52] The ends could not always justify the means. When famine hit the Volga region's peasantry in 1891, Mikhailovski's anti-Marxist campaign reached an intense pitch. How could Marxists regard capitalism as a 'progressive' stage in the country's development, he enquired, when it produced such appalling distress? Mikhailovski charged that Marxism worked with a deterministic model of historical change; he challenged the claims of 'scientific validity' made for the world-view of Marx and Engels.[53]

These considerations were unpersuasive to many young activists. Marxism gained in popularity. The youngsters despised the language of compromise and indeterminacy. They sought to re-examine agrarian socialism now that its original economic rationale was, in their reckoning, mistaken. But they did not drop every single element in the narodnik tradition, a tradition which had never been a homogeneous entity in any case. Agrarian–socialist ideas were a notable ingredient in Russian Marxism's constitution. This should not surprise us. The writings of Marx and Engels, voluminous and impressive as they were, did not amount to a definitive and unambiguous prescription for their followers; and there was always a need, in particular, for adaptations to national circumstances. The agrarian socialists had already attempted to confront the problems of Russia's historical development. They had been harrassed by the same police state. The nascent circles of Marxist activists did not despise the traditions elaborated by the narodnik enragés of the 1860s and 1870s; it was commonly accepted by the generation of the late 1880s that earlier generations could offer guidelines of practical and theoretical value. The first political material read by Vladimir Ulyanov was narodnik in content. His brother had been a notable narodnik. And the first political groups attended by Vladimir too were to hold narodnik ideas. It would be passing strange if Russian agrarian socialism were to have left no trace in the thinking of his mature years.

Yet it is hard to demarcate precisely the notions taken by him from the narodniki. Even less surely can the process be dated. He made a few brief references in the 1900s. He professed respect for the courage of the narodnik activists and their organisational techniques.[54] This has been well publicised. He made an additional and much less famous acknowledgement in 1894. It occurred in a comment on populist economics. While making basic criticisms, he nevertheless perceived virtues. He specified several useful narodnik contributions to socialist theory.[55] He praised their approval of the need to expand national industrial and agricultural output. He highlighted their admiration for up-to-date forms of technology. He paid tribute to their zeal to spread learning and science among the people.[56] He was ever eager to commend Chernyshevski in particular; he was to declare, in 1909, that this hero of his had grasped many essentials of a materialist philosophical standpoint.[57]

Ulyanov's express statements, furthermore, are almost certainly not an exhaustive list of the narodnik influences upon him. The argument must remain tentative, based as it is upon coincidences between the ideas of Vladimir Ulyanov and various prominent narodniki; yet the similarities are too strong to be dismissed as merely accidental. Like Petr Tkachev, not only was he drawn to notions appearing to rest upon scientific principles. He also yearned for a similar condition of all-conquering certitude.[58] He attached enormous significance to the need for socialist intellectuals. He concurred with Tkachev's vision of the intelligentsia as the educator, organiser and guide of the 'masses'.[59] Ulyanov, like Lavrov, placed a high value on the potentiality of individual thinkers; and, like Chernyshevski, he assumed and emphasised that exact truth about the world was in man's capacity to acquire.[60] He admired the Land And Freedom organisation. He too placed emphasis upon discipline and hierarchy and centralism.[61] His strategy, with its accent upon a worker-peasant alliance, had obvious populist resonances.[62] But there were further echoes as well. Both Tkachev and A. I. Zhelyabov had said that socialism would be introduced only through violent popular upheaval; and Tkachev had also anticipated that an epoch of socialist dictatorship would be required to extirpate all elements of the old regime.[63] In Tkachev's opinion, mass terror would be needed for the task.[64]

Such notions pervaded the thought of the future Russian Marxist Vladimir Ulyanov. They would become interfused and bonded with other notions derived directly from Marx and Engels. It would be a powerful compound; and, because so many of these populist ideas in any case had trace elements in Marx's own works, it is ultimately impossible to discern which tradition influenced him more deeply in various particular matters. The two traditions were never totally separate.[65] Time would elapse before Vladimir's debt to populism would fully manifest itself. He was still only seventeen years old. But he had made his start in politics. And, as he spent that summer of 1887 poring over his executed brother's books, he was taking his first large strides towards the formation and elaboration of his outlook upon the world.

2   Roads to Freedom

KAZAN

The Russian government's dilemmas were abundantly evident in the contortions of its educational policy. School and university curricula were state-controlled. Officialdom held that several branches of the humanities and the sciences induced modes of thought pernicious to a political system steeped in traditional privilege and ritual. Aleksandr III re-introduced obstacles to the access of non-noble adolescents to higher education. Sons of landowners were adjudged inherently more loyal to the regime. The emperor also empowered the Ministry of Education to tighten up the student disciplinary code. It was not unusual for ex-army officers, with their robust approach to punishment of disobedience, to obtain posts in university administration. Yet this line could not be pursued too far. Economic and military reconstruction was unrealisable without an expansion of educational facilities. Any industrialising state faces this fact of life. And the tsarist political police was under-equipped to organise surveillance of all undergraduate groups and gatherings. In any event, the government scarcely wished to provoke the hostility of literate young people gratuitously. The sanctions against insubordination remained insufficient to deter. But the rules and restrictions affecting undergraduates were still oppressive; and students were acquiring a reputation for rebelliousness.[1]

Unsurprisingly, the police opposed Vladimir Ulyanov's entrance to university. Sasha's hanging was still recent news, and the authorities might have continued to make life difficult for the Ulyanov children except for their headmaster F. M. Kerenski's intervention. He described his pupil's academic excellence. His mother promised to move house to be near to him. Objections were waived. Vladimir handled the correspondence about his brother Dmitri's transfer to school in Kazan.[2] He found rooms for himself in the city in August 1887. He started to attend lectures. The family were to take up residence in town in November.

The Volga region, where Vladimir had so far spent all his days, was

30

of growing economic importance; it also witnessed political unrest. Kazan was the most unruly city on the river's banks. The administration was Russian, but Tartars constituted a substantial minority of the inhabitants and were unreconciled to tsarist dominion. His stay in Kazan must have intensified Vladimir's awareness of the 'nationalities question' in the empire.[3] Kazan was also a place chosen by the government since the 1860s to which to exile arrested revolutionaries.[4] Underground political groups were active. A young person in revolt against the regime could without difficulty contact kindred spirits there. Students in Kazan, as elsewhere, were required to swear not to enrol 'even in legally permitted societies, without the explicit sanction of the nearest authority in each individual instance'. Vladimir took the oath, but only as a tiresome formality.[5] The government had banned all students associations based upon the criterion of geographical origins. Such associations survived in Kazan. Vladimir joined the Samara–Simbirsk association, and made a quick impact. The other members elected him, though only a first-year student, as their representative on the secret council uniting all such associations inside the university. This council met in November to discuss ways to support the anti-tsarist disturbances organised by the students of Moscow university. A demonstration was arranged for 4 December.[6] Scarcely had he become an undergraduate than Vladimir Ulyanov was immersed in potential trouble. He knew the risks. As brother to a would-be regicide, he was a marked man.

His activities were not confined to academic matters; he also involved himself with a group of revolutionaries led by Lazar Bogoraz. The plan was to reconstitute the People's Freedom organisation. Bogoraz was no mere talker. His group was arranging to produce pamphlets and proclamations; it communicated with activists in St. Petersburg.[7] The beliefs of the group are known only sketchily. Circumstantial evidence suggests that its members wanted a terrorist campaign; and that they doubted whether 'the people' was capable of carrying out its own political revolution.[8] Aleksandr Ulyanov would probably have felt happy among them. This is not complete surmise. It has come to light that a former associate of Aleksandr's was on close terms with an associate of Lazar Bogoraz's.[9] The resemblance in ideas extends to a further matter. Bogoraz's group was like Aleksandr's in wishing to maintain contacts with local Marxist activists. Fraternal solidarity among revolutionaries of all varieties was approved.[10] Bogoraz himself is a shadowy figure. Though being the group's leader, he did not lead unopposed. Disagreements about policy divided the membership.[11] It would be instructive to possess the details, but apparently nothing has been recorded for posterity.

Vladimir Ulyanov's role in the group remains obscure. It cannot have been very weighty. Shortly after joining Bogoraz, he had to concentrate his attention upon the Samara-Simbirsk student association. The Kazan demonstration of 4 December caused an uproar. It was met with the official suspension of lectures. A hundred students were arrested, Ulyanov being among them.[12] When asked why he had risked such trouble, he reportedly replied: 'What is there to think about? My road has been laid out by my elder brother.'[13] Ulyanov behaved recklessly. Along with others, he announced his withdrawal from the university in protest againt 'existing conditions' in academic life.[14] The rector already intended to expel him. The Ministry of Internal Affairs meted out a sentence typical for first offences of this kind: Ulyanov was exiled to Kokushkino, the estate recently inherited by his mother upon the death of Dr Blank. The police were instructed to keep him under surveillance.[15] His mother wrote letters begging that he be re-admitted to his studentship; but to no avail. He continued independently with his reading in jurisprudence. At the same time he returned to his brother's book collection and worked through tomes of Russian revolutionary literature. He read and re-read Chernyshevski's novel *What Is To Be Done?* Its impact upon him was profound. As Ulyanov was to confide to a friend, Chernyshevski 'ploughed him over and over'.[16] We have seen that Vladimir Ilich borrowed some political and philosophical attitudes from Chernyshevski. He also experienced a powerful emotional influence. Chernyshevski's novel leant dignity and heroism to socialist ideals. Such was Ulyanov's admiration that he took the dangerous step of writing to Chernyshevski (but he received no reply since the exiled oppositionist was already mortally ill).[17]

The Ulyanov family was allowed to move back to Kazan in September 1888. Vladimir remained banned from the university and denied permission to go abroad to complete his studies. He again contacted local revolutionaries. Bogoraz had fled to Rostov; but Ulyanov managed to track down M. P. Chetvergova, an ex-member of People's Freedom. He attended her political circle.[18] Chetvergova's group, like Bogoraz's, had contacts outside Kazan. It associated itself with the terrorist leader M. V. Sabunaev, who was travelling the country making arrangements for a convocation of all the local groupings.[19] Both Chetvergova and Sabunaev are dimly-known personages. But quite possibly their ideas were similar to those of Aleksandr Ulyanov.[20] Again we cannot be sure about the nature of

Vladimir's contribution to the group. Obviously, however, this eighteen-year-old former Kazan student was in serious jeopardy of arrest.[21]

And, if caught, he would not have been punished as leniently as before. His mother in fact had a deterrent effect upon him for the last time. Worried by his involvement with revolutionaries in Kazan, she sold up the family house and purchased a landed estate at Alakaevka in Samara province. They moved in May 1888.[22] The police broke up Chetvergova's group mere months later; had it not been for his mother's action, Vladimir would probably have joined the others in prison. Ulyanov brought his legal textbooks and his political reading material to Alakaevka. In the winter of 1888–89 he reportedly began to study Karl Marx's *Das Kapital*.[23] The effect upon him was enormous. Marx was shortly to emerge as the focus of his political world; there would be no other writer, not even Chernyshevski, who would be so revered by Ulyanov. It is impossible to say whether intellectual appreciation was as yet accompanied by an attraction of the emotions. But this was not long in coming. Ulyanov's collected writings will be combed in vain for traces of adverse comment on Karl Marx. The tone is uniformly not just approving but adulatory. He did not abandon non-Marxist authors. Darwin's books too seem to have appealed to him at this time.[24] But Marx was obviously becoming the towering intellectual force in his thinking. Expulsion from Kazan University gave him leisure for cultural exploration. Steadily his political viewpoint was clarifying itself.

His mother's transportation of the family to Samara province did not prevent him from striking up friendships with local revolutionaries; and many of these, like N. S. Dolgov and M. P. Golubeva, were veterans of the terrorist wing of the agrarian-socialist movement.[25] But Vladimir nursed doubts about the strategy of People's Freedom. He joined A. P. Sklyarenko's narodnik group in Samara. Sklyarenko was only a little older than Ulyanov; he had once been influenced by the ideas of People's Freedom but he too was entering a period of reconsideration which would lead him to Marxism. Ulyanov found himself among congenial colleagues in his own period of intellectual ferment.[26]

MARX AND ENGELS

Marx's ideas and Russian populism, while coinciding in several important areas, diverged in others of equal significance. The young Vladimir's debt to Marx is hard to define with precision. They did not know each other personally. Marx died in 1883. Such impression as he made upon Ulyanov was achieved through his books. Our sources are exiguous. The winter of 1888–89 is probably the correct date of Ulyanov's first reading of *Kapital*, but we cannot be categorical: a few accounts suggest that it was in fact earlier.[27] Ulyanov was a bibliophile. He read fast, he read voraciously. We do not possess the record of his initial encounter with Marx. *Das Kapital* is unlikely to have been the only book. Ulyanov's earliest extant writings offer some clues. Citations made by him in his articles of 1893–95 suggest that, if *Kapital* was the most closely scrutinised text, *The Communist Manifesto* (written by Marx together with Frederick Engels) and Engels's *Anti-Dühring* were also works of influence.[28] It is quite likely that these same books were familiar and important to Ulyanov in 1889. If we are uncertain about chronology and bibliography, moreover, we must be still more cautious about thematic influences. Ulyanov the anti-autobiographer has left no account. In order to gauge how he initially reacted to Marx it is necessary to make guesses based upon indirect comments made by Ulyanov in his own early writings. It was, furthermore, an evolving relationship. From the end of the 1880s until his death in 1924, Ulyanov was an assiduous Marxologist; he was engaged more intensively in the study of Marx and Engels than of any other theorist (including the populists).[29] He continually returned to the works of his great inspirers in order to receive inspiration afresh. We must therefore tread tentatively in our assessment of Marx's impact upon Ulyanov while he was yet a young man.

The economics of Karl Marx were an enduring interest of Ulyanov's. The analysis of capitalism was especially attractive. Marx had described in *Das Kapital* how industrialists, introducing new forms of machinery and a new division of labour into their factories, had inaugurated transformations of epochal significance. Capitalism enormously expanded the production of goods. It spread educational facilities more widely and raised the level of popular consciousness.[30] Unlike the narodniki, Ulyanov condoned capitalist development. He also shared Marx's enthusiasm about capitalism's organisational principles (whereas the populists, though welcoming modern inventions in technology, did not accept the need for a hierarchical distribution of duties inside factories).[31] Ulyanov also approved of large-scale social units. The characteristic agrarian-socialist affection for the small, self-contained community found little echo in Ulyanov's writings. And perhaps *Kapital*, with its withering critique of proposals to preserve 'communalistic' social relationships once capitalist development had begun, leant further strength to his Russian follower's standpoint.[32]

Ulyanov did not eulogise capitalism. His aim was to indicate that the modernisation of the Russian economy would afford advantages exploitable by socialists in the future. For capitalism was not to be regarded as a cul-de-sac. It was the penultimate rather than final epoch in global social change. *Das Kapital* exposed capitalism's internal contradictions. Capitalism operated upon principles of competition: the capitalist maintained his business by hiring labourers to work in his factory, to maximise his competitiveness he was obliged not only to extract as much labour power as possible from his work-force but also to invest an increasing proportion of his revenue in the acquisition of the latest types of equipment.[33] Inexorably some capitalists would be more successful than others. Economic power would fall into fewer and fewer hands. The general effect would be that the capitalist system would periodically get the supply of goods out of balance with the demand for them. Massive economic crises would recur.[34] The solution would be for the working class to establish a 'dictatorship of the proletariat'.[35] Both culturally and politically, the workers would be well-suited to such a role. Of all social classes, they had least interest in a private-enterprise economy; they should be encouraged to engage in 'class struggle'. This would necessitate a lengthy political campaign. On the whole, the narodniki had denied that a parliament, even if it were to be set up in Russia, was a suitable forum of activity for revolutionaries. Marx had no such self-denying ordinance. Nor had Ulyanov.[36] He also enthusiastically concurred (and here Tkachev was fully with them) that force was the midwife of radical political change. Only when the working-class dictatorship had swept away all remnants of the capitalist system would a more relaxed regime be initiated.[37] And the transition would then be made to communism itself. Eventually a new society would be created which would take as its guiding rule: from each according to his ability, to each according to his needs.[38]

Such a denouement is a common theme in Ulyanov's work. He did not expect it to be realised immediately. *Kapital* and *Anti-Dühring* postulated that inherent laws governed the workings of a socio-economic formation such as capitalism. Marx, in addition, sketched a majestic sequence of stages in historical change. Feudalism gave way to capitalism. And capitalism would be supplanted, ultimately, by communism.[39] A social and cultural stage could not simply be 'leaped over'. Again this was an attractive pattern of thought to Ulyanov, who aimed to counter the narodnik contention that Russia had an exceptional destiny in store if only the political will was shown by the revolutionary movement.[40]

In general, Ulyanov argued that Marxism offered a satisfactory basis for the explanation of social relations. It was 'scientific'. Marx himself had frequently contrasted himself with those other socialist theorists who, founding their ideas upon moral inclination, produced only 'utopian' programmes. Ulyanov propounded this view avidly.[41] He maintained that scientific analysis, not sentimentality, should direct policy; and that the bedrock of such an analysis was provided in the writings of Marx and Engels. Ulyanov spoke of *Kapital* as incontestable truth. It was not, in his opinion, open to refutation.[42] This did not mean that no questions about society remained to be answered. Marx and Engels had laid the foundations. It was up to their followers to deploy and adapt their ideas in the light of different conditions. Each country was bound to be in some sense unique; and political circumstances, too, could not help but change over the years. Thus no specific recommendation of policy was automatically applicable to a universal pattern. Marxism had to be handled 'creatively'.[43] On the other hand there were limits, in Ulyanov's presentation, to the experimentation allowable. Even in his first published writings, he was quick to raise the cry of delinquence and even heresy whenever his interpretations of the Marxist canon were challenged.[44] 'Orthodoxy' was to be his unfailing demand.

There were many Marxists who objected to his interpretations. This was understandable. Marx was an exceptionally broad-ranging thinker; he never formulated his exuberant analysis into a single, final, uncontradictory synthesis. Engels's *Anti-Dühring* was an attempt at such a formulation. It probably made Marx's ideas appear more clear-cut than they really had been.[45] The complexity and inchoateness of Marx's Marxism were recognised even in the years shortly after his death; and these qualities are even more obvious now that we possess several important tracts which lay unpublished until the 1920s and 1930s.[46]

It has been pointed out that Marx allowed for a variety of routes of social development in the epochs prior to socialism; and that he used the concept of 'Asiatic despotism' rather than 'feudalism' to designate a number of societies in the East.[47] It has been shown too that he did not discount the practicability of a peaceful transition to socialism where political freedom existed. He speculated upon such an outcome in Britain and the USA.[48] Doubts about Lenin's version of Marxism exist in further areas. It has been noted that Marx never treated *Kapital* as completely incontrovertible; and that, moreover, it is in the nature of scientific propositions that they are capable of being tested. For all the divergences between Marx and Engels (and these are too often exaggerated, because Marx had the opportunity to criticise the *Anti-Dühring* before publication), there is nothing in Engels's literary output which suggests belief in the possibility of attaining knowledge of eternal validity.[49] Ulyanov, furthermore, played down the working class's ability to develop its own socialist ideas. Marx was not so pessimistic.[50] In addition Ulyanov had a penchant for political violence. He certainly repudiated individual repudiating terrorism as a primary tactic of overthrowing the Russian autocracy; but he nonetheless was to approve of mass terror, even before the events of 1917–18, as a positive means of eradicating all vestiges of the ancien regime once a revolutionary government was esconced in power. It is doubtful that Marx always felt so unambivalently.[51] Ulyanov's Marxism was, accordingly, a legitimate version in most respects. But not in all. This was not unusual; indeed it was typical for Marxist thinkers to be selective and to modify, alter and inadvertently distort Marx's notions in order to produce an interpretation which seemed to them to be most suitable for their time, their country and their own political preferences.

RUSSIAN MARXISM AND RUSSIAN POPULISM

This meant that debate among Russian Marxists could not be confined to the generalities of Marxism. The discussion also had to come to grips with details. Russia's particularities required consideration. Marx himself caused problems. On certain issues of immediate political relevance he gave a degree of succour to the narodniki. In 1877 he wrote to the populist Mikhailovski denying that *Das Kapital* prescribed a model of historical development for all countries. Russia, he stated, might take a different path from Western Europe's.[52] In 1881 the Russian Marxist Vera Zasulich approached him for clarification. The reply was depressing, at least for her. He repeated that the Russian peasant commune might well be usable as a vehicle for making a direct transition to socialism.[53] He encouraged the sociologist M. M. Kovalevski to pursue his researches on communal practices. In his

later years, Marx himself collected notes on Russian village traditions.[54] This was not the only encouragement he gave to narodnik
attitudes. He admired the terrorists of People's Freedom. Both he and
Engels felt that the assassination of the emperor might so destabilise
the political situation as to detonate revolution in Russia. Engels after
Marx's death continued to sanction terrorist activity.[55] He was not
initially attracted, moreover, by the Russian Marxists emerging in
the 1880s; he treated them as somewhat bookish specimens who
lacked the revolutionary instincts of the courageous narodnik
undergrounders.[56]

Mikhailovski made play with his correspondence with Marx; and
Zasulich found her own response from Marx so embarrassing that she
withheld it from public knowledge.[57] Yet Marx had not rejected her
unconditionally. His remarks were qualified. He affirmed that once
the Russian economy had embarked upon the capitalist road of
development there would be no means of preventing capitalism from
taking a hold; and he felt in any case that a commune-based revolution
in Russia would fail without aid from revolutions in industrially-
advanced countries elsewhere.[58]

Marx's self-disentanglement from the populist embrace did not
wholly dispel the admiration for him felt by many narodniki. N.
Danielson was a persistent suitor. It was he who, in 1872, had made the
first translation of Marx's *Kapital* into any foreign language; and his
ensuing correspondence with Marx and Engels is replete with attempts
to persuade them that the narodnik belief in the impracticability of
capitalist development in Russia by no means contradicted Marxian
economics. In addition Petr Tkachev, theorist of narodnik terrorism,
was also one of Europe's most distinguished Marxologists in the 1870s.
Marx's economics commended itself to the populists in general.
Tkachev's respect went further. He liked also what he took to be
Marx's politics. He argued that Marxism, properly interpreted, did not
discount the possibility of countries taking a direct path from feudalism
to socialism without an intermediate capitalist stage; he claimed that
Germany itself had had such an opportunity in the sixteenth century.
This was unacceptable to Engels. Tkachev seemed to him to place
altogether too much emphasis upon the capacity of revolutionary
leaders to change history's course. Engels and Tkachev engaged in
public dispute in 1874. It was an intriguing spectacle, not least because
it provided the first sight of Marxism's co-founder being castigated as
having drawn incorrect conclusions from his own works.[59]

But even this did not irretrievably damage the reputation of Marx and Engels among populists; Mikhailovski's anti-Marxist tirades were not universally approved. A case of continuing sympathy is found in Vladimir Ulyanov's narodnik brother Aleksandr. In writing a new draft programme for People's Freedom in 1887, he expressly described the Marxists in Russia as comrades.[60] His ideas too had a Marxist aspect. He regarded the eventual achievement of socialism as 'inevitable'. He called for the nationalisation of the land and of industrial enterprises. He conceded that the peasantry was not a uniform social class and that a petite bourgeoisie was already being formed in the countryside; he stated also that urban workers would have to be the main conveyors of the idea of revolution to the people. He did not idealise the peasant. Nor did he have a simplistic view on how to organise political activity. He perceived a need for an alliance with middle-class groupings such as the liberals in order to bring down the autocracy. He supported terrorism. But he did so not because he though it would destroy tsarism but rather with the ambition of pressuring the government to grant political freedoms. Aleksandr Ulyanov bestrode two periods in revolutionary endeavour, and he appealed for revolutionary unity on the grounds that the disagreements between Marxists and his own group of narodniki covered questions that were not 'essential' ones.[61]

Such appeals, however, fell upon increasingly deaf ears among Marxists after the late 1880s. Aleksandr Ulyanov was still too populistic for them. For all his eclecticism, he believed in the direct transition from feudalism to socialism; he also wanted to base the future society upon the unit of the village commune. And he did not abandon the narodnik view of capitalism as a retrogressive historical stage.[62]

These were attitudes justifiably taken by Russian Marxists to be quintessentially opposed to the thrust of *Das Kapital* and *The Communist Manifesto* (which had claimed a much greater portion of Marx's time and mental effort than his letter to Mikhailovski). Nevertheless other populist ideas lived on in Russian Marxism. In some aspects, their influence was stronger upon others than upon Vladimir Ulyanov himself. Agrarian policy supplies an example. Mikhailovski accused the Russian Marxists of callous disregard for the sufferings of the peasantry in the 1891 famine; they were charged with condoning any phenomenon, however oppressive to the mass of the population, so long as it helped capitalist development. The Marxist N. E. Fedoseev rejected this claim. He described his own programme as involving not the expropriation of most peasant households but rather the preservation of a large social class of independent small-holders.[63] An analogous rejection was made by P. P. Maslov in the 1890s. Maslov criticised governmental financial policy to allow agricultural prices to soar; it was his view that cheap food was essential for society's well-being and for capitalist development.[64] Some Marxists went further than Maslov. Activists such as A. I. Rykov would argue that, when the autocracy was overthrown, all gentry-held land should be handed over to the peasantry.[65] This was a traditional populist demand. Narodnik ideas were far from being moribund. In fact, by the turn of the century, there even appeared Russian Marxists (among whom the most notable was L. Nadezhdin) who called for the restoration of terrorism as a primary tactic of struggle against the monarchy.[66]

Ulyanov shrugged off such suggestions. He did not support calls for the lowering of agricultural prices; he did not, at least in the 1890s and indeed until 1905, favour the proposal to transfer all agricultural land to the peasantry. Nor did he approve of the use of assassinations as a primary revolutionary tactic. Populistic though he was in certain leanings, he was unpopulistic and antipopulistic in others.

GEORGI PLEKHANOV'S MARXISM

He was not without assistance from other Marxists in elaborating his Marxism; and the Russian who most influenced him was Georgi Valentinovich Plekhanov. In his younger days Plekhanov had been a leader of Black Repartition and been forced to flee to Switzerland in 1880. He saw that the chances of preventing capitalist development were receding fast; and he was shocked by the peasantry's abstention from wholesale revolt. He gradually accepted Marxist political positions. Controversy ensued. Russian Marxism received its baptism of fire in a struggle with agrarian socialism. This made the early Russian Marxists keen to demonstrate the validity of their self-description as Marxists; and their edginess was exacerbated by the statements made in the 1880s by Marx and Engels. Perhaps it was only in 1892, when Engels at last declared that capitalism had decisively gripped the Russian economy,[67] that the coolness towards the experiments in Russian Marxism fully vanished. Plekhanov in any case addressed himself mainly to a Russian readership. Attacking People's Freedom, he ridiculed the notion that a small band of conspirators could effect a revolution. Premature attempts by socialists to seize power in Russia had to be averted.[68] According to Plekhanov, the next stage in the country's political transformation would be not an agrarian-socialist government but a government representing the interests of the rising bourgeoisie. This would come about only through bloody revolution. Parliamentary democracy was attainable in the empire only through the forcible overthrow of the absolute monarchy.[69]

Plekhanov's *Socialism And Political Struggle*, written in 1883, put this case at length; he expanded his reasonings in 1885 with *Our Disagreements*. Both books were acclaimed in most respects by all young Russian Marxists. Ulyanov reiterated its arguments.

He also sided with Plekhanov over those matters in his books that sparked off Russian Marxism's earliest internal dispute. Plekhanov saw that it went against the grain, for most socialists, to propose the emplacement of the middle class in power; and he knew his policy to sanction the further immiseration of most, though not all, peasants. Plekhanov was unflinching. He argued that the economic trends were irreversible;[70] and Ulyanov ranged himself with him against the Fedoseevs and Maslovs who took a less indifferent attitude to the peasantry's plight.[71] In addition, Ulyanov approved of Plekhanov's insistence that capitalism was no longer a distant projection. It had arrived in Russia. *Das Kapital* contained little about the peasantry; but Plekhanov endeavoured to show that Marxian categories of analysis were applicable to the changing economic relationships in the depths of rural Russia.[72] Plekhanov used data from V. E. Postnikov and other zemstvo statisticians. He was an aggressive, sarcastic debater (and this must have been an element in his attractiveness to Ulyanov, who was to become notorious for his polemical zeal). He was especially skilled in drawing attention to the long-term economic effects of the Edict of 1861; there was nobody who put the view more vividly that the government's reforms were a watershed in capitalist development. His two early books were a crucial contribution to the Russian Marxist doctrine that capitalism was on the verge of pervading all economic relations in town and countryside.

Georgi Plekhanov was not alone in his thinking. Other ex-narodniki joined him in 1883 to propose the adoption of a Marxist programme for Russian socialists. Among them were Pavel Akselrod, Vera Zasulich and Lev Deich. Plekhanov and his associates called themselves the Emancipation Of Labour Group.

They saw urgent tasks to perform; they did not intend to wait upon events.[73] European history contained many examples of slow, steady processes of change interrupted by unexpected explosions of discontent. The Paris Commune had been precisely such a phenomenon. In 1871 the workers of the French capital threw up the barricades and installed their own administration. The Commune lasted only weeks, being suppressed by troops dispatched from Versailles. But it lived on in the memory of Europe's revolutionaries. The Emancipation Of Labour Group wished to be in a position to take full advantage of any similar situation which might arise in Russia. Plekhanov drew attention to *The Communist Manifesto*; he pointed out that Germany, at the time of its publication in 1848, had been at a level of economic and political development comparable with Russia's in the 1880s. What had been sauce for the Prussian goose was sauce for the Russian gander. The Emanicipation Of Labour Group perceived no reason why they should not eventually be able to form a mass political party like the German Social-Democratic Party. By the mid-1890s, the German social-democrats had won the loyalty of millions of their nation's workers; they were sending more and more representatives to the Reichstag. The German Social-Democratic Party was Marxist in ideology and was the main force inside the Second International (which united Europe's socialist movement). Plekhanov's perspective was optimistic. Even Russian economic backwardness was to be regarded as an asset: it would mean that socialist ideas could be disseminated among Russia's working class at an earlier stage in the country's economic transformation than had been possible in Britain, France or Germany.[74]

Such ideas were endorsed by Ulyanov and the young generation of Marxists. They admired a further argument. This was that industrial workers were the 'vanguard' of the social forces opposed to the Russian monarchy. They were to lead the 'democratic revolution'. They would need allies, since the proletariat still constituted a minority of the population. They would have to tug the middle class, the peasantry, the non-Orthodox religious groups and the non-Russian nationalities into a coalition. Only the working class, however, had the potential to act as an unambiguously revolutionary body. All the other classes and groups were likely to make compromises with tsarism. Plekhanov's colleague Akselrod therefore urged that industrial workers should maintain 'hegemony' over the anti-monarchical movement in Russia.[75]

The Group said little about the immediate steps to be taken. Plekhanov called upon the socialist elements of the intelligentsia to guide the workers towards Marxism; and, again, Ulyanov was to warm to Plekhanov's belief in the intellectual's capacity to attain exact knowledge of society – a belief that was not universally accepted by Marxists inside and outside Russia.[76] But Plekhanov offered no counsel about the organisational forms of the political party which would eventually be founded. Nor did he describe the means to be employed to overthrow the monarchy. He assumed generally that mass action would be needed; he criticised People's Freedom for suggesting that assassination campaigns should be the primary tactic.[77] The Emancipation Of Labour Group thought that the workers, as the vanguard of the anti-monarchical forces, would be in a position to demand comprehensive reforms from the succeeding middle-class government. The Russian Marxist programme should call for a system of parliamentary elections based upon universal, secret-ballot suffrage. Freedoms of conscience, expression, organisation and assembly should be declared. The professional army should be abolished; there should be a 'general arming of the people'. Plekhanov wanted legislation protecting the rights of factory workers at the place of employment; he also desired to lift the restrictions upon the peasantry's right to leave the village commune at will. He sought the abolition of redemption payments.[78] His Group felt that such a programme would provide the political and economic framework necessary for the maturation of Russian capitalism. It would also equip socialists with the chance to propagate their ideas and construct a mass political party.

Plekhanov claimed to have sketched a programme in line with the contours of European Marxism as it was widely interpreted in the years after Marx's death. For the most part, his claim was just. But there remained elements that did not fit the pattern.

This was discernible in his refusal to make an absolute rejection of assassinations as a method of fighting the autocracy. He opposed terrorism as a primary means of bringing down the regime, yet still regarded it as an acceptable auxiliary tactic.[79] Such a viewpoint was not in keeping with the outlook of Karl Kautsky and other theorists of the German Social-Democratic Party in the 1890s (even though Marx himself had approved of an assassination campaign in Russia).[80] There were further contrasts. Plekhanov certainly expected the overthrow of the autocracy to be followed by a period of bourgeois government. This was entirely unexceptionable doctrine. But his programme also demanded a plenitude of rights for workers and peasants; he even expected the bourgeois government to give financial aid to their self-organised co-operatives.[81] His capitalism was not going to be of an untrammelled variety. His untypicality does not end here. It is equally visible in his treatment of the subsequent measures for the eventual dismemberment of capitalism itself. *Our Disagreements* emphasised the need for a 'working-class dictatorship'.[82] This accorded with Marx's call for 'the dictatorship of the proletariat'. Plekhanov was somewhat more categorical than Marx; for Marx had not entirely discounted the possibility of a peaceful transition to socialism. In any case, phrases like 'dictatorship' were already an embarrassment to the German Social-Democratic Party in the 1890s. Instead, Kautsky tended to emphasise the benefits of universal suffrage.[83] Ulyanov was on Plekhanov's side. The version of Marxism produced by Plekhanov seemed to his young follower to be both entirely acceptable in doctrine and wonderfully suited to the political tasks facing Russian Marxists in the years ahead.[84]

ACTIVISM IN SAMARA

It took time for the Marxist circles in the Russian empire to acquire their organisational identity. Plekhanov arranged to have his pamphlets smuggled back from Switzerland. In 1886 he made contact with Marxist activists in St. Petersburg led by the Bulgarian D. I. Blagoev. But Blagoev was quickly arrested, and Plekhanov's role as a practical leader became negligible for the rest of the decade.[85] Nevertheless his own intellectual odyssey towards Marxism was being repeated by many revolutionaries. Poles and Jews were in the forefront. Their groups, located in the empire's western regions, led the way in forming disciplined, cohesive underground local organisations. Indeed the Bund, as the Jewish Marxist party was called, shortly enrolled thousands of workers.[86] But revolutionaries of Russian origin also were bestirring themselves in the same direction: towards Marxism.

Among them, in Samara, were Vladimir Ulyanov and A. P. Sklyarenko. The Volga city of Samara was not as politically volatile as Kazan; but, from the standpoint of the revolutionaries, it compensated for its quiescence by its intellectually more bracing discussions. Local journals in the 1890s contained articles by writers of national renown.[87] Evening debates were a feature of the city's clandestine political activity. Sklyarenko's group was invited to contribute to narodnik meetings; and these invitations were accepted. They offered the chance to win further recruits to Marxism. Nobody has pinpointed when Sklyarenko's organisation made its own crossing over to Russian Marxist doctrines. Vladimir Ulyanov was reportedly even more enthusiastic about the new ideas than Sklyarenko and to have been the force behind the group's transformation. He proved his mettle in debate with leading terrorists who visited Samara in search of supporters. M. V. Sabunaev made such a trip in December 1889. He was persisting in his endeavour to re-establish a network of People's Freedom groups; and apparently he argued, like Aleksandr Ulyanov, that revolutionaries of different persuasions should not exaggerate their differences. Accounts of the meeting in Samara suggest that Ulyanov revealed himself as a devastating critic of Sabunaev's strategy.[88] He seems to have become his group's most trenchant polemicist. When P. I. Rossinevich repeated Sabunaev's attempt in March 1891, it was again Ulyanov who took up the intellectual cudgels.[89]

Yet it remains a matter of speculation whether he had opted decisively for a Plekhanovite position in this period. Autobiographical fragments are again scarce. No activist with even the barest sense of self-preservation would jot down such details at the time; but later in life Ulyanov was to date his revolutionary career as having started in 1892–93.[90] It is possible that this signified the time of his conversion. Could it be that in 1890 and 1891 he detected the inadequacies in agrarian-socialist views without yet embracing a Russian Marxist perspective? Such a condition was not unusual in those years. It would certainly have allowed him to take issue with the Sabunaevs and the Rossineviches. But it would not have forced him to avoid contact with the terrorists; indeed he was happy to have the chance to discuss politics with veterans of People's Freedom exiled to Samara. He retained the agrarian-socialist interest in the mechanics of the 'seizure of power'.[91] Yet Ulyanov, as M. P. Golubeva's memoirs indicate, refused to put high hopes in the peasantry: 'He could in no way understand on what kind of "people" we expected to base ourselves, and he began to explain at length that the people was not some single and undifferentiated entity, that the people was constituted by classes with differing interests.'[92] These were formative years in Ulyanov's career. It is frustrating that the published sources are so sparse.

Nonetheless Ulyanov's life was not yet wholly absorbed in political activism. Though modest in size, his mother's estate at Alakaevka required someone to run it; it was natural for her to turn to her oldest surviving son. His encounter with economic management was brief. He was reticent about the reasons, except for an opaque later remark that 'relations with the peasantry became abnormal'.[93] It would be instructive to know more about the episode. Ulyanov was having his

first working contact with non-privileged sections of the rural population; and we may wonder whether the experience simply confirmed his
convictions about them or altered them in some way. Once more the
sources fail us.

Ulyanov made no other attempt at the practical application of his
economics until becoming leader of the Soviet government; hencefor-
ward his knowledge of the world of toil was to come through books and
from activists with first-hand acquaintance with economic affairs in the
village and town. He had not abandoned hopes of a lawyer's career.
His mother's pleas to the authorities were rewarded on 17 May 1890
with official notification that he could register himself as an external
student attached to the university of his choice. The fates were with
him. The police department in Samara, though aware of his friendship
with 'persons of doubtful reliability', were unable to supply concrete
proofs of 'anti-state' behaviour.[94] He selected Petersburg as his
university city. He spent three months there on a study-trip, leaving
Samara in August 1890. On his return, in October, he undertook the
reading which would enable him to sit the final examinations in spring
and autumn 1891. He acquired digs in St. Petersburg in March. He had
no involvement in political activity (although he used the chance to
look up his brother Aleksandr's friends and to enquire about the last
months of his life). It was not a happy sojourn. Yet another tragedy
afflicted the Ulyanov family. Vladimir's favourite sister Olga, herself a
student in St. Petersburg, caught typhoid and died on 8 May 1891.
Hers was the third funeral that it fell to twenty-one years old Vladimir
Ulyanov to organise.[95] But he resumed his studies with his already
proven powers of detachment and resilience; and, when the exam
results were published in November 1891, he received the Russian
equivalent of a first-class honours degree.[96]

In January 1892 he started work as a temporary assistant barrister in
the offices of A. N. Khardin, a Samara lawyer who was also his chess
partner. He seems to have been an effective defence counsel. In July he
obtained papers for permanent employment; he showed outward signs
of being a young man who, after a flirtation with revolutionism, had
settled down to mundane respectability. A discreet watch was kept on
him by the police, but nothing compromising could be ascertained. In
fact his political commitment was as strong as ever. The descriptions of
governmental abuses given in Anton Chekhov's short stories set off a
charge of emotion in him: 'I felt quite literally sick; I couldn't stay in
my own room, I got up and went outside.'[97]

Throughout 1892 the Sklyarenko–Ulyanov group continued their meetings. They began to expand their membership, welcoming newcomers like I. K. Lalayants. Their common thirst for study was prodigious. They combed their way through *Kapital* and *Anti-Dühring*; they were also attracted by Engels's *Condition of the Working Class in England*. They maintained an interest in works by non-Marxist writers. It is likely that Ulyanov was familiar with the writings of Ricardo, Guizot and Ashley. The group also kept abreast of events in the German Social-Democratic Party. Kautsky's *Die Neue Zeit* sometimes arrived in Samara, and Ulyanov would pounce on copies eagerly. Pamphlets by Plekhanov too would occasionally reach him.[98] The labour of self-instruction proceeded. And, as confidence increased, the Samara activists sought to do something of their own to strengthen the plausibility of Russian Marxism in general. Plekhanov's economics were a sketch of trends. Ulyanov and Sklyarenko agreed on the need to conduct more detailed work on agrarian statistics. They commenced research on the contemporary peasant economy; and this led Ulyanov not only to investigate zemstvo statistical handbooks but also to grasp every opportunity to talk directly with peasants. His brother-in-law Mark Elizarov was a peasant's son with a clerical job in Samara. Elizarov introduced him to rural inhabitants. So too did A. A. Preobrazhenski.[99] Ulyanov's own work as a lawyer, which not infrequently involved the defence of individual peasants, gave him further insights into the operation of the village commune.[100] He began to write articles. Alakaevka provided an enclave of calm for his studies. Determined to organise his work effectively, he marked out an area in the garden to serve as his office; the family called it Volodya's Corner.[101]

Reportedly, by the end of 1892, he had drafted three articles intended to expose weaknesses in Vorontsov's economic standpoint. There is a story too that Ulyanov and Mikhailovski met face to face in debate in the summer of that year, and that Mikhailovski came off worsted. The tale is probably fictitious.[102] But there is no denying that Ulyanov had by now emerged as a competent exponent of Marxism. He was firm in conviction, savage in discussion. It remained for him to prove that he was not only a promising economist but also a practical political leader.

3 Arrivals

ST. PETERSBURG

Industrialisation poses problems everywhere it is attempted; and not the least of them is the question about the political place of the workers. Public debate raged through the nineteenth century in Britain. It commenced later in Russia, but by the 1880s it was in full spate. Official tsarist attitudes were authoritarian. But they possessed an admixture of paternalism; the government hoped that the working class, like the peasantry, would continue to revere the emperor as 'the little father'. The revolutionaries were striving to reverse this subordinate status. The narodniki, though conceiving of the workers as peasants temporarily removed from the land, increasingly treated the working class as the prime force to pull down the autocracy. Marxists put the working class even higher in their scheme of things; the proletariat was expected by them to refashion the whole of society in its own image. All cities in Russia witnessed the struggle for the workers' loyalty. But naturally the competition was at its most ferocious in Petersburg: not only was it the seat of government; it also contained a large number of vast factory complexes. The profit motive had triumphed over notions of town-planning, and the result was an interspersing of gaunt industrial blocks with palaces and administrative buildings. There was little residential segregation on a class basis. The discrepancy between the lifestyles of the upper orders and the oppressed manual labourers was therefore superabundantly visible. It was a matter that the authorities ignored at their peril.

Ulyanov decided to pull up his Volga roots and move there. His mother, now in her late fifties, was well capable of tending to her affairs independently. He had yet to make acquaintance with his first factory worker. His theories were still untested by practical observation of industrial urban life, and he desired to rectify the situation. He arrived in the capital on 31 August 1893 and quickly started work in the lawyer's offices of M. F. Volkenshtein.[1]

Political considerations held his thoughts. On his way from Samara he had stopped off in Nizhni Novgorod and contacted a Marxist circle led by P. N. Skvortsov and S. I. Mickiewicz. Skvortsov told him how and where to link up with Marxists in the metropolis. Ulyanov also made a stop-over in the town of Vladimir in order to meet N. E. Fedoseev; but Fedoseev was in prison and the meeting did not take place.[2] Ulyanov's initiative did not secure him an automatic welcome in St. Petersburg. He had been put in touch with the group founded in 1892 by S. I. Radchenko. Its members opposed the use of terror in any form as a means of bringing down the autocracy; and they apparently learnt that Ulyanov, like Plekhanov, was not absolutely hostile to assassinations. They interviewed him carefully. No doubt he reassured them that he did not share the narodnik-terrorists' belief in terror as the primary immediate tactic. They allowed him to join.[3] He must have convinced them that he no longer supported People's Freedom; otherwise it is inexplicable why he did not try to enter the organisation of populist terrorists already in existence in the capital. Ulyanov nonetheless took some months to make his influence felt upon the Petersburg Marxists. Radchenko's priority was to spread propaganda in the workers' educational circles. Propagandists were scarce. Yet it was not until autumn 1894, fully a year after the move from Samara, that Ulyanov became exercised by pedagogical activity.[4] Nor did Ulyanov participate in the group's negotiations with other workers' organisations in the winter 1893–94. The 'organisation man' of future years was not yet known for his administrative talents.

Ulyanov's initial pre-occupation, in fact, was with his books. He was completing his self-education as an economist. He analysed the latest agrarian statistics. He returned to the first two volumes of *Das Kapital*, correcting mistakes in the Russian translation as he went.[5]

He also encouraged Radchenko's group to hold its own discussion sessions. This gave him the chance to shine. In October 1893 G. B. Krasin delivered a paper on Russian economic trends; but it was Ulyanov who showed himself to be the more cogent critic of agrarian socialism.[6] Pursuing his investigations, he completed an article entitled *New Economic Directions in Peasant Life*. The general content differed little from Plekhanov's earlier material. A particular point was nonetheless noteworthy. Ulyanov re-organised zemstvo statistical data so as to show that it was the peasant households with the greater acreages which were achieving the higher agricultural productivity.[7] This was a technical refinement beyond Plekhanov's aspirations. A second point of interest is discoverable in another article written by Ulyanov in 1893, *Concerning the So-Called Question of Markets*. In it he argued that narodnik writings were pre-occupied by discussions on consumer goods and had ignored the goods used in further stages of production. This was in his view a crucial neglect. He maintained, against the narodniki, that the growth rate in output of producer's goods was always greater than the rate for goods made for consumers; and that the market for capitalist development did not depend upon the existence of a massive affluent peasantry.[8] Ulyanov's contribution was already a significant extension of Plekhanov's original claims.

It was not unusual for Marxists to take their intellectual self-preparation so seriously;[9] and nobody in Radchenko's group said that Ulyanov was neglecting his duty. Disputes about socialist theory gained in importance in the Petersburg labour movement in the mid-nineties. Agrarian socialists and Marxists clashed. Workers were asked to choose between the two rival views on the future. They did not rush to choose.

Among the working class there lingered ambivalent feelings about intellectuals. In 1889, three workers had established a Central Workers' Circle to provide popular educational facilities. Student-intellectuals were invited as teachers under the workers' control. Strikes broke out in the Thornton textile factory in the winter of 1890–91. The Circle created a Central Workers' Fund to help strikers financially and to print leaflets. A trade union was in the making. Both agrarian socialists and Marxists contributed teachers for the Circle's activities. Arrests in 1891 and 1892 failed to catch all the Circle's activists, and Radchenko persisted with his attempt to make it a stronghold for Marxism.[10] Success was not easily obtained. Radchenko believed in the primary role to be played by intellectuals in the fight for socialism; and his organisational code, with its heavy emphasis upon secrecy, impeded even the operation of the education circles. On the other hand, the workers as students were unattracted by narodnik–terrorist talk of immediate insurrection. Their foremost demand was for cultural and political tuition. This gave the Marxists a distinct advantage over People's Freedom; and the course of training offered by Radchenko's group gained dozens of recruits in 1893 and 1894.[11] Ulyanov too involved himself, offering himself as tutor to a workers' circle in autumn 1894.[12]

It was around this time, however, that Marxists elsewhere in the empire began to reform their tactics. Courses tended to isolate the worker-students from the rest of their work-mates. The circles had little contact with factory life. Jewish and Polish activists pressed the need to conduct 'agitation' among ordinary workers. This would involve speeches and pamphlets on particular issues. Activists should campaign against low pay, unsafe machinery and management abuses; they should organise strikes. A handbook, *On Agitation*, was printed in Vilno to summarise the tactics. The assumption was that strikes would attract an attempt at repression by the government and therefore would steadily draw the working class into political opposition to the regime. *On Agitation* was carried to St. Petersburg in September 1894 by Yuli Osipovich Martov (who was shortly to become a close collaborator of Ulyanov's); and he brought news of the success of the tactics in western regions of the empire.[13] Radchenko's group baulked at first, not wanting to be deflected from their instructional programme. But opinion had swung round in favour by the end of the year. The group awaited its opportunity. And when strikes occurred in a number of armaments works in January 1895 it was Ulyanov who composed the proclamatory leaflets.[14]

He combined this work with maintained interest in economics. In spring and summer 1894, writing furiously, he finished a three-part manuscript called *What Are 'the Friends of the People'?* It filled out the analysis offered in his previous work. It was also his first attempt to attack the interpretation of Marx's ideas by the narodnik Mikhailovski; Ulyanov very reasonably stressed Marx's affirmation that Russia's chance of experiencing a unique social transformation would vanish once capitalism had started to develop.[15] This development, Ulyanov declared, had now commenced. He had his manuscript reproduced in a few dozen copies on a duplicating apparatus. In August he was informed of a more sophisticated machine available in Vladimir province, and he took a trip out from St. Petersburg to arrange for the production of a further hundred copies.[16] This time-consuming practicality galled him when he contemplated the ease with which certain other exponents of Marxian economics in the capital managed to publicise their views. Petr Bernardovich Struve, a young graduate, had already achieved fame through his contributions to open debates at the Free Economic Society. In September 1894 Struve's book *Critical Remarks* sneaked past the censorship and was published legally. Through their common friend Aleksandr Potresov, Ulyanov met up with Struve around New Year 1895. Ulyanov wanted help with publication of his economic studies. An agreement was struck to produce a symposium of articles. At the last moment, in April 1895, the censor intervened and nearly all the copies were burned before they could be sold.[17]

ULYANOV, STRUVE AND PLEKHANOV

Vladimir Ulyanov's relations with Petr Struve were an alliance of convenience. It catches the eye that Ulyanov, who in the 1900s was often portrayed as the incarnation of implacable irreconcilability, did not appear in this light to his early comrades in St. Petersburg. Many indeed thought him too ready to be reconciled. What business, they asked, had a Marxist revolutionary to talk with those self-proclaimed followers of Marx like Struve who seemed to have an aversion to the very goal of socialist revolution?[18]

The answer clarifies the singular stance in matters of theory assumed at the time by Ulyanov. His interest in Struve was not limited to publishing opportunities. It was also political. Struve was at the centre of a group of writers. His associates M. I. Tugan-Baranovski, S. N. Bulgakov and N. A. Berdyaev were already emitting glimmerings of the contributions they would each make to Russian public life. They were very independent thinkers; they felt no compulsion, unlike many other Marxists like Ulyanov, to anchor all their statements to the writings of Marx and Engels. They were a well-heeled bunch. With the single exception of Plekhanov, they were the best-known Marxists in the Russian empire in the 1890s. Word of their emergence reached the Emancipation Of Labour Group in Geneva. Initially Plekhanov hoped to combine with them in publishing ventures. Struve, Tugan-Baranovski and Bulgakov were sophisticated economists and had deployed their learning against Vorontsov. Tugan's material was most remarkable. Working on developmental economic theory, he invented a series of mathematical schemata to represent the interrelationship of capital and labour in an industrialising society. Like Ulyanov, he argued that capitalism could grow largely through the production of industrial machinery and other producer's goods and would not have to depend predominantly upon the creation of a mass consumerist market. Capitalism would not be inhibited by the pauperisation of the majority of the peasantry. Neither Struve nor Tugan were at all worried that the country's material progress would be achieved at enormous social expense.[19]

These arguments were an essential reason for Ulyanov's approaches to Struve's group; he liked their unflinching acceptance of what they believed to be the logical outcome of capitalist development. The issue was the principal item of debate until the late 1890s. Ulyanov disagreed about details in their depiction of the pattern of capitalism's growth;[20] but he evidently derived intellectual benefit and perhaps also a degree of psychological support from his discussions with Struve, Tugan and Bulgakov.

The conditionality of Ulyanov's alliance, however, was manifest from the start. Struve agreed that the working class was the most dependable instrument for removing the monarchy; and he yielded to no one in his belief in Russia's need for political freedom. But he made no unambiguous recommendation of violent methods to that end. This reluctance pervaded his strategy. He refrained, too, from condoning the use of force to advance socialism's cause in the more distant period when the autocracy had been dismantled. He preferred evolution to revolution. He expected capitalism to give way to socialism not through bloody upheaval but as the result of peaceful, transitional measures. Struve believed in the virtues of reform. But how could a 'bourgeois state' be made to inaugurate a programme for the death of capitalism? Struve anticipated the question. In *Critical Remarks* he denied that the state always needs must be the guardian of the interests of the propertied classes;[21] he implied that its powers were autonomous enough to allow it to carry through radical reforms regardless of opposition by industrialists. In general, moreover, Struve made no direct criticism of capitalism itself. He noted Marx's suggestion that a socialist transformation of society would begin to be politically feasible only when the capitalist economy faced crisis and ruin. Struve opposed this approach. For him it was intolerable that socialists should aim to come to power at a time of economic disruption. He emphasised capitalism's progressive role. *Critical Remarks* was a song of praise for its capacity to raise levels of production, create conditions of plenty, introduce educational facilities and modernise the country's culture.[22]

Plekhanov was disconcerted. *Critical Remarks* was already moving towards a repudiation of the *Communist Manifesto*. This movement was to continue. In the late 1890s Struve and Tugan-Baranovski would argue that many fundamental ideas of Marx and Engels were wrong. Struve would reject Marx's labour theory of value as being simplistic; Tugan would assert that recent empirical data undermined the credibility of Marx's predictions about the rate of return of investment under capitalism.[23] Plekhanov was to look on them as mere 'Legal Marxists'. He was to treat them as outriders for a pan-European 'revisionist' movement threatening to disfigure Marxism by making it indistinguishable from liberalism. Indeed Struve was to become a leading inspiration for the Russian liberal party, the Constitutional Democrats.[24]

Yet Plekhanov desisted from waging war upon Struve and company in 1894. He even agreed, yielding to Potresov's persuasion, to contribute articles to collections organised by Struve. His objections remained in force. He showed no displeasure when he heard of attacks upon Struve by other Marxists in Russia. Ulyanov was the most notable aggressor. In mid-1894 he already referred to Struve as 'mister': a term of conscious literary abuse among Marxists.[25] Ulyanov flailed out at Struve's sins of omission, most notably his failure to state the need for 'class struggle'.[26] He depicted Struve as a prophet of the politics of civil peace. Ulyanov anticipated a faster and more violent transition to socialism. Taking Struve to task, he stressed the revolutionary perspective of Marx's writings. Struve was also alleged to have underestimated the extent of industrial growth already achieved in Russia. Ulyanov highlighted the 'bourgeois direction' of his country's economy. 'Did it not,' he asked, 'express itself completely clearly even in the 1860s? Did it not dominate too in the entire course of the 1870s?'[27] He knew, of course, that industrialisation still had a long way to go. Russia still lagged behind Britain, Germany and the USA. Yet Ulyanov called attention to the fact that, at the time of the writing of the *Das Kapital*, even England (which was the most industrially-advanced nation in Europe) had a factory labour force which constituted a mere twelfth of its population.[28] Revolutionaries in Russia could take heart from this. Ulyanov refused to accept that Marxists should confine their political appeals to factory employees. He looked further afield; his stirring contention was that industrial workers were 'merely the upper layers of the immense mass of the peasantry which already lives through the selling of its labour power more than by its own economy'.[29]

Struve found Ulyanov's description of Russian reality hopelessly hyperbolical. The two spent many evenings in conversations; it was Struve's hope that, if Ulyanov succeeded in obtaining an exit visa, Switzerland would demonstrate to him what a true 'bourgeois order' looked like.[30] Arguments out of books were clearly incapable of achieving this. But Ulyanov's confidence was boosted not only by the discovery that he was Struve's equal in his knowledge of Marxian texts but also by his feeling that he would be welcome as an ally by the Russian Marxist he most admired, Plekhanov.

His presentiments were correct. And yet it behoves us to note that the views of Ulyanov and Plekhanov were not identical even in the 1890s. Plekhanov did not assert that capitalism 'dominated' the Russian economy; he merely said that 'it can become and is becoming' the dominant force.[31] Nor did he enthuse about talk of the revolutionary potentiality of the peasantry. Since leaving Black Repartition, Plekhanov had come to regard the peasants as being too easily drawn towards support for the political status quo. He also disliked Ulyanov's insulting remarks about middle-class liberals. It was Plekhanov's contention that Marxists should exhibit all possible tact in order to attract the liberals into an all-out war against the autocracy.[32] Already, too, Plekhanov objected to Ulyanov's depiction of Russian feudalism. Ulyanov claimed that Russia's feudal traditions had been motivated by essentially the same conglomeration of social forces as in the West. For Plekhanov, this ignored the state's primary role in entrenching feudalism in Russia in centuries past. He judged that Russian feudalism held important features in common with Asiatic despotisms.[33] These differences of opinion would gather in significance in the years ahead. But, for the moment, the two men happily put them aside and sought the fulfilment of their common immediate aims. Together, they would confront agrarian socialism; and they would try to minimise the advances made by 'revisionist' Marxism.

THE EMERGING LEADER

Vladimir Ulyanov at the age of twenty five was recognised by his comrades as 'a person of great calibre'.[34] And he knew his own worth. But he was not vain; and others noted that this gave him the self-assurance to listen to fellow activists rather than merely impose his opinions upon them.[35] He was mature beyond his years. The impression was enhanced by his physical appearance: he was losing hair on the dome of his cranium and bore a close resemblance to his deceased father. He was nicknamed Old Man by workers in his education circle (who also informed him that his loss of hair came from reading too many books).[36] He retained a severe demeanour. He was a demanding teacher, expecting his charges to tackle *Das Kapital* almost as soon as they could read and write.[37] Study and writing had confirmed his intuition that he had found his vocation as a full-time revolutionary. It was an intensely serious calling for him, and never in the years ahead would he allow the slightest frivolity get in the way of his pursuit of political goals. But fun was not alien to him. Chess, hunting, walking and reading novels and philosophy were his pleasures (although Potresov claimed that Ulyanov was the only man in the world who

derived positive enjoyment from refusing a second beer).[38] Nevertheless everything took a subordinate place to politics. Revolution was
Ulyanov's career and his dream.

His mother's monthly allowances were crucial.[39] The job with
Volkenshtein's was a cover; Ulyanov hoped it would shrug off the
police's attentions. He limited himself to some minimal work as a
part-time consultant and gave up court appearances as a barrister.[40]
Life was comfortable. Summer holidays in summer 1894 were spent
with cousins in Moscow province. This was a further sign of the gap of
privilege separating him from the industrial workers (who, if they
visited the countryside at all, did so to help their families with the
harvest). His only personal trouble was his health. In March 1895 he
was stricken by pneumonia. Fortunately it was a mild bout and his
mother, hurrying to Petersburg, nursed him over the worst of it.[41]

It was in the capital that Ulyanov met Nadezhda Konstantinovna
Krupskaya. She was a Marxist activist belonging to the political milieu
joined by Ulyanov, and was present at those early sessions where he
attracted respect as an economist. She never forgot her first impression. It was aural: Ulyanov's sarcastic laughter. Krupskaya detected
something 'wicked and dry' in it.[42] She was attracted to him, and he to
her. In 1894 he was her usual escort home after political meetings.
Contrary to the jibes later made at her expense, Nadezhda Konstantinovna was not a bad-looking girl; but she suffered from a worsening
thyroid complaint which, in middle age, was to bulge out her eyes.
Ulyanov himself was physically agreeable in the eyes of very many
women. The relationship started slowly. It seems to have been
conducted entirely within the ambit of contemporary proprieties.[43]
Neither he nor she spoke much about the days of their courtship. But
Ulyanov was obviously the dominant partner. He was clearly going to
make a reputation for himself in politics, and he confided to her that he
was incapable of becoming emotionally entangled with anyone not
sharing his general beliefs.[44] Nadezhda was not intimidated by him.
She is often presented to us as 'the constant, trusty friend' of Ulyanov,
as if she were a canine companion rather than a spouse.[45] But she did
not always do his bidding. And there were certain areas, such as
educational theory (and perhaps educational practice too), where she
probably thought herself his better.[46] Ulyanov was contented. His first
steady girlfriend was someone who could hold her own in political
debate and whose commitment to enduring the travails of a revolutionary's existence was no smaller than his own.

Ulyanov's liking for Nadya, as he called her, did not prevent him from being away from her for several months. For years he had desired to see foreign countries. As early as 1888, after his expulsion from Kazan University, he had applied for permission to pursue his undergraduate studies abroad. In March 1895, finally, his request was granted.[47] He remained under surveillance after his move from Samara but, whether through an insufficiency of policing resources or because Ulyanov's time had been taken up more by literary work than by underground activism, he evaded detection.

His real aim was to contact Plekhanov's Emancipation Of Labour Group in Geneva. He had a plausible alibi. It was conventional for persons of his social station to travel round the rest of Europe on trips devoted to education or amusement. Paris, Berlin and Florence bustled with affluent Russian visitors. Ulyanov's appetite for tourism did not diminish with the years. There was hardly a cathedral town of northern France or a Swiss mountain resort not explored by him on his travels. On 25 April 1895 he took a train from the Russian capital with a ticket for Switzerland.[48] Plekhanov, despite their differences over many issues, was Ulyanov's idol; nobody alive, except Frederick Engels (who died that August), evoked commensurate respect from him. He journeyed to pay homage. Awe mingled with affection; Ulyanov would later recollect that he had had the feeling of 'being in love' with Plekhanov.[49] Such a metaphor is extreme, especially for a man of Ulyanov's reticence. It is therefore all the more suggestive of the profound importance attached by Ulyanov to the world of ideas. It is interesting in a further sense as well. Throughout his career he displayed vigour, even daring, in his intellectual development; but he felt insecure in his convictions unless he could corroborate them with citations from the works of his heroes. In the 1890s he made no pretension to sit upon the high pedestal occupied in his imagination by Georgi Plekhanov. Only Marx and Engels sat even higher.

Indeed Ulyanov's intellectual style looked like an exaggeration of Plekhanov's own. True, he could still feel nervous in face-to-face disputes. In Moscow, at a political gathering, he delivered a caustic denunciation of Vorontsov's economics. At the end of the meeting he was told that Vorontsov had been in the audience. Confusion overwhelmed him. He raced from the room.[50]

And yet he was unaffected by such sensitivities when it came to debates in print; his literary mode sounded its characteristically aggressive notes at the outset of his career.[51] Indulgence to opponents appeared to him as mere quietism. As yet he identified populism as the main polemical enemy; his comments on Struve though combative,

still lacked the unbridled offensiveness of his ridiculing of the
narodniki. He was unashamed about his pugnaciousness. Why mollify
criticisms when you know you are right? Why not emasculate the
arguments of your antagonists if this can persuade others to accept
your own? Ulyanov was convinced, in every fibre of his body, that
Marxism supplied the only mode of social investigation which could
produce 'correct' answers to analytical and practical problems; he
spoke of it as if it were a faith and not open to re-examination and
possible refutation. It was also part and parcel of his mental make-up
to suggest that, however complicated a political situation might
appear, there was always only a single policy adoptable by logically-
thinking revolutionaries. Correctness, in his view, was the twin sibling
of consistency; and no sharper charge did he level at his opponents
than that they wore their opinions lightly. In instincts, mannerisms and
technique it is remarkable how closely Ulyanov the rising theorist and
activist resembles Lenin the experienced premier of the Soviet
government.

TO SWITZERLAND AND BACK

And so to Switzerland. The mission entrusted to him in St. Petersburg
was to put communications between Geneva and Russia on a more
regular basis. He was to promise financial assistance, drawn from local
membership dues, to the émigrés. It was hoped that a Russian Marxist
newspaper might be set up in Geneva. A Moscow activist, E. I. Sponti,
was in Switzerland at the same time and with similar intentions. At last
the disparate groups were coming together to lay the ground-work for
a political party. On 2 May 1895 Ulyanov arrived in Lausanne and
obtained Plekhanov's address. He spent the month in conversations
with Plekhanov and Akselrod. He stayed for a week with Akselrod's
family in the mountainous countryside outside Zurich. Both his elders
were favourably impressed by Ulyanov. He seemed precisely the type
of undergrounder needed by the movement: accomplished in socialist
theory and adept at administrative business. They compared him
favourably with Sponti, who appeared to retain an excess of narodnik
insurrectionary impatience (and who, unlike Ulyanov, had the temerity
to carp at the Geneva group for not writing material accessible for
ordinary workers). Plekhanov, Akselrod and Ulyanov found it easy to
come to terms with each other. A plan was drawn up. Plekhanov and

Akselrod would act as newspaper editors in Western Europe while Ulyanov headed a co-editorial committee in St. Petersburg.[52]

Ulyanov spent the remainder of that summer in excursions around continental Europe. He was blithely unaware that the police in St. Petersburg had just broken his cover and reported that he stood 'at the head of a circle involved with revolutionary propaganda among workers'. The purpose of his trip abroad was ascertained.[53] Ulyanov continued with his tour: in June 1895 he moved to Paris and visited Marx's son-in-law Paul Lafargue; in July and August he transferred to Berlin, working daily in the Prussian State Library. Plekhanov secured him an interview with German Social-Democratic Party leader Wilhelm Liebknecht.[54]

He returned to Russia on 7 September.[55] Marxists in St. Petersburg were by then optimistic about starting a mass working-class movement. Factory strikes were in the offing. Yuli Martov campaigned for the unification of all clandestine groups in the capital. Radchenko's and Martov's organisations combined activity. The Bureau selected to direct the new grouping included V. I. Ulyanov, Y. O. Martov and G. M. Krzhizhanovski. The priority was to produce a series of agitational leaflets and get them scattered around as many plants and works as possible.[56] Despite a search at the border, Ulyanov had succeeded in smuggling home half a suitcase of literature from Switzerland. This was still far from enough. The Petersburgers negotiated with adherents of People's Freedom in hiding in Finland and in possession of typographical facilities. Apart from Martov, Ulyanov was the only fluent writer in the group; and the switch of plans towards leaflet-printing augmented his importance. When textile-workers went on strike in November, he wrote a rousing leaflet addressed *To the Working Men and Women of the Thornton Factory*. He helped, too, to produce a pamphlet entitled *Russian Factory Legislation*. This was not work he did by shutting himself away in his rooms. The effectiveness of a leaflet or pamphlet depended upon the writer's acquaintance with specific conditions in the factories where copies were to be distributed. Ulyanov compiled his information directly from the workers themselves. He visited working-class streets to ascertain the progress of strikes in the Thornton textile factory and the Laferme tobacco factory. For the first time he was involved in day-to-day underground activism.[57]

This necessitated frequent changes of residence in order to keep one move ahead of the police. Yet Ulyanov had not fogotten his agreement with Plekhanov and Akselrod. The Petersburg organisation still wanted to assist the foundation of an émigré newspaper, and Ulyanov wrote and sent material to Akselrod in November.[58] But his organisation also wished to set up its own news-sheet. It was to be called *Rabochee Delo* (or *Workers' Cause*). Ulyanov was to be editor.[59] Workers were still wary of calls to rise against the autocracy. Ulyanov's leaflets were deliberately apolitical (though he assumed that economic strife would draw workers into politics). Newspapers, on the other hand, would reach out to a more sophisticated readership, attracting both intellectuals and labourers with political awareness. Therefore *Workers' Cause* would propose the formation of a workers' political party.[60]

On 8 December 1895 the Department of Police acted. The proofs of *Workers' Cause* were confiscated; forty Marxist activists, not far short of the entire St. Petersburg organisation, were arrested. Ulyanov was among those caught. So lucky in avoiding the police's clutches when in Samara, he now faced his first lengthy spell of incarceration. He was put in cell 193 by himself. Interrogation began on 21 December; physical coercion was forbidden under prison rules (and least of all would officers break them in the case of Ulyanov, who was not only of the gentry estate but also a legal expert). He was to remain in prison for fourteen months.[61] Anyone joining a revolutionary group had to accept risks; Ulyanov was philosophical. He took a detached, almost 'economic' view of his fate. For he would worry, when hearing of a comrade's imprisonment, not so much about the ensuing material and emotional hardships as about the 'waste' incurred by the loss of an activist's contribution to the cause.[62] Not that his own activism was extinguished in jail. No longer free to organise support for St. Petersburg strikers, Ulyanov concentrated upon expanding his economic writings into a full-length book with a view towards demolishing agrarian–socialist theories once and for all. He had monastic peace for his studies. He took precautions against becoming physically unfit. The daily exercise walk in the yard was obviously inadequate, and Ulyanov adopted a daily regimen of press-ups and trunk-rolls. For recreation he used the prisoners' wall-tapping code to play chess with other inmates.[63]

But research was his pre-occupation. The regulations allowed twice-weekly visits from relatives and friends; and Ulyanov got his sisters to borrow textbooks and journals from libraries. He was interrogated again in early 1896, but the interruption to his labours was negligible.[64] In prison he was a full-time writer.

He also had plentiful time to reflect upon the fortunes of the labour movement. A few leaders such as Martov and Radchenko had eluded the police in December 1895 and perpetuated the existence of their organisation (which they renamed the Union of Struggle for the Emancipation of the Working Class). Difficulties had increased. The organisation had greatly relied upon the Central Workers' Group, which was the successor of the Central Workers' Circle, for establishing contact with factory workers; and the arrests had involved many leaders of this Group. The remaining middle-class activists could less easily stay in touch with workers. But the Union of Struggle pressed on, undaunted by the arrest of Martov in January 1896. Fedor Dan took over the leadership. The Union's disparagers commented that the few leaflets composed in 1895–96 were the merest drop of water in the stream that turned the mill of labour discontent; it was pointed out that the great textile strike of summer 1896 took the Marxist activists by surprise. Employers, moreover, would seldom make more than nugatory concessions. Count Witte as Minister of Finances instructed provincial governors to stand firm against disobedient workers. Yet police reports demonstrated that, although Marxist activists were not always the instigators of unrest, they and their leaflets were welcomed by the work-force once industrial conflict had begun.[65]

PRISON THOUGHTS

Ulyanov heard of these events from his prison cell; he was kept informed by legal newspapers and his permitted visitors. Plekhanov's vision was apparently being justified by the march of history. It was Ulyanov's acute expectation of the autocracy's imminent demise that led him, in the winter of 1895–96, to review the party programme projected by Plekhanov a decade previously. Ulyanov found nothing in it to reject. But he thought it failed to provide the comprehensive range of policies vital for a political party aiming to be in the thick of the final battles against the Romanov dynasty. The main goal of Plekhanov, in his project's agrarian section, had been to facilitate capitalist development by abolishing both redemption payments and compulsory commune membership. This had Ulyanov's assent. But in order to secure active peasant support he proposed an enticement: the party should call for the restitution to the peasantry of the so-called 'cut-off strips'. This was the term for the segments of peasant-cultivated land which had been lost to the gentry under the Emancipation Edict of 1861. Such a policy, according to Ulyanov, would arouse the oppressed inhabitants of the countryside from political torpor.[66] It was not, by a long chalk, as comprehensive an appeal to the peasantry as the populists had made: Ulyanov was not promising the transfer of all agricultural land. But he hoped that the strips would be attraction enough.

He added little that was new to the section to be aimed at factory workers. This did not signify neglect of urban issues. From the end of 1896 his mind was exercised by the many problems encountered by Marxists in disseminating socialist ideas in the towns.

The outbursts of working-class discontent posed a nagging question. The Marxist activities had to decide how much control they should seek to obtain over the labour movement. The issue became acute in Petersburg in early 1897. Factory strikes had led dozens of workers to join the Union Of Struggle; and, because most intellectual organisers had fallen prey to the police, the working-class recruits had come to constitute the majority of the organisation. The newcomers wanted to alter the perspectives of the Union Of Struggle. In particular, they disliked the idea of broadening the current fights over wages into an immediate struggle against the autocracy; and they desired to put workers in full charge of strike funds. Some talked of founding a newspaper written and edited entirely by factory labourers. Workers were to take over the leadership inside both the party and the trade unions; they were determined to keep the intellectuals under control.[67] Such demands exasperated Radchenko. He was reluctant to admit any worker to a leading position in the Union Of Struggle. He was an intellectual élitist. It was his assumption that working men and women lacked the skills and free time necessary for effective underground administration. Radchenko and his colleagues from the early 1890s were dubbed the Veterans; the newcomers to the Union Of Struggle, who attracted experienced activists like K. M. Takhtarev and A. A. Yakubova to their side, became known as the Youngsters.[68]

Ulyanov entered this discussion. As luck would have it, in February 1897 the authorities were winding up their investigations into the case of the Union Of Struggle. Ulyanov was sentenced to three years' exile in eastern Siberia. Permission was granted for prisoners to be released for a few days in St. Petersburg to gather their belongings prior to departure. Apart from seeing his family, Ulyanov again contacted the Union Of Struggle. He sided with the Veterans in most respects. Neither he nor Radchenko believed that socialism was a doctrine which would be acquired by the working class unless socialist intellectuals provided ideological guidance. On the other hand, Ulyanov did not expect this state of affairs to last forever; in fact he enthusiastically welcomed individual workers into the direction of the Union Of Struggle so long as they possessed the requisite level of education and training, and he assumed that such promotions would shortly increase as the result of the Union's pedagogical activities. But he agreed with Radchenko that workers should not run the Union simply because they were workers.[69] The discussion between the Veterans and the Youngsters was ill-tempered, neither side being willing to make a compromise. At stake stood the choice of the path for the labour movement to follow in the hazardous conditions of nineteenth-century Russia. But no binding decision was taken by the Union Of Struggle before the exiles left St. Petersburg for Eniseisk province in Siberia on 17 February 1897.[70]

Middle-class convicts making such a trip would seek to render it as comfortable as possible firstly by undertaking to pay the rail-fare (and thereby securing an upholstered compartment) and secondly by requesting to live out their Siberian term in the comparatively hospitable climate of the city of Krasnoyarsk rather than the frozen wastes of villages further to the north. The first but not the second request was satisfied in Ulyanov's case.[71] His mother made a successful third plea that, because of his recent pneumonia, he should be allowed to stop over with relatives in Moscow for a week en route to exile. He even managed to study for a day in the Rumyantsev Museum Library. On 23 February he boarded the train for Siberia, accompanied as far as Tula by his mother and sisters Mariya and Anna.[72]

It was not until April that he was officially informed that his place of exile was to be Shushenskoe village near the small town of Minusinsk. He was permitted to spend the previous weeks in freedom in Krasnoyarsk; and, pressing on with his economic treatise, he visited local libraries to arrange borrowing facilities. Shushenskoe was not a total disappointment. It was not very far north of Krasnoyarsk, and postal communications were reasonably frequent. His tireless mother offered to come to live near him. He would not countenance it, earning a rebuke from his sister Mariya for his 'terrible inhospitality'; but he pointed out that the trip to Shushenskoe was 'a pretty bothersome affair and not very pleasant'.[73] Officialdom in Eniseisk province was not inordinately oppressive. The political exiles were granted leave to visit each other in their various villages. Occasional sojourns in Minusinsk were sanctioned. The government made Ulyanov a monthly allowance of eight roubles; this was not a large sum but it bought a sufficiency of food, and in any case his mother continued to supplement his account.[74] His period of exile was not laden with gloom. He set aside a portion of each day for leisure; unlike many contemporary revolutionaries he recognised the importance of keeping fit. His acquaintances disagreed about the identity of his favourite sport: was it country walking or skating or gamebird shooting? In essence they were all correct. For everything he did, at the time of doing it, elicited from him the same passionate intensity. He overbrimmed with primal enthusiasm, treating fellow exiles as a mass resource for competitive 'relaxation'. If fortunate, they might get away with a quick game of chess. But friends learnt to beware of him on days when he had more than his normal store of surplus energy to burn; they knew he was quite likely to insist upon a wrestling contest or some other such horseplay.[75]

Politics, though, laid claim to most of his waking hours. Initially he dreaded exile; he made the quip that prison had provided an excellent environment for a writer.[76] But his family in Russia kept him well-stocked with books and journals as required. In 1897 he researched indefatigably. He was cut off from regular, detailed news about Marxist groups in the empire as a whole. Nobody writing to him could include politically sensitive remarks. For information about fresh developments he relied upon those activists falling into detention in Eniseisk province later than himself. Such arrivals were few in Ulyanov's first twelve months of residence in Siberia (although it was in this fashion that he received the compliment from Plekhanov and Akselrod that 'he wrote better than anyone else in Russia for the workers').[77] The frustrations were endless. Yet they were not overwhelming, if only because he appreciated the usefulness of the time vouched to him to reflect upon his achievements and set-backs in St. Petersburg and to apply his conclusions to the needs of the Marxist movement in the Russian empire.

4 Capitalism in One Country

'THE DEVELOPMENT OF CAPITALISM IN RUSSIA'

Socialist scholar–politicians had become notable figures in Russian public life by the turn of the century. Mikhailovski and Plekhanov were outstanding in the older generation; and younger men like A. A. Bogdanov, V. M. Chernov, P. P. Maslov and V. I. Ulyanov were already set fair to emulate them. The combination of scholarly accomplishment and political eminence was not a uniquely Russian phenomenon. The German socialists had their Kautsky, and the Italians would later produce their Gramsci. The emergence of this species of political leader is not easily explicable. But it would appear to be no coincidence that the countries which bred such specimens were embarking upon economic transformation. Their young intellectuals grew up in societies where the contrast between the old and the new was sharply delineated. Opposition to the political establishment might lead them to take up arms. Equally, they might be induced to take to the pen. Activists sensed that radical alternative policies were unlikely to attract sufficient following unless they could be shown to be rooted in a 'scientific' understanding of the world. Books on history, philosophy and economics were therefore popular with the Russian reading public. The day of the literary essay was drawing to a close. As the expansion of higher-educational facilities took place after 1861, so the number of readers who would countenance tackling drier and more scholarly tomes on matters of immediate interest rose dramatically. The learned journals of the 1890s were full of such material.

The book to confirm Ulyanov's claims as a scholar was *The Development of Capitalism in Russia*. The manuscript was completed in October 1898. Ulyanov's erudite footnotes referred to over six hundred books and articles. The argument was carefully constructed.[1] The text of the first edition ran to 480 pages. 1200 copies were put on sale. It was published legally under the pseudonym of V. Ilin. Each chapter contains lengthy sections written in a style characteristic of academic treatises; but his many derogatory remarks about Mikhailovski and Vorontsov testified to lively political aims. He was launching an offensive on a limited front. Subsequent generations would often regard *The Development of Capitalism* as a comprehensive textbook on the country's economic transformation in modern times.[2] But in fact Ulyanov stated narrower intentions: he wished to examine the process of formation of the Russian domestic market for capitalism.[3] The particularity of Ulyanov-Ilin's theme is discernible in the gaps, which he freely acknowledged, in his treatment. Peter the Great, who launched Russia's first industrialising drive in the eighteenth century, is mentioned only once. Count Witte attracts only fleeting references. No attention is given to Russia's balance of trade with foreign countries, to governmental loans raised abroad, or to foreign industrial ownership in St. Petersburg and the Donbass.[4]

These lacunae were intentionally provocative. It was a nostrum of Plekhanov, Struve, Tugan and Ulyanov that capitalist development would not be impeded by the expropriation of the mass of the peasantry. They pointed to the boost to industrialisation given by the countryside. Many poor peasants worked for low wages in urban factories; and some richer peasants bought agricultural equipment from the towns. All these writers argued also that capitalist relations were beginning to characterise the internal workings of the village commune.[5]

Nonetheless Plekhanov, Struve and Tugan had ventured little further in sketching the agrarian sector's importance for capitalist growth; they descried connections between urban and rural phenomena but interpreted them as but one factor among many which explained Russia's industrial drive. Ulyanov found this too tentative. Russian agriculture, in his view, was no second-level influence upon industrialisation. Rather it was the provider of an essential and basic domestic market for capitalist goods. His general presentation of economic development resembles a picture of an ecological chain. The habitat of huge mammals like the elephant is sustained by the existence of millions of microscopically small insects; and, in Ulyanov's opinion, the growth of large-scale heavy industrial production depended upon the rise of a minority of the peasantry to financial prosperity. He argued that their demand for agricultural machinery took up a vital share of the market for industrial goods. Wealthy peasants were set upon emulating those gentry landowners who created capitalist farms (unlike most landords, who rented out land to peasants rather than

farm it themselves). And these farms too gave impetus to manu-
facturing industries to produce machinery for a modernised agriculture. The implication was plain. Russian industrialists could promote
the country's economic advance even without the props of governmental contracts and foreign loans. They had a domestic market of
their own. And, if only the many semi-feudal restrictions upon
industrial competition were removed (which was as near as Ulyanov
could come to call for revolution without annoying the censorship
office), there would be no limits to the potential of Russian economic
growth.[6]

The Development of Capitalism offered a picture of steady, irreversible change. Ulyanov implied that social differentiation was a unilinear
process; and that it brought ever-increasing gains in agricultural
efficiency through the application of machine-powered equipment on
larger and larger tracts of soil. Big was not only beautiful: it was also
cost-effective. The extension of territory owned by rich peasants
involved them in the buying out of poor peasants. But the landless
would be able to better their situation. They would earn more money
in wages than they had obained as inefficient peasant cultivators.[7]

This vista was the most inspiriting of all those painted by Russian
Marxists. Capitalism, according to Ulyanov, still confronted an epoch
of maturation but Russia was already a capitalist country. The social
structure had been altered fundamentally. He conceded that factory
workers, miners and railwaymen had reached only one and a half
million in number. But there were also a million workers in the
construction trade; and a further couple of millions were employed in
timber-felling and other less skilled occupations. There were about
three and a half million hired labourers in the agricultural sector; there
were also around two million workers employed in 'putting-out'
industry in their own village homes. Hired labour was therefore the
condition of ten and a half million souls out of 125 millions. Even this
computation did not exhaustively comprehend the 'proletariat and
semi-proletariat'. Poor peasants with land were in practice hardly
distinguishable from landless rural labourers: both groups had
recourse to employment by gentry landlords and rich peasants. From
Ulyanov's tabulations it therefore emerged that 'proletarians and
semi-proletarians' constituted over sixty-three million souls. This was
over half of the entire imperial populace.[8] Censorship difficulties
prevented him from spelling out his political conclusions; but the
experienced Marxist reader could detect that Ulyanov's analysis was
directed against Struve as much as against Mikhailovski. Russian

industrialisation, according to Ulyanov, was at a more advanced stage than was generally allowed.[9]

Ulyanov hoped to spark off a controversy; his friends relished the possibility of a literary furore ignited by his book's sarcastic asides.[10] Its reception, upon publication in 1899, was in fact rather quiet. Russian Marxist theorists could appreciate that Ulyanov, in marked contrast with Struve, did not praise non-socialist economists like List or Sismondi. But no reviewer properly enthused about the work. Plekhanov refrained from comment, perhaps displeased that the younger man had not modified his views on the nature of Russian feudalism. Nor did Struve enter the debate. Indeed he had been acting as Ulyanov's literary agent: the united front of Russian Marxism in all its variants had still not been completely broken (although Struve did permit himself a brief sally, in late 1899, against the Marxist movement's increasingly hagiographic deployment of Marx's texts).[11] At the time the only Marxist to write a lengthy review of the book was P. N. Skvortsov, who had himself written on the peasant commune[12] and now spared Ulyanov no criticism.[13] Ulyanov composed a suitably aggressive retort.[14] The dispute faded away. Ulyanov's economic studies had not caught the reading public's imagination like Struve's *Critical Remarks.* But the balance sheet was not at all depressing. For his book, though not a best-seller, at least had solidly confirmed his status as a Marxist writer of seriousness and distinction.

But how cogent is its analysis? His definitions are problematical. He was particularly vague about what he meant by capitalism; the nearest he came towards a verbal formulation was his comment that 'the degree of the domestic market's development is the degree of capitalism's development in a country'.[15]

Skvortsov's main theoretical criticism had been that Ulyanov left no room for the occurrence of economic crises.[16] This remark especially riled Ulyanov. The susceptibility of capitalism to periodic economic crises was a cornerstone of Marxism, and Skvortsov expressly accused Ulyanov of misrepresenting *Das Kapital.* The charge was that *The Development of Capitalism* assumed the existence of an economy whose various sectors and sub-sectors operated in harmony with each other.[17] Thus supply appeared always to equal demand. 'Proportionality' seemed achieved. In truth, Ulyanov's book scarcely mentions disproportionality; its main message is indeed devoted to the ease of capitalist development in Russia. But Ulyanov, when taken to task by Skvortsov, convincingly disclaimed any intention of proving the practicability of proportional co-operation between branches of the economy.[18] Such a demonstration was in fact Tugan-Baranovski's goal.[19] And in 1898 Ulyanov published articles not only in riposte to Skvortsov but also against Tugan. He argued that the instability of capitalism resided not only in the difficulties of regulating supply and demand as between economic sectors. It also derived from conflicts of social interest. The growth of capitalism, Ulyanov emphasised, inevitably caused unrest among the ever more numerous body of the working class. Workers would always need to consume more than the capitalist system could permit.[20]

Both Tugan and Ulyanov claimed to have understood Marx better than the other did. Their arguments continue to be debated (as do those of the three volumes of *Das Kapital* itself). For our purposes, though, it is perhaps most useful to note the differing political lines lurking behind the theoretical positions. Tugan was centring upon the technical perfectibility of capitalism, Lenin upon the revolutionising effects of capitalism's growth.

Skvortsov made other points of a more practical import. Above all, he called attention to mediaeval economic history. It was Skvortsov's contention that a national market in grain had existed long before the advent of capitalism; and that Ulyanov's account of nineteenth-century phenomena failed to show why they should be defined as specifically capitalist.[21] This criticism was later to be repeated by several writers ranging from liberals like N. N. Chernenkov to agrarian-socialist sympathisers such as A. V. Chayanov. *The Development of Capitalism*, in their opinion, was excessively taken up with macro-economics. It paid insufficient attention to the internal workings of the peasant commune. Differences of wealth among the peasantry were a centuries-old phenomenon and were not exclusively a sign of capitalist development. Ulyanov had assumed that kulak families would accumulate riches from generation to generation. Chernenkov and Chayanov, however, showed how accumulation was obstructed by those Russian peasant customs of inheritance which made household elders divide their possessions among all their sons. Dismemberment of agricultural units was the consequence. They also demonstrated that, in many regions, it was not so much the entre-preneurial spirit that made a particular household rich as the relatively large number of its young male members. More sons meant greater labour-power and greater entitlement to communal land.[22]

These were criticisms that could not lightly be brushed aside; and Ulyanov's later critics inside the Russian Marxist movement itself were to make much of them. In fact Ulyanov later admitted that his case was not entirely watertight; he blamed the absence of inter-generational peasant statistics (and he continued to make this argument even though his own data on horse ownership between generations undermined his contention that a steady division of the peasantry into rural proletariat and rural bourgeoisie was under way).[23] In any case, he would also prove willing to concede in his post-1905 writings that his book had grossly over-stated the extent of Russian agrarian capitalist development. This was damning self-criticism. But it was balanced by a penetrating counter-thrust against his critics. His very reasonable argument was that the cyclical trends described by them might impede but would not ultimately halt the maturation of rural capitalism in Russia.[24] Thus he stuck proudly by his book as an analysis of general trends. In addition, recent empirical research has tended to corroborate his assertions about the huge importance of agriculture's contribution to Russian industrialisation; and about the increasing commercialisation of grain output in the years before the turn of the century. And peasants, it is now agreed, were already producing about four fifths of the empire's grain marketings in the late tsarist period.[25]

And so *The Development of Capitalism* is a work of great weaknesses and great strengths. Few writers in the field of general economic developmental theory would nowadays be so inattentive either to state intervention (although, admittedly, he rectified this in his later writings) or to foreign loans. Nor is it proven that agricultural efficiency always rises proportionately with size of landholding; or even that landless labourers are usually better off than poor peasants. Ulyanov's vision of an ineluctable process of industrialisation appears sanguine in the light of the difficulties experienced today by Third World countries seeking economic modernisation. On the other hand, his work has its merits too even on this theoretical plane. His thoughts on capitalism's underlying susceptibility to crisis have an impressive subtlety. His analysis of the process of industrialisation also has lasting value; he was especially effective in showing the significance of rural handicraft production for the consolidation of capitalist relationships. He was clearly no mean economist.[26]

THE PARTY IN RUSSIA

The intrinsic qualities of Ulyanov's scholarship give the lie to suppositions that his book's economic optimism originated exclusively from a populistic zeal, albeit transmuted into a Marxist form, to foreshorten the schedule for revolutionary change (even though the foreshortening instinct was undoubtedly a deep-seated part of his make-up).[27] But this does not mean that he was economist first, and political activist second. He was both at once. His unashamed distortion of Vorontsov's views point to this. So, too, does the fact that he was formulating ideas on political strategy years before the completion of his economic *magnum opus*.[28]

The precise path of his approach to the intellectual formulations of *The Development of Capitalism* will, for want of the requisite personal details, always remain mysterious. His reticence continued after publication. It was accompanied by a certain nervousness; he was not yet the completely confident littérateur of later years. Fortunately for Ulyanov, 1899 was also the year when Karl Kautsky published *The Agrarian Question*; and Ulyanov delightedly noted that he had analysed industrialisation in a manner not dissimilar from his own.[29] This was not the only cause of his feeling of well-being. Nadezhda Krupskaya was arrested by the police in 1897. She was sentenced to exile. In January 1898 Ulyanov wrote to the authorities requesting that his 'fiancée' be permitted to join him in Shushenskoe. Such engagements between revolutionaries were often fictions enabling members of a group to congregate while serving sentence. Affection as well was involved in this case. At any rate, the authorities took Ulyanov at his word but insisted upon marriage. Nadezhda gave her consent.[30] Her mother accompanied her to Shushenskoe. There was a last-minute hitch: no wedding rings were available. But a factory-worker in exile with them found a piece of copper and hammered out two home-made ones for the bride and groom; and on 10 July 1898 Vladimir Ilich Ulyanov and Nadezhda Konstantinovna Krupskaya were joined in wedlock.[31] It was a union which provided him with emotional support for the rest of his life. More immediately, Krupskaya as a new exile conveyed information about the underground Marxist movement. She and Vladimir sat up for long nights discussing the drafts of his treatise, helping with his translation assignments (which included a Russian-language edition of Sidney and Beatrice Webb's *History of Trade Unionism*), and talking about revolutionary strategy in Russia. He did not bother to try to escape from Siberia. Knowing that his term of exile would be completed by 1900, he waited patiently and concentrated on thinking, planning and writing.

Ulyanov and Krupskaya had been among those St. Petersburg Marxists who believed that the time had arrived to found a political party. Stirrings towards unification occurred simultaneously elsewhere; and the *Workers' Newspaper* editors in Kiev summoned other clandestine groups to a congress in Minsk in March 1898. Nine delegates arrived. They claimed mandates to represent groups in St. Petersburg, Moscow, Ekaterinoslav and Kiev as well as the entire Jewish Bund. *Workers' Newspaper* representatives also attended. This effort was not praised everywhere: the group in Ivanovo-Voznesensk suspected that the Kievan comrades had omitted to invite it because of known political disagreements. Groups in other places expressed unease. But the *Workers' Newspaper* leaders maintained that the call for a congress would have been futile if they had not been able to operate with exceptional powers of discretion.[32] Ulyanov was to become notorious for his heavy-handed manipulation of Congress arrangements. Evidently he was reinforcing a pre-existing tradition.

A sense of historic occasion, however, permeated the proceedings. A party was being born. A name had to be found for it, and the delegates agreed on the Russian Social-Democratic Labour Party. Thus they aligned themselves with the German Social-Democratic Party. The Minsk Congress sought an end to the Russian autocracy and the creation of a democratic republic. Factory workers would lead the opposition to the regime. The delegates committed the Russian Social-Democratic Labour Party to political perspectives hammered out by Plekhanov and Akselrod for more than a decade.[33] The Congress also approved a notional party structure and elected a Central Committee to guide party affairs in periods between Congresses. The Central Committee's powers were defined broadly. It was to be allowed to co-opt further members for the contingency that the police might succeed in arresting those already elected. But the rights of local groups (or committees, as they were thenceforward to be known) were to be safeguarded. Activists in the provinces were permitted free choice of policy so long as they kept inside the ambit of the party programme. The obvious drawback was that no official programme existed. Approaches had been made to Plekhanov but he had not yet supplied a draft. Next best to a programme was a brief manifesto of the party's intentions. Literary composition was entrusted to Struve; and he discharged it dutifully: it was his last act as a Marxist; his political sympathies would shortly impel him to declare himself a liberal. Finally, the Congress recognised *Workers' Newspaper* as the party's official organ.[34]

Russian Marxists, whether at liberty or (like Ulyanov) in exile, believed they were beginning to have their government on the run. The emperor Nikolai II had succeeded to the throne of Aleksandr III upon his death in 1894. He urged liberal constitutionalists to give up their 'puerile dreams'. The only serious manifestation of social unrest occurred in working-class quarters of industrial cities. As yet the government was not pushed to political reforms. But the crescendo of strikes in 1895–96 compelled ministers to acknowledge that some concession to the grievances of workingmen had to be made. A factory law was promulgated in 1897. Jubilant social-democrats, as the Marxists increasingly called themselves, noted that the maximum working day was to be reduced to eleven-and-a-half hours. Stricter regulations about child labour were enacted. Safety standards were announced. Factory inspectors were accorded functions in the supervision of industrial relations. Lobbying by employers had led to a dilution of the law's clauses; and Russian labour legislation had some distance to go before it gave the freedoms prevailing in Western Europe. But Russian workers had extracted their first instalment. They had accentuated weaknesses in the autocracy's position, and the outbreaks of industrial conflict in 1898 showed their determination to be accorded both higher wages and greater dignity of treatment. There were 215 strikes in that year.[35] The Russian Social-Democratic Labour Party aimed to tug political advantage out of an economic strife that appeared to follow a path of inexorable embitterment.

The police had had no prior intelligence about the First Party Congress. When news reached the government, the order was given to arrest all social-democratic supporters at large. Five hundred were incarcerated by January 1899. The victims included eight out of the nine delegates to the Congress; and the three-man Central Committee was destroyed before its members could co-opt others to take their place.[36] The practical constructions of the Party Congress lay in ruins. Even if Ulyanov had evaded capture in 1895 and survived to make his influence felt in Minsk, he would almost certainly have still joined his comrades in prison and exile.

PROJECTS FOR THE PARTY

News of the Congress in fact reached Ulyanov in May 1898. Before finishing *The Development of Capitalism*, he had resumed his deliberations about the party's programmatic and organisational requirements. Politics and economics co-existed in his thoughts. Ulyanov had written an entire pamphlet in late 1897, and had it published in Geneva as *The Tasks of Russian Social-Democrats*; and in 1899 he produced a series of draft articles ending with his *Project for Our Party's Programme*.

From the outset, he re-affirmed his admiration for the earlier attempts by Plekhanov and Akselrod; his own aim was only to offer 'particular editorial changes, corrections and additions'.[37] He again endorsed the view that the next stage in Russia's political development would be not a socialist seizure of power. Capitalism had yet to mature in Russia. Ulyanov also approvingly cited Akselrod's contention that only the working class could act as 'the advance-line fighter' against the autocracy. He refused to predict the precise mode of assault to be used: he thought it futile to discuss whether it would be a general strike or an armed uprising. The point was to get on with preparations for the struggle.[38] Mildly remonstrating with Plekhanov and Akselrod, he sought the inclusion of paragraphs describing the course of capitalist development in their country. He wanted, too, a more obvious emphasis upon the need for 'class struggle'. And, in order to combat those like Peter Struve in Russia or Eduard Bernstein in Germany striving to revise Marxism, Ulyanov wanted to insert a statement on the inevitability of 'the growth of poverty, oppression, enslavement, humiliation and exploitation' under the capitalist order.[39] He stuck to the Geneva Group's picture of the state structure to be set up upon the autocracy's dismantlement. He repeated the call for a general arming of the people. He added a stricture of his own. So as to reinforce the democratic nature of the civil administrative institutions it would be essential to introduce the elective principle to the tenure of public office. Bureaucrats should no longer be appointed from above.[40] Plainly, if ever such a revolution took place, it would produce a government more nearly under popular control than any state in history. Ulyanov then added a list of social reforms. The maximum working day should be lowered to eight hours; every worker should be guaranteed a break of at least thirty six hours per week. Child labour and night work should be banned altogether. Industrial courts should be instituted, and these should allow for equal representation to employers and employees. Officers of the factory inspectorate should be elected to their jobs. Employers should be made responsible before the law for accidents occurring at the place of work. Such limitations on the rights of industrialists, Ulyanov maintained, were vital if workers were to obtain the cultural environment necessary for them to take full advantage of the political reforms envisaged by the party.[41]

In his proposals for the countryside, Ulyanov cited Akselrod's recommendation that social-democrats should adopt 'the revolutionary side' of Russian agrarian socialism.[42] Narodnik ideas, he repeated, were not automatically unacceptable. At the same time Ulyanov declared that his programme, despite outward resemblances, did not seek the ultimate goals of agrarian-socialist 'utopianism'. His measures were designed to foster the consolidation of rural capitalism. They were also meant to attract the peasantry into associating itself with the worker-led revolution; but their net economic result would be to nurture the system of exploitation of peasant by peasant.[43]

Nonetheless there lingered a nervousness among many Russian Marxists about appearing too 'populistic' on the agrarian question. Discussions were becoming heated. It was in this period, around the turn of the century, that several activists like A. I. Rykov and theorists like L. Nadezhdin amplified their demand for the expropriation of all gentry-held land; and that Nadezhdin proposed a policy of land nationalisation.[44] Ulyanov still baulked at such ideas; he felt that they would place excessive power in the hands of what, after all, he presumed would be a bourgeois-led government.[45] Peasants might well end up worse oppressed than ever. Yet he ceased now to be quite as cautious as his elders in Geneva. He remained committed to the return of the cut-off strips; and he demanded not only the abolition of redemption payments but also the restitution to the peasants of all monies paid to the state under this system since 1861. The fiscal system should also be changed. Tax collectors were to deal with individual peasant households, not whole communes. Ulyanov opposed the dismemberment of capitalist latifundia. But he was bent upon curtailing the rights of those landlords who rented out land to the peasantry. He proposed the creation of special courts to allow households to secure reduction of 'excessive' rents. Absentee land-lordism would be attacked. He also called for the formation of 'peasant committees'. Ulyanov's intentions were two-sided. He did not want only to facilitate a rise in agricultural output: he desired equally to effect the entrance of the peasantry into political life.[46]

Thus he exhibited a concern for details in his draft party programme. His practicality led him also to consider the party's organisational condition; there was little point in speculating about the post-autocratic future if the party was in no fit shape to guide the working class and the peasantry in the present. The police had broken up the Petersburg Union Of Struggle as well as the Central Committee. In Ulyanov's opinion, the Russian Social-Democratic Labour Party was an organisational mess.

As early as 1897, in *The Tasks of Russian Social-Democrats*, he asserted that 'the struggle with the government is impossible without a strengthening and development of revolutionary organisation and conspirativeness'.[47] In *The Essential Question*, written in 1899, he refined his proposals. It was his belief that the party's overriding priority should be to introduce a 'division of labour' into its affairs.[48] He loved to use analogies from the economic field. Functional specialisation would permit the party to train experts in agitation, pamphleteering, fund-raising and spy-hunting. It also made for greater safety from arrest. Specialisation would mean that information about the names and whereabouts of other activists would be less freely available.[49] Such an 'economy of forces' should be welcomed. But in order to consolidate this transformation it would be necessary, too, to implement the concept of centralisation. Democratic control from below was desirable in principle. But the enforced clandestinity of operations restricted the scope for 'heavily-attended revolutionary meetings'.[50] Hierarchical discipline was a priority. Ulyanov did not go completely overboard into organisational authoritarianism. Not quite; for he recognised the validity of a further problem. It centred upon democratic control. He defined the difficulty as being 'how to collocate the need for the full freedom of local social-democratic activity with the need to form a single and therefore centralist party?'[51] But, significantly, he left his cumbersomely-phrased question unanswered. His preoccupation was to get the party to accept his arguments for specialisation and centralisation; everything else was a secondary issue which could be tackled in the due course of time.

Such an approach was shared by many former comrades in the Union Of Struggle. It also appealed to numerous activists currently associated with *Workers' Newspaper* and *Workers' Banner*.[52] Plekhanov and Akselrod did not demur. And Vladimir Ulyanov justifiably represented his programmatic and organisational proposals as a valid development of the doctrines of Plekhanov. He contended unremittingly that assassinations should not be viewed as a primary tactic of assault on the autocracy. Again Nadezhdin was causing problems. He suggested that narodnik terrorism had not been as politically misguided as other Russian Marxists had been wont to declare. But Ulyanov stood by Plekhanov. Neither Ulyanov nor Plekhanov opposed terrorist acts in principle. Ulyanov clarified his position. It was, he said, possible to envisage assassinations as a 'defensive' tactic.[53] He seems to have had in mind the killing of persons, such as police spies, capable of breaking up party organisations.

AGAINST 'ECONOMISM'

In his Shushenskoe writings he had sketched a party programme and a plan of party organisation. He had barely mentioned a further issue: what was to be the relationship between this party and the urban working class? His past career gave evidence of his beliefs. Like Plekhanov, he saw the party as the political guide of the industrial labour force. The party should not necessarily tack to the wind of popular moods of the moment; it should seek to pull workers along in its wake.[54] Ulyanov had not altered his mind in Siberia. If anything, he was even more strongly convinced of the leading role to be played by the party. It had to canalise the rising flood of discontent into revolution. He urged social-democrats to set about 'the education, disciplining and organisation of the proletariat'.[55] The imagery is trenchantly hierarchical; it bursts through all the qualifying language of the sentences around it. Discipline was always a key theme in his thought.

In summer 1899 such views were suddenly subjected to a criticism even more severe than by the attack already made by the Youngsters in St. Petersburg. The critics were E. D. Kuskova and S. N. Prokopovich. As Russian social-democrats in emigration, they had studied the Belgian labour movement and been impressed by the material and social amelioration obtained through legal methods. Kuskova wrote a brief article which became known as her *Credo*. Its suggestion was that workers should forget about revolutionary politics and struggle exclusively for their own economic well-being. The fight against the absolute monarchy could safely be left to the middle class. This was anathema even to those who had sided with the Petersburg Youngsters; for they, while acceding to workers' demands to influence party policy, had never envisaged that this would result in a lengthy abstention from political conflict. The apoliticism of Kuskova's *Credo* horrified Veterans and Youngsters alike from the old Union Of Struggle. Both Kuskova and Prokopovich were scholars rather than organisers; they had no following in Russia, and Prokopovich was arrested in 1899 when he attempted to return from emigration. The campaign for their ideas, which were dubbed Economism by their adversaries, seemed defunct.[56] But not to Plekhanov. Emigré political developments worried him. His example in forming the Emancipation Of Labour Group in Geneva had been followed by dozens of Russian emigrants in other major cities of Europe such as Paris and Berlin. In 1898 they banded together into a European organisation proclaiming itself as the League Of Russian Social-Democrats Abroad. The First Party Congress in Minsk had recognised the League as the party's official foreign branch. Plekhanov's authority was on the wane. His tetchiness towards the younger émigrés was bad enough; but he also maintained few lines of communication with social-democratic organisers in Russia itself. Irritation with Plekhanov and Akselrod helped to push the Berlin section of the League temporarily towards Economism in 1898.[57]

A counterattack was mounted by Plekhanov; and his criticisms took little heed that the league's dalliance with 'Economism' did not last into 1899. The League's newspaper was called *Workers' Cause*. So far from advocating an apolitical strategy, every issue carried the slogan: 'The social emancipation of the working class is impossible without its political liberation.'[58] It smuggled May Day leaflets back to Russia in 1899, calling for the promulgation of political liberties. *Workers' Cause* supported political demonstrations in Russia whenever they occurred. In other respects, however, it differed from Kremer's *On Agitation*. Editor B. I. Krichevski believed that the fight for higher wages would gradually transmute itself into political struggle against the autocracy; he also highlighted what he saw as the cultural immaturity of the broad strata of the Russian working class. *On Agitation* by contrast had not spoken of gradualism. It had urged Marxists to grasp opportunities to politicise the labour movement; and it was free from Krichevski's evident belief that peasant newcomers to the factories were improbable material for the organisation of the growing opposition to the monarchy.[59]

Plekhanov was wrong to treat Kuskova and Krichevski as politically indistinguishable. Yet he had a point when he said that *Workers' Cause* had rejected the early consensus that the workers should lead Russia's democratic revolution[60] Plekhanov campaigned simultaneously against another social-democratic newspaper. Its name was *Workers' Thought*; it had been founded in St. Petersburg itself and, though subsequently printed abroad, had kept links with the metropolis. Arrests of older leaders gave it a dominant position inside the Union Of Struggle. The first editor was a certain Kok. He made the newspaper a forum of discussion of the viewpoints of the workers themselves. Letters about management abuses filled its columns. Kok and his collaborator K. M. Takhtarev (who had been a Youngster in the social-democratic dispute in 1896) castigated what they perceived as the malignant influence exerted by the middle-class intelligentsia upon the labour movement.[61] This to Plekhanov appeared a betrayal

of Marxism. His suspicions were confirmed in 1899 when *Workers'*
Thought produced a Supplement. It contained an article by the
German revisionist social-democrat Eduard Bernstein arguing for an
'evolutionary' rather than 'revolutionary' interpretation of Marxian
ideas. The accompanying editorial endorsed Bernstein's approach.
Workers should involve themselves in politics, but should pursue their
ends by exclusively peaceful means.[62]

Ulyanov, hearing of the controversy in August 1899, took
Plekhanov's part. A copy of Kuskova's *Credo* had reached Eniseisk
province; and a little was known about Kok too. Ulyanov was as
infuriated as Plekhanov. Among the exiles he was the pre-eminent
intellectual; he was also their most inspiring organiser: it was he who
wrote letters of cheer to comrades like Martov who had been placed in
less comfortable villages much further to the north.[63] He wrote a
declaration of protest against Kuskova and Kok. *Workers' Thought*
was accused of Economistic ideas (even though its enthusiasm for
Bernstein signified a rejection of apoliticism). He was not trying to be
fair; he was trying to crush Plekhanov's opponents.[64] Sixteen social-
democratic exiles in the locality appended their signatures to
Ulyanov's protest.[65]

This dispute was the first truly open breach in Russian Marxist unity;
and the question was instantly posed why Plekhanov and Ulyanov
risked such a rupture. Their whole strategy had been founded upon the
assumption, correct as events were to show, that the autocracy's fall
was inevitable and would not long be postponed; they had also rightly
predicted that workers, chafing against economic oppression, would
eventually turn to the politics of revolution. So why worry so much
about the *Credo*? Neither Plekhanov nor Ulyanov wrote down their
justification for the benefit of posterity. But doubtless they felt
strongly about the need for preventive action; they observed Bernstein's continuing influence in the German Social-Democratic Party
and desired to pre-empt any such development in Russia (however
unlikely it was to occur). If anything, Plekhanov at this moment was
even less tolerant than Ulyanov. Both agreed on the offensive against
the 'Economists'; but Plekhanov also wished to terminate the state of
semi-truce with Struve. Ulyanov resisted a severing of organisational
links.[66] Struve in 1899 still held that the workers were the major
political force against the autocracy; and Plekhanov was asked to
refrain from precipitate action. But even Ulyanov's patience was
wearing thin. He had never been known for his tolerance. It is difficult
to imagine either Ulyanov or Plekhanov doing as Fedoseev had done

in writing respectful letters to Mikhailovski.[67] Admittedly, they
rejected 'dogmatism'. Both considered Marxism to be a creative
science.[68] They justifiably felt that their own adaptation of Marxian
policies to Russian circumstances showed that they were not vapid
regurgitators of hackneyed German ideas. But their protestations of
open-mindedness were not universally valid. And Ulyanov in particular, in the years ahead, would increasingly write and behave as if he
alone among the exponents of Russian socialism understood Marxism
correctly.[69]

RELEASE FROM EXILE

Until the First World War, however, Ulyanov's focus was upon
Russian Social-Democratic Labour Party; he commented about
disputes racking the German Social-Democratic Party, but resisted the
temptation to intervene vigorously. Plekhanov proffered advice to
Kautsky. Ulyanov experienced inhibitions. For him, Kautsky and
Plekhanov were now the world's two greatest living Marxists.

   Ulyanov's deference had its instrumental side. He knew Kautsky to
be a supporter of Plekhanov's political strategy for Russia. He knew
too that Kautsky, as a man of the pen, would be pleased by Ulyanov's
proposed remedy for the Russian party's nagging ills. Ulyanov wanted
to establish a central party newspaper. This ambition absorbed his
attention as he left Shushenskoe and exile on 29 January 1900.[70] He
had pondered a great deal about journalism while in Siberia. A
clandestine political newspaper would have immense possibilities. It
would allow the party to give a thorough airing to all its troublesome
problems. There was too much uncertainty about policy. Ulyanov had
remarked in 1894 that the existence of many contradictory opinions
was a sign of the social-democratic movement's strength.[71] This was no
longer his claim. Now the purpose of debate, he said, was primarily to
set a clear line for the party. Every member had to know where the
party stood. He presented the plan as if intending to act impartially as
editor-in-chief. The impression was effaced by his other statements.
He saw his projected newspaper as an organiser of party life; its
function would not be to preside over free discussion but to use all
means at its disposal for the victory of Ulyanov's ideas.[72] He had
started the venture in Siberia, inviting Yuli Martov and Aleksandr
Potresov to join him in an editorial 'troika'. Both accepted. As they

were the first to admit, they had entered the ambit of Ulyanov's magnetism of personality; he seemed to them to be a born leader.[73]

Practical details had yet to be settled. No decision had been taken even about the newspaper's geographical base, whether in Russia or abroad. The order for Ulyanov's release from exile forbade residence in metropolitan, industrial or university towns of the empire. He chose to live in Pskov, nearly two hundred miles from Petersburg.[74] It was a prudent selection, since he could expect to meet dozens of former political prisoners there.

But it meant separation from Krupskaya. Her own term of exile was not due to expire until 1901 and, when Ulyanov left Shushenskoe, she was permitted to take up residence in the Urals town of Ufa. All his pleas for her to be transferred to Pskov came to nought. They travelled together by the Trans-Siberian line to Ufa. Staying with her a few nights, he contacted local social-democrats.[75] He stopped over in Moscow, Nizhni Novgorod and Petersburg too; by the time of his arrival in Pskov on 26 February he had greatly expanded the number of his acquaintances and assured himself of assistance from dozens of activists.[76] The next problem was funding. In St. Petersburg he had met Vera Zasulich, in the course of her mission to Russia on behalf of the Geneva Emancipation Of Labour Group; she announced the Group's approval of the project but could not offer financial subsidy.[77] Ulyanov and Potresov had made a start on getting the necessary monies. A. M. Kalmykova, a wealthy sympathiser with the revolutionary cause, donated two thousand roubles. Yet tens of thousands were needed to pay for paper and printing. Negotiations were opened with Struve and Tugan. Martov had always viewed Struve with distaste, and tried to dissuade Ulyanov from meeting him. Ulyanov, however, insisted. He pursued a paradoxical aim: one hand beckoned Struve to supply money and literary material to a journalistic enterprise; the other waved at him contemptuously, promising that editorial space would be reserved for criticism of his policies. To Martov's amazement, a preliminary deal was struck. Struve's initial reservations were overcome by the concession that he would be allowed to contribute articles in his own right, albeit under the title of discussional articles and without official imprimatur.[78]

By late spring 1900 Ulyanov and Potresov were convinced that police surveillance would make it difficult to set up the presses in Russia; and their fear increased when, on 21 May, Ulyanov was arrested while making a trip to St. Petersburg. Upon release, Ulyanov made hurried last contacts with potential agents for the newspaper. He paid a quick visit to his wife in Ufa. And on 16 July he crossed the border.[79] As he alighted on the station platform in Zurich some days later, he could hardly contain his elation; he looked forward to closer collaboration with Georgi Plekhanov. Plekhanov lived in Geneva. Akselrod's house was near Zurich and Ulyanov spent a while there before moving on. The two got on splendidly, as if they had been lifelong friends. The only unpleasantness, which was to appear important to Ulyanov solely in the light of ensuing events, occurred in connection with Plekhanov. Akselrod too adored Plekhanov. His devotion, moreover, had undergone the trial of its object's vanity. Plekhanov would not be crossed even in trivial matters. Akselrod groped towards the main point. Plekhanov liked the idea of the newspaper; he approved of its proposed name, *Iskra* (or *The Spark*). But he did not fancy the plan to base it in Germany: he preferred Switzerland. Indeed he was holding out for Geneva. No reason was offered. Ulyanov was being braced to accept a dictatorial reluctance to let slip a chance to dominate a major social-democratic publication.[80]

Plekhanov and Ulyanov came face to face in late July. If anything, Akselrod's warnings turned out to be too mild; both Ulyanov and Potresov were astounded by their elder's prickliness. 'I tried to observe caution,' Ulyanov recalled, 'by avoiding the "sore spots"; but this constant keeping oneself on one's guard could not help but reflect itself heavily upon one's mood.'[81]

There were rows about the Jewish Bund, with Plekhanov indicating objections to its inclusion in the Russian Social-Democratic Labour Party. Plekhanov was touchy about Kautsky (who, Ulyanov surmised, had not opened the pages of *Die Neue Zeit* to him as often as he felt he deserved). Worse than his tantrums were his acts of duplicity. Plekhanov was loathe to collaborate with Struve. Ulyanov conceded to Plekhanov the right to edit the terms of Struve's involvement with *Iskra*; but the days passed by in Geneva, and still Ulyanov had not received Plekhanov's version. Ulyanov tried to do the final editing for himself. Still Plekhanov quibbled, and only when harried by an exasperated Ulyanov at a formal meeting did Plekhanov divulge his true motives: he did not want Struve's participation under any conditions whatever.[82] Outraged, Ulyanov retired to Steindl's Wiener Grand-Café and tried to get his anger off his chest by committing his account to paper. The language is revealing. No other piece of prose by Ulyanov carries us so directly to the heart of his emotions. He had, he stated, lost his 'feeling of being in love' with Plekhanov. He believed that he and Potresov had been treated 'like children', indeed like 'slaves'. It was 'an unworthy thing'. His sense of humiliation was overpowering. The conclusion he drew, however, was hardheaded: 'It is necessary to behave to everybody "without sentimentality", it is necessary to keep a stone in one's sling.'[83]

There is little reason to challenge Ulyanov's estimation of the low cunning in Plekhanov's behaviour; but perhaps he himself was more boisterous and intimidating than he admitted. In any case, the dispute was already prising Plekhanov away from his refusal to have dealings with Struve. But other matters remained divisive. Ulyanov wanted to base the newspaper in Munich with himself and Potresov as chief editors. Plekhanov threw one of his fits. And, when faced down by the two young 'careerists' (as Ulyanov felt sure he now thought of them), he submitted his resignation from the project.[84] Ulyanov and Potresov fell for the ploy and begged him to reconsider. Plekhanov laid down fresh conditions. He demanded double the voting power of any other editor. Ulyanov and Potresov instantly gave in. But hours later they saw how they had been duped, and they took a leaf out of Plekhanov's book: they resigned. Akselrod duly padded round to see them and duly took Plekhanov's side. Zasulich was so distressed that friends worried that she might kill herself. Another meeting was held with Plekhanov. Again he attempted to get his way with the help of hysterics. Ulyanov and Potresov were unperturbed this time. Plekhanov announced his intention to withdraw entirely from public life. The young men left the room. They refused to be fooled.[85]

As yet, though, their victory was Pyrrhic: *Iskra* would not be published. They therefore reverted to an honourable compromise; they proposed to Plekhanov that they all jointly print a collection of articles. If this worked out well, they stated, they would retract their *Iskra* resignation. Plekhanov conceded the necessary ground.[86] Subtle manoeuvrer that he was, Ulyanov had made the vital discovery that the way to defeat Plekhanov over *Iskra* was to avoid open pitched battles and to conduct a war of attrition. Plekhanov's bullying days were over. Compelled to make that first retreat, he was already too disorientated to stop further backward movement. A triumphant Ulyanov packed his bags and departed for Munich on 24 August 1900.[87] The squabble over location fizzled out. Nor was Ulyanov troubled by worries about the composition of the editorial board. Formally there would be six editors. The older émigrés would be represented by Plekhanov, Akselrod and Zasulich; and the newcomers by Ulyanov, Potresov and Martov. In practice, however, geography would have an influence. The three hundred miles separating Geneva from Munich were bound to put Ulyanov into an authoritative position. There he would also be able to conduct negotiations with potential subsidisers like Struve without being badgered to distraction by Plekhanov. Ulyanov had carried off the spoils. Though inexperienced in committee work, the novice had picked up the necessary skills and techniques with consummate ease; and Plekhanov, whose glacial manner had chilled all who had approached him as fellow Marxists, was having to treat his former disciple as a leader of equal worthiness and power.

5 Straightening Sticks

'ISKRA' IS FOUNDED

The need to establish a political party was unquestioned among Russian Marxists at the turn of the century. Not even the so-called Economists objected. Russian social-democracy was following European precedents; German and, to a lesser extent, British socialists had already established influential parties. In France the situation had changed somewhat. Parties had come into disfavour with large sections of the French working class, and many intellectuals too distrusted them: the result was a campaign to base the workers' movement upon the *syndicats* operating at the factory level. Syndicalism dispensed with parties. Such an attitude had little attraction for the majority of Russian Marxists, at least until after 1905. It was generally recognised that parties were essential for the overthrow of tsarism; even those early narodniki who had been suspicious about the need for specifically political activity had nonetheless concurred that the party was the most appropriate vehicle for socialism's advance. This commitment was still stronger among the Russian Marxists. And, although the debate was as yet at an embryonic stage, there was widespread agreement about the practical shape to be taken by the party. The undemocratic system of power in Russia compelled certain responses. Russian Marxists would have to operate clandestinely. Their party would have to be centralist. It would naturally emphasise discipline and hierarchy; and some of its leaders would have to live and work abroad.

There, however, consensus ended. No agreed guidelines existed as to how the initiative for forming the party should be undertaken. The dissolution of the Central Committee left the options open. Ulyanov, joining the émigrés of Russian social-democracy in 1900, was ready and willing to snatch whatever opportunities came his way (or could be manipulated so as to do so).

His first task was to get his newspaper into production. *Iskra* had a print-run of a few hundred copies; and, compared with the legal conservative dailies of Petersburg, it seemed a Lilliputian affair. But Ulyanov was not so unrealistic as to expect *Iskra* to be read by every Russian factory worker. He had a narrower readership in mind. He wanted to reach the organisers of existing Marxist groups. The variety of Marxism's manifestations had never been greater. Not all the precepts of Plekhanov had gained universal approval before the turn of the century; and now the opposition was becoming better organised. *Iskra* was created to rally the groups still faithful to Plekhanovite standpoints. The first issue was made on 11 December 1900.[1] The lay-out was clear and there were no misprints. Ulyanov's name did not appear. Anonymity was customary for most contributors (although the Russian political police already knew who was on the editorial board). Ulyanov wrote a good deal of the copy: three lengthy articles flowed from his pen for the initial publication. Truly *Iskra* was Ulyanov's child.[2] Reportage on the labour movement was blended with discussion of political strategy. Disquisitions on philosophy and sociology were left to the sister journal *Zarya* (or *Dawn*), which appeared three times between 1901 and 1902. Ulyanov and his fellow writers expected a lot of their readers; they assumed an acquaintance with the current arguments and lexicon of European Marxism. *Iskra* had a cosmopolitan ambience. Ulyanov, while recognising the need to communicate with activists based in Russia, nevertheless lapsed frequently into French quotations and Italian catch-phrases. This was not exhibitionism (though doubtless it was authorially enjoyable). *Iskra* wanted to demonstrate its intellectual weightiness. Its accent did not fall only upon practical policies; questions of theory, too, were prominent. Slogans peppered every page. Ulyanov succeeded in producing twenty nine issues of *Iskra* in its first two years and in maintaining substantial uniformity of content. Repetitiousness was treated as a virtue. Clarity was all-important. *Iskra* called again and again for 'the overthrow of the autocracy' and the consolidation of 'the democratic revolution'.[3]

Neither Ulyanov nor Plekhanov would brook rival journalistic enterprises. K. M. Takhtarev, taking over the editorship of *Workers' Thought* from Kok, proposed in 1900 to put the newspaper under Plekhanov's direction. Plekhanov spurned the suggestion. Takhtarev was given to understand that Plekhanov could not break a prior commitment to *Iskra*.

But this alone would hardly have held Plekhanov back. Plekhanov's mind was probably also mulling over the likelihood of Takhtarev's policies changing abruptly again in the future (as indeed they did very shortly).[4] Ulyanov continued to point to the Economistic orientation of *Workers' Thought* and *Workers' Cause*. In fact no Russian social-democratic publication was preaching 'Economism' in 1900: political struggle against the monarchy was a commonly recognised priority. Not a few activists in Russia already objected to *Iskra*'s defamatory methods. *Southern Worker* did so with particular anger. This was a newspaper founded in Ekaterinoslav in 1900; it aimed to fill the gap caused by the arrest of the editorial board of Kiev's *Workers' Newspaper* in 1898. *Southern Worker* had initially held Ulyanov in esteem. It had even invited Ulyanov, Martov and Potresov to serve on its editorial board; but the 'troika' refused. *Southern Worker*'s subsequent effort to unite the warring sections of the party was regarded by *Iskra* as a futile attempt to reconcile the irreconcilable.[5] Nothing short of total victory would satisfy Ulyanov and Plekhanov. Their natural abrasiveness was strengthened by their fear lest the party should prove incapable of fulfilling its self-ascribed historic destiny. Their minds were therefore transfixed by the dangers of 'tailism'.[6] They despised those, like Kuskova, who implied the need to stand at the tail, not the forefront of the revolutionary movement.

They also knew that social disorder was increasing in Russia. The years of economic boom had ceased in 1899; whole industries were hit by a world trade recession. The immediate effect was a decrease in the number of strikes.[7] Yet discontent remained. The students in the universities organised demonstrations in 1899. Gradually their example began to be followed by workers. A May Day demonstration in Kharkov in 1900 halted production in the factories; troops were used to restore imperial order. Strikes picked up in number in 1901, and May Day demonstrations could not be prevented in St. Petersburg, Tiflis, Simferopol and Kharkov. In November 1901 the workers in Rostov-on-Don conducted a week-long series of marches and public meetings. The city was sealed off militarily and hundreds of demonstrators were taken into custody.[8] Not only the towns were turbulent. Disturbances were increasing in the countryside. Provincial governors warned that peasant passivity could no longer be taken for granted.[9]

Iskra reported on a political system in decay; its editorials triumphantly described the manoeuvres forced upon the government. S. V. Zubatov, in charge of the political police in Moscow, had argued that the prohibition of trade unions undermined the regime's stability by delivering discontented workers into the hands of the revolutionaries. His recommended solution was the creation of labour organisations under covert police control. The new unions would be kept clear of politics, confining their activity to economic wrangles between workers and employers. The Moscow scheme was copied elsewhere in 1900.[10] The government also cautiously began to reconsider agrarian policy. Even Witte, the arch-industrialiser, urged change. The commune no longer appeared to guarantee conservative restraint. In 1899 the emperor abolished joint responsibility for taxes in those communes where land tenure had not been subject to repartitions. In 1901 he appointed a commission to investigate all aspects of the peasant question in European Russia; and in 1903 joint fiscal responsibility was ended even in areas where the commune frequently repartitioned the land among its households.[11] The belief was taking hold in court circles that prudence called for the fostering of a social class of independent peasant smallholders. Another attempt was being considered to prevent revolution by means of reform from above.

'WHAT IS TO BE DONE?'

Ulyanov, writing for *Iskra*, poured his greatest effort into consideration of the party's condition. *The Urgent Tasks of Our Movement* appeared in the first issue; it resumed the organisational proposals of his Siberian period. But he wanted to expand his argument in a full book. The result was *What Is To Be Done?* It was printed in spring 1902. He had meant to have it finished earlier but his newspaper responsibilities slowed him down.[12] The book contains over fifty thousand words; its central points are clearly made, even though the language signals the haste of its composition. Its contents have frequently been misunderstood. *What Is To Be Done?* has been viewed, by numbers of apologists and detractors alike, as a univeral practical blueprint. Ulyanov has been said to have tendered a schema of organisational mechanics fit for all socialist parties in all times and in all countries. In fact he announced restricted aims. His immediate recommendations were addressed specifically to Russia and presented not as an eternal panacea but as solutions to 'the painful questions of our movement'.[13]

All the same, Ulyanov's analysis comes encased in general theoretical propositions. Leadership is the dominant theme. The urban working class is to lead the democratic revolution; but it will not discharge its historic duties unless given direction by the social-democratic party. Left to themselves, workers cannot develop socialist ideas. They will limit themselves to an apolitical quest for marginal improvements in their material conditions. Socialist 'consciousness' has to be introduced from without. The job of educating the working class in the first instance falls inevitably to those middle-class intellectuals disaffected from the capitalist order.[14] Only the intelligentsia possesses 'scientific' knowledge. Armed with the 'correct' theory, the party will be able to implement the 'correct' forms of organisation. 'Incorrect' strategies like 'Economism' inhibit unification. For the party should strive after centralisation and discipline; it should operate with the techniques of clandestinity elaborated by Russian agrarian socialists in the 1870s.[15] Working-class members, being habituated to the regulations of factory life, will accept the need for hierarchical subordination. Leadership, leadership, leadership. In proffering his prescription for the Russian party, he yet praised the looser organisational arrangements possible for the German social-democrats. He attached, however, a remark of theoretical significance. He declared that even in Germany, where a measure of political liberty prevailed, socialists were unable to ignore the necessity of maintaining a stable core of talented, experienced leaders. 'Primitive' democracy simply could not work.[16]

Floating buoyantly in the jerky course of his prose were sentences of rousing clarity. 'Give us an organisation of revolutionaries,' he exclaimed, 'and we shall turn all Russia upside down'.[17] He extolled the revolutionary fire and administrative competence of the early narodniki.[18] His earnestness was unmistakable. 'Without a revolutionary theory', he asserted, 'a revolutionary movement can not even exist'.[19] Science was a weapon of political struggle. Disciplined cohesion and strict recruitment stipulations were others. Ulyanov declared that the party organisation should 'consist mainly of persons engaged full-time in revolutionary activity'.[20] Electivity to party offices was fine in principle. But in Russian political conditions it was 'an empty and dangerous plaything'.[21] This conclusion was not intended to discourage or depress. It was offered as a realistic assessment which would advance Russian social-democrats nearer to their ultimate goals. Ulyanov wanted to inspire. Indeed he announced it as his slogan: 'It is necessary to dream.'[22]

The book possessed a high emotional charge. It was also a polemical extravaganza; Ulyanov virtually boasted of his 'uncomradely methods', and confessed that his work included 'exaggerations'.[23] But the *Iskra* board supported him. Its public posture of unanimity was belied by reservations expressed privately. Plekhanov and Akselrod had criticisms to make in 1901. Their substance is unknown; yet it was serious enough for Plekhanov to feel annoyed that Akselrod would not help him to take the matter further.[24] Akselrod's refusal is mysterious. Possibly he wanted to avoid the fragmentation of the newspaper board; and he may also have been loathe to castigate a work which at any rate attacked revisionism in Marxism. Potresov was less inhibited. He told Ulyanov that the book gravely underestimated the 'spontaneous' development of socialism among working-class people.[25] Such comments, however, were kept within the family of the *Iskra* board. And Ulyanov in any case did not lack admirers elsewhere. N. Valentinov testified to the book's electrifying effect. He instantly felt that Ulyanov had supplied Russian social-democrats with something that had been unavailable: an up-to-date comprehensive rationale for the party's existence. Ulyanov delineated the immediate tasks ahead gave and a justification for immediate optimism.[26] A. A. Bogdanov and A. V. Lunacharski too were attracted. They liked the book's stress upon what could shortly be achieved in Russia; they approved of its contempt for bookish theorising (which they associated with the Swiss-based émigrés). *What Is To Be Done?*, for them, was a highly estimable account of the modes of activity appropriate to circumstances in contemporary Russia.[27] No practical advice since *On Agitation* had won such praise. Ulyanov's sympathisers ignored the book's darker side. Some, such as L. B. Kamenev, apparently found his arguments on 'socialist consciousness' entirely acceptable.[28] Others, like Bogdanov, in fact firmly believed in the workers' capacity for political self-development; but, for the moment, they were caught up by the sheer enthusiasm and apparent practicality of *What Is To Be Done?*[29]

Yet the book also had many critics. Its controversial approach was quickly perceived; and the main reason why it did not straightaway evoke enormous controversy was that the dispute about the party programme held greater attention in 1902–1903.[30]

Among the early adversaries was B. I. Krichevski. He assailed Ulyanov's views on consciousness. He believed that the book accorded importance to the party at the working class's expense; and that, moreover, it envisaged the central party apparatus as the military high command of the revolution.[31] Krichevski's writings in 1902 initiated a tradition. Years passed before all the possible implications of the book were teased out; probably not even Ulyanov had fully appreciated them at the time of composition.[32] The conflict steadily sharpened in 1903. It already touched upon a matter which profoundly annoyed Ulyanov. The principal opponents were A. S. Martynov and V. P.

Akimov. Ulyanov's attitude to organisation, they asserted, was not Marxist at all. They described it as narodnik. In their view, Ulyanov had not merely utilised secondary elements of populism but had restored the nucleus of Tkachevian organisational doctrine. These were grievous charges. The critics claimed that the book's recommendations would effectively exclude workers entirely from the party. Ulyanov was arraigned for proposing to create a conspiratorial organisation, isolated from the mass of the people and constituted by the middle-class intelligentsia. Such a party of 'professionals' would try to seize power through the bomb-throwing plots beloved of narodnik terrorists; it would ignore the Marxist tenet that social revolutions occur only when whole classes of the population become involved in the struggle.[33]

In fact, Ulyanov maintained his hostility to narodnik social theory. He could note also that his works had for years involved a conventional contemporary Marxist perspective of the stages of political changes: bourgeois democracy followed by the dictatorship of the proletariat.[34]

Angered by his critics, he wrote his *Letter to a Comrade About Our Organisational Tasks*. He disowned any desire for a party of middle-class activists. He wanted workers to be recruited too.[35] But he reiterated that every member should give a commitment to active participation in party life. Membership would cover a large scale of degrees of activity. Ulyanov expected the full-time revolutionaries in each local committee to be privy to more secrets and to exercise greater authority than their colleagues. The more full-timers in the committees, the better it would be for the party as a whole. But the rank-and-file members also had their duties; and unless the party could attract thousands of such entrants it would remain an ineffective force against the autocracy. Ulyanov envisaged the local party structure as a series of concentric circles. The core would be provided by full-timers; the middle circles by part-time activists; the outer circles by rank-and-filers.[36] The onus of commitment and authority would increase in proportion to the member's nearness to the innermost circle. Local committees had to be allowed some autonomy. The Central Committee should not arbitrarily appoint officials from above, even though the need for clandestinity ruled out the full application of the elective principle.[37] The central party apparatus would not be all-powerful and unchecked; and, by the same token, it was unjust to accuse him of aspiring to be party despot. He objected to personalised arguments. He also re-affirmed that he accepted individual terrorism as a 'defensive' tactic only.[38]

The *Letter* showed that he did not want a middle-class clique of militarily-disciplined conspirators. Yet Akimov still had telling points to make. He emphasised the prominent contribution made by the workers themselves in the Russian empire to the formulation of socialist ideas.[39] Akimov, had he so desired, could also have adduced English data. Brandishing the Webbs' researches, Ulyanov had declared that socialism could never have existed without direction by middle-class intellectuals (and that Karl Kautsky had said something similar in 1901).[40] But neither the Webbs' data nor later scholarship proved any such thing. English artisans and labourers in the early nineteenth century had elaborated varieties of socialism without the imposition of ideas by an intelligentsia.[41] Certainly, socialism has subsequently failed to attract the British working class as a whole; but the reasons for this lie in the country's pattern of socio-economic development, not in the irresolution of intellectuals.

Ulyanov's critics continued to contrast him with Marx and Engels. Martynov quoted extensively in order to show that Marx had assumed that workers of themselves moved towards socialism because of the nature of the capitalist system which oppressed and exploited them.[42] In 1869, Marx had stated: 'Trade unions are the schools of socialism. It is in the trade unions that workers educate themselves and become socialists, because under their eyes and every day the struggle with capital is taking place.'[43] These predictions of Marx's remain unfulfilled, as the English case shows. Nevertheless the point at issue here is different. It is that Marx emphasised the spontaneous growth of socialist consciousness whereas Ulyanov's book asserted a requirement for rigorous guidance by the intelligentsia. Martynov's case was powerful, but not completely invulnerable. Marx had also spoken about the virtues of communists who 'have over the great mass of the proletariat the advantage of clearly understanding the line of march, the conditions, and the ultimate general results of the proletarian movement.'[44] Evidently his concepts were not as clear-cut on spontaneity as Martynov supposed and, for that matter, Marx had not tried to produce a 'theory of the party'. Even so, Ulyanov had undoubtedly dispensed with an inconvenient but basic portion of the Marxian heritage. He was more pessimistic than Marx about workers. Undeniably, he had highlighted the 'elemental' force of the massed working class; he had said too that the party could not impose an insurrectionary time-schedule upon the urban crowds. Nonetheless he emphasised a 'negative' side. Workers who were not party members, in his portrayal, were good at destroying regimes through direct action on the streets; but this seemed to exhaust their virtues, save only that they took easily to discipline because of their factory training.[45] Justifiably, his critics complained of his underestimation of the organisational achievements of ordinary workers. They objected to his assertion that trade unions built up without assistance from the intelligentsia were bound to be amateurish, fragmented, localist affairs. Again the Webbs could be cited against him.[46]

What Is To Be Done? and *Letter to a Comrade*, moreover, were most evasive on a final matter raised by critics: how can it be ensured that the central party apparatus does not run out of control by the party? Ulyanov was concerned predominantly with the implementation of hierarchical command. He had no scheme for formal democratic accountability beyond the regular convocation of party congresses; this left the central apparatus with enormous latitude for organisational manipulation. It would be many years, not until the time of his last illness, before he would consider such commentary as anything other than the mental meanderings of those who had fallen under the spell of 'bourgeois' sociologists'.[47]

THE RUSSIAN POLITICAL ARENA

Iskra's editors aimed to rally support among Russian social-democrats and convoke a Second Party Congress; their intention was to get their strategy accepted as that of the party as a whole. Thus they would entrench themselves as party leaders. Thus, too, they expected to head the Russian revolutionary movement in its entirety. For Marxism had held sway over oppositionist thinking and activity in the 1890s.[48] The narodnik terrorists were disunited and ineffective; their agrarian socialist rivals who concentrated upon mass propaganda made little headway among peasants and workers. Meanwhile the liberals appeared as endless talkers. Social-democratic activists formed the most effective clandestine groups; even the catastrophe of 1899, when the police rounded up five hundred undergrounders, was a sign of the Marxist movement's gathering strength. No other political trend possessed so large a network of leaders. Marxist theory had also made a mark on the legal press. Books on Russian historical development were available in the shops of major cities. And the clandestine printing-presses made increasing quantities of political material available to activists and sympathisers. Their pre-eminence in the camp of the forces of opposition to the monarchy seemed unchallengeable; and it corroborated their belief that the 'vanguard' class in the democratic revolution was bound to be neither the middle class nor the peasantry but the factory workers.

This complacency was shattered at the turn of the century. The liberals moved towards forming a party. Their spokesman was Struve. By 1900 he was talking wholly negatively about Marxism. Ulyanov was surprised by his truculence. They met in Munich. The purpose of their discussions, which continued until mid-February 1901, was to cement their earlier agreement over joint publishing activity. A late-night session in December 1900 finally convinced Ulyanov that he would have to trim his demands; but, even so, he wanted to avoid loss of face: he made sure that Struve saw him laughing dismissively as they parted.[49] Neither Ulyanov nor Struve divulged whether they made a financial settlement. Nonetheless Struve now regarded liberalism as an independent movement in clandestine Russian politics. In 1902 he founded his journal *Liberation*. Its campaign for constitutional change was to do much to swing sections of the industrial bourgeoisie and the professions into a posture hostile to the autocracy.[50]

The *Iskra* editors were still more worried by the emergence of another political grouping. Agrarian socialism was again attracting support; its intellectual troubles in the late 1880s and early 1890s, when all its vivacity seemed to have been bequeathed to Russian Marxism, had not really been death-throes. In 1901 the new leaders established the Party Of Socialist-Revolutionaries.[51] The outstanding theorist and organiser was Viktor Mikhailovich Chernov. His ideas hearkened back to the narodniki. He refused to accept the argument of Russian social-democrats that the peasantry and the factory workers in Russia could be categorised as distinct classes of the population. Socialist-revolutionaries treated them together as 'the toiling people'. Unlike the narodniki of the 1880s, Chernov recognised that capitalist economic development was practicable in Russia. In fact he accepted that capitalism would and should exist for several more years; and he refrained from calling for the immediate introduction of socialism after the fall of the autocracy. The next stage in the country's political development would be a democratic republic. Even so, the socialist-revolutionaries intended to press for the 'socialisation of the land' without delay. Landed property would thereby be abolished. Agricultural soil would not be nationalised but transferred into 'the possession of the entire people'. This would not be socialism; the land would be divided up among those working on it but they would continue to produce for private profit. Chernov anticipated a lengthy epoch of propaganda before Russia would move from the 'bourgeois' to the 'socialist' phase.[52]

Not all his comrades agreed with him. A grouping which became known as the Maximalists wanted to instal a socialist government as the immediate successor to the Romanovs. They were less sceptical than Chernov about the rapid acceptability of socialist ideas to the Russian peasantry. They also re-introduced political terrorism. Both factions looked to the workers as well as the peasants for potential recruits.[53]

Iskra rejected Chernov's projects as being unscientific. All that Ulyanov would say in favour of the socialist-revolutionaries was that they did at least recognise that social differentiation was presently occurring in the village commune; he scorned their notion that governmental action could halt the process.[54] Agrarian capitalism was inevitable. So that, although Chernov's populism moved even closer to Russian Marxism than Aleksandr Ulyanov's had done, a gap still remained. *Iskra*, however, worried about the attractiveness that slogans like 'land and freedom' might have for urban workers. The Party of Socialist-Revolutionaries might snatch hegemony of the revolutionary forces. Young intellectuals in the Volga region were beginning to rally to Chernov's ideas, impressed as they were by the recrudescence of peasant turbulence after the quiescence of the 1890s.[55] In the Economist controversy, *Iskra* had been fighting heretics. The socialist-revolutionaries could be a more potent enemy: they were infidels. They inserted a dangerous element of subjectivism and diffuseness into debates among revolutionaries.[56] Indeed the internal life of the Russian Marxist movement itself already gave cause for concern. L. Nadezhdin, after emigrating to Switzerland, had formed a group called *Freedom*; he made his call for an immediate terrorist campaign ever more forcefully. *Iskra* had begun life fighting a 'right-wing' foe, which it dubbed Economism. From mid-1901 it was struggling on two fronts inside the party. The vehemence and frequency of its articles against *Freedom* show just how seriously the 'left-wing' threat was regarded.[57]

Ulyanov came to the fore as the implacable harrier of heretic and infidel. In March 1902 the security of *Iskra's* typesetting facilities in Munich could no longer be guaranteed, and the editorial board by a majority vote (with Plekhanov and Akselrod constituting the minority) decided to move premises to London.[58] Ulyanov's influence was increasing. This was partly the result of the low level of literary productivity of three of the six editors: Akselrod, Potresov and

Zasulich.[59] It also derived from his own superabundance of hard work and verve. His colleagues found him fastidious in life-style; Martov, Potresov and Zasulich set up their commune in the English capital, but nothing would induce him to become enveloped by what he saw as their bohemian muddle.[60] Krupskaya emigrated in 1901. She kept house for him, freeing him to study daily in the British Museum. He was turning into an excellent administrator. He was industrious in keeping tabs on the Russian underground; he and Krupskaya maintained a voluminous correspondence by means of invisible inks and laboriously-translated codes. He welcomed newcomers into emigration, especially those like Lev Davydovich Trotski who could be asked to write for *Iskra*.[61] Ulyanov revelled in his position of *primus inter pares*.

And with such a team, Ulyanov was in a fine position to campaign to win supporters in Russia; he saturated *Iskra* with the strategical and organisational concepts developed in *What Is To Be Done?* In a literal sense the book made his name. He had signed it with the pseudonym of 'N. Lenin' (which he had first used in 1901 in a letter to Plekhanov).[62] The book won him a fame among underground activists rivalled only by Plekhanov. Although he was to employ at least 160 *noms de guerre* in his career,[63] it was as Lenin that he ascended to general prestige inside the Russian Social-Democratic Labour Party; his *Iskra* writings consolidated a reputation already acquired as Marxist economic theorist and Petersburg activist. Ulyanov-Lenin moved to establish a tightly cohesive party. His old underground friends served him well. Men like B. I. Gorev, P. A. Krasikov and V. P. Nogin were sent into Russia to campaign for *Iskra*.[64] They made extensive tours, outdoing rival newspapers in energy and resources. Police at the border became efficient at intercepting packages of *Iskra*; but more devious routes of transport were found to expedite their arrival.[65] The pugnacity of Ulyanov-Lenin in Western Europe was emulated by his followers back in Russia. A Congress was to be called with all speed, and *Iskra*'s supporters were to ensure that provincial committees selected pro-*Iskra* representatives. Ulyanov-Lenin was unrestrainedly militant: 'A fight perhaps causes irritation to a few persons, but thereby it clears the air; it defines relations directly and precisely; it defines which disagreements are basic and which secondary, defines where there are people taking a completely different road and where there are true party comrades dissenting only about particularities.'[66]

THE PARTY PROGRAMME

It worried Ulyanov-Lenin that the *Iskra* board had not yet drafted a party programme; in 1901 he pestered Plekhanov to undertake the job. Plekhanov was respected as the party's primary theoretician. Ulyanov-Lenin was reluctant to make the first draft. Plekhanov, however, saw his own priority of the moment as being to crush Struve in philosophical debate.[67] Only late in the year did he succumb to Ulyanov-Lenin's badgerings.

Plekhanov offered up his manuscript around New Year 1902, and the six editors of *Iskra* met on 8 January to discuss it.[68] Ulyanov-Lenin turned up with an armful of proposed corrections. The other four watched in bemused horror as combat commenced. Plekhanov had always played the schoolmaster in disparaging Vladimir Ilich's prose style. Revenge was now exacted. The master was corrected magisterially. Plekhanov was taken to task for implying that the proletariat constituted a majority of the Russian population.[69] Ulyanov-Lenin was a harsh examiner. He laughed at Plekhanov's assumption that no consumer goods were available to factory workers.[70] Plekhanov's draft lacked punch. Why say 'discontent', asked Lenin, when you can say 'indignation'?[71] Months of contention followed, with Akselrod vainly calling upon the protagonists to mitigate their comments about each other. Plekhanov was asked to compose a second draft, which he completed by March. Lenin was no less displeased. Plekhanov's project was still repetitious and abstract; it was 'not the programme of a practically fighting party but a *Prinzipienerklärung*, it's more a programme for students'.[72] Zasulich lost patience. She could not see why Lenin was so aggressive when Plekhanov, for once, was obviously not averse to compromise. Lenin backed down. Even so, he continued to snipe at Plekhanov with remarks such as the following: 'I bow and give thanks for this little step towards me'.[73] No wonder that it was not until 1 June 1902 that the agreed programme of the *Iskra* board could be published.[74]

The final version was close to Lenin's draft of 1899; the sections on factory legislation were largely his creation, and the agrarian sections too bore his imprint.[75] Akselrod was content with the final product. Even Plekhanov was pleased. He teased Lenin over his inelegant use of brackets and punctuation marks, but the tensions eased between the two men in late 1902; both were willing to profess contentment with the *Iskra* programme. The party was to struggle for the greatest possible extension of civic freedoms in the post-autocratic state. It would call for the universal suffrage, for an elective administration, for a people's militia, for the secularisation of the state, and for the right of national self-determination. Its social goals would include compulsory universal education and a state pension scheme. The party would press for workers to obtain an eight-hour working day, more effective safety regulations, representation on arbitration tribunals, and the general opportunity to organise themselves in defence against employers; and for peasants to be allowed to form their own local committees as well as to possess the 'cut-off strips'. Lenin and Plekhanov presented a common front. They anticipated the maturation of the Russian capitalist economy under a bourgeois government constrained to concede political and social reforms which would facilitate the eventual coming to power of the social-democratic party.[76]

The front was a triumph over personal jealousies. It also was achieved despite disagreements over questions of substance. Plekhanov's preamble stated that 'capitalism is becoming more and more the dominant mode of production' in Russia. Lenin pressed that capitalism was 'already the dominant' mode.[77] Plekhanov accepted the amendment. As yet, in 1902, no differences in practical policy were hinged upon the contrasting phrasings; it was only in 1917, when Lenin began to call for the inception of the transition to socialism, that his higher estimation of the level of Russian economic development came to obtain direct political significance.[78]

No serious dissension was easily detectable in the discussion about the methods to be employed when socialism was introduced. Broad consensus existed. Both men expected that the social-democrats would take power only after a period of 'bourgeois rule' (which would follow the autocracy's overthrow). Both also characterised the transition to socialism under the term of 'the dictatorship of the proletariat'. Plekhanov mentioned this in his first draft.[79] When Lenin attacked his offering as being generally too 'noisy', Plekhanov substituted 'the political power' of the proletariat for 'dictatorship of the proletariat'.[80] But Lenin had in fact liked the original phrase, and encouraged its restoration. He noted that this was in line with their common interpretation of Marx's thinking.[81] Initially Plekhanov resisted the restoration; in his opinion there was no distinction between the two formulations under discussion since, as he proceeded to argue, 'in politics he who holds power is the dictator'.[82] But he saw no sense in further dispute and soon accepted Lenin's view.[83] Plekhanov would not foreswear the necessity of the working class to resort to force 'for the defence of its own interests and for the suppression of all social movements directly or indirectly threatening such interests'. Other classes in the population would have no guarantees of democratic civic rights.[84] Accordingly dictatorship, for both Lenin and Plekhanov, would be a stern business; neither leader committed himself to the principle of universal suffrage.

Again, however, the *Iskra* board's visible accord was not devoid of hints of fundamental disharmonies in later years. These nuances were partly a matter of tactical differences. But they also impinged upon basic political problems. Perhaps in 1902 they were too obscure for the potential significance to be discerned.

Firstly, Lenin was keener than Plekhanov to mention the party's suspicions about the peasantry. Rural attitudes were a mixture of progressive and reactionary qualities. The future socialist government, declared Lenin, should certainly attempt to persuade the peasants to accede to the abolition of private-enterprise practices. But it would be necessary to 'use power' if persuasion failed;[85] and therefore Lenin deplored Plekhanov's lack of reference to the peasantry's 'conservativeness'.[86] Plekhanov made no objection. He had in any case, ever since turning to Marxism, taken a dimmer view of the peasants than others like Lenin. Only Zasulich on the *Iskra* board objected to the proposed deployment of power: 'On millions of people! Just try then! . . .'[87] A further problem indicated a more serious implicit division between Lenin and Plekhanov. It concerned mass terror. *What Is To Be Done?* contained a passage lauding the narodnik Tkachev's standpoint on the subject as 'magnificent'.[88] Plekhanov approved the dictatorship's right to turn to violence in the case of political resistance; but he was not an enthusiast for terror: he never commended the execution of persons, regardless of their actions or opinions, just because they happened to belong to a particular social class. Lenin's approach was far cruder. He did not specifically threaten to organise a post-revolutionary terror. But, to put it mildly, his position was hardly typified by vehement opposition to such a policy; and his approval of this kind of terror was to re-surface from time to time well before the grim days of 1918.[89]

Iskra's leaders were anyway pre-occupied by the defence of their proposed programme from attack by other social-democrats. Dispute ensued between *Iskra* and its rivals. There was agreement that *Iskra*'s legislative schema for the post-autocratic republic was mostly acceptable; everyone in the party welcomed the extensive political and social rights to be demanded for the workers.

But controversy attended other matters. Martynov was a prominent critic. For him, the social-democratic party should be a workers' party aiming to represent the interests of the working class alone; its programme had no need for a section directed towards peasants. In any case, the party's general premise was that the overthrow of the absolute monarchy should lead to the removal of all remnants of feudal practice inhibiting capitalist economic development. Martynov asked how this would be assisted by the mere grant of the 'cut-off strips' to the peasantry. The assistance would be trivial.[90] P. P. Maslov, Lenin's old adversary in agrarian questions, pursued the point. He asked what was to stop *Iskra*'s peasant committees from seizing not only the 'cut-off strips' but the entire land. Maslov, unlike Martynov, recognised the party's need for an agrarian policy. His own proposals went further than Lenin's. He wanted the large gentry-owned latifundia to be transferred to local governmental agencies after the monarchy's overthrow.[91] Lenin's replies were caustic. He re-stated, answering Martynov, that the peasantry was doomed as a social class; and that it was 'tailism' to sit back and let the bourgeoisie dominate agrarian reform. He was less persuasive in retort to Maslov. He re-affirmed, bluntly and without further argumentation, that the implementation of his own ideas would deliver a deathblow to feudalism in Russian agriculture.[92] He also repeated his attitude to governmental ownership of land after the forthcoming revolution. His position was exactly as it had been when he had opposed L. Nadezhdin's demand for nationalisation as dangerously premature. He announced his abhorrence of 'idiotic experiments in state socialism'.[93]

Practical policies were not the only source of dissension from *Iskra*'s programme. General theory was involved. Neither Martynov nor Akimov accepted the down-playing of the workers' capacity for political self-development, and they harrassed Plekhanov as fiercely as they had Lenin over *What Is To Be Done?*[94] Martynov let the matter rest at that.[95] Not so Akimov: he was disturbed by other breaks with the conventional European understanding of Marxism which were made by *Iskra*; he especially objected to the demand for a proletarian dictatorship.[96]

THE SECOND PARTY CONGRESS

Russian social-democracy was riven by divisions over nearly every basic problem of revolution in 1902. Terrorism, peasants, organisation, workers, historical stages: all these vexed questions coiled around each other to produce an entanglement of programmatic uncertainty.[97]

The *Iskra* leaders strove, by means of the forthcoming Party Congress, to shape and fix official social-democratic opinion in their mould. The organisational controls were to be in their hands. The Congress's outcome would be affected by the composition of the delegations. *Iskra*'s plans were nearly frustrated in March 1902. Social-democratic leaders back in Russia, notably those belonging to *Southern Worker*'s editorial board and to the Bund, joined with the League Of Russian Social-Democrats Abroad to convoke a meeting in Bialystok. *Iskra* dispatched Fedor Dan. The meeting elected a three-person Organisational Committee to arrange a Congress.[98] Dan was one of the three; his presence would ensure that *Iskra* was not left uninvolved. Most attenders, however, were quickly arrested. Dan was among the victims. The sole member of the Organisational Committee remaining at liberty was K. Portnoi, a Bundist and *Iskra*'s enemy. Lenin had to resume the initiative quickly. He encouraged measures to call a further meeting in Pskov in November. Portnoi was persuaded to attend; and thus the Pskov sessions had some form of descent from the earlier meeting in Bialystok. An Organisational Committee was again chosen, this time with *Iskra*'s supporters in command. A further series of arrests weakened *Iskra*'s position in the winter of 1902–1903; but the determination of the agents on tour in Russia bore fruit. Party committees in Nizhni Novgorod, Saratov and Rostov announced loyalty to the theoretical and organisational principles of *Iskra*. Such victories were not always permanent; opponents were able in places like Ekaterinoslav to stir up worker members against the *Iskra* agents' contempt for elective practices. But the campaign was going *Iskra*'s way in spring 1903. And the Organisational Committee used its authority, in cases of dispute among local social-democrats, to validate the mandate of the faction siding with *Iskra*.[99]

The Second Congress itself began on 17 July 1903. The first venue was Brussels; but the attention of the Belgian police was aroused, and the Congress adjourned to London. Two days were consumed by exchanges about the Organisational Committee. The Bundists complained that their groups, which united tens of thousands of party members, were granted only five voting places at the Congress while tiny groups in central Russia had received a place apiece.[100] The critics' target was Lenin. But Plekhanov exonerated his colleague: 'Napoleon had a passion for making his marshals divorce their wives: some gave in to him in the matter even though they loved their wives. Comrade Akimov is like Napoleon in this respect – he desires at any cost to divorce me from Lenin.'[101] And the Congress, with its built-in *Iskra* majority, sanctioned the Organisational Committee's actions.[102]

The question of the Bund came next on the agenda. Bundist leader M. I. Liber put the case that the Jewish population of the empire confronted special problems, not least the pogroms; and that the Bund should therefore be granted broad organisational autonomy inside the party. Martov and Trotski, Jews themselves, opposed. Passions ran high. Yet the resultant voting had never been in doubt: the Bund's proposal was rejected by forty six delegates against five.[103] The Congress turned to decide the party programme. Lenin, already pleased by the Bund discussion, took as prominent a role in debate as Plekhanov. *Iskra*'s project was taken as the basis for discussion.[104] Martynov headed the critics, assailing *Iskra*'s editors for implying that workers could not come to socialism without the guidance of middle-class intellectuals. Lenin admitted to exaggerations: 'We all know now that the Economists bent the stick in one direction. In order to straighten the stick it was necessary to bend it over in the other direction, and that is what I did.'[104] Plekhanov backed Lenin. He defended, too, the reference to the 'dictatorship of the proletariat'. After the socialist takeover of power in the distant future, Plekhanov argued, a social-democratic government might well not immediately feel safe to submit itself to electoral competition at regular intervals.[106] The Congress accepted the general analysis afforded by the *Iskra* board.

The delegates then considered the programme's specific policies. The section on factory legislation was greeted with acclaim. The agrarian section was less warmly received. Seven speakers criticised it, and only Trotski spoke in Lenin's favour.[107] Most critics harried Lenin for offering too little to the peasantry: an interesting occurrence in view of attacks on him for being a crypto-populist. But Lenin's suggestions were accepted by a thumping majority. The *Iskra* project, with few amendments, became the official party programme.[108]

The travails of Congress were just beginning. Its commission drafting the party rules was at odds; the Iskra team itself was divided. Martov disliked Lenin's proposal on the conditions of party member-ship. He took Potresov and Trotski with him. Lenin wanted to define a party member as someone 'who recognises the party programme and supports it by material means and by personal participation in one of the party's organisations'.[109] Martov's formulation ran slightly differently. His member would be someone 'who recognises the party programme and supports it by material means and by regular personal assistance under the direction of one of the party's organisations';[110] and Martov recommended his own definition as being less authoritarian and exclusive than Lenin's. The precise literal contrast is elusive. So much so that many would attribute the disputes to vapourisings induced by the over-heated expatriate political atmosphere. But there was also a fundamental issue at stake; Lenin and Martov each knew what the other meant in broad terms. Martov wanted a slightly more 'open' party than Lenin. His current priority was to maximise the recruitment of factory workers to the party, whereas Lenin's was to take precautions against infiltration by persons with no intention of active participation in party life. The Congress decided in Martov's favour. Twenty eight 'softs' took his line while Lenin could muster only twenty two 'hards'.[111]

The split in *Iskra*'s ranks lasted the rest of the Congress. Lenin proposed a tripartite structure for the supreme party apparatus. The central newspaper, *Iskra*, would be based abroad and produced by three editors. The Central Committee, which was to supply organisational guidance to local committees, would be a three-person team located in Russia. Co-ordination between *Iskra* and the Central Committee would be ensured by a Party Council with five members – two to come from *Iskra*, two from the Central Committee and one to be elected directly by Congress.[112]

Martov found the proposal anything but innocuous. A three-person editorial board could only mean the removal of Akselrod, Potresov and Zasulich. Plekhanov and Lenin would lord it over *Iskra*. Martov's speech caused a surprise, since he had assented to Lenin's proposal before the opening of the Congress.[113] Angry exchanges occurred. Outside the hall there was trouble when A. V. Shotman threatened to beat up an *Iskra* 'hard' who had gone over to the 'softs'. Lenin raced out to tug back Shotman with the admonition that 'only fools use their fists in polemics'.[114] Non-violent dirty tricks, however, were not ruled out. Lenin's supporter S. I. Gusev circulated a forged list purporting to contain Martov's nominees for the central party apparatus; it included, as a ploy to discredit Martov, several advocates of the 'Economistic' ideas already condemned by the entire *Iskra* faction.[115] Lenin strove to weld the 'hards' together. He made the rounds of the delegates, ascertaining their political stance and jotting them down as either 'hards' or 'softs' in his notebook. A meeting of 'hards' was held on 3 August. Still Martov did not despair of restoring harmony. There were many issues which saw both groupings inside *Iskra* united. In particular it was their common wish that the party should be centralised, disciplined and clandestine; the 'softs' felt no less strongly than the 'hards' that Russian political conditions disallowed the formation of an open mass party on the model of German social-democrats. But Plekhanov and Lenin would not compromise. In order to keep their supporters' loyalty in quarantine they denied the floor to Martov at their grouping's session.[116]

The Congress sanctioned Lenin's tripartite central structure. Plekhanov and Lenin thereupon had a stroke of luck. The Bundists walked out on 5 August, affronted by their treatment by the Congress. These would certainly have sided with Martov. In the event, the *Iskra* ballot gave places to Plekhanov, Lenin and Martov.[117] Martov declined to serve as the solitary 'soft'. His supporters knew that the battle was lost for the Central Committee, and they refused to cast votes. The 'hards' coasted home. The Central Committee was to consist of G. M. Krzhizhanovski, F. V. Lengnik and V. A. Noskov. Plekhanov's own position was reinforced by his simultaneous election as the Congress's representative on the Party Council.[118]

Even now the marathon was not ended. On 10 August the delegates discussed the party's attitude to other anti-autocratic political groups. This was the Cinderella debate of the Congress. The earlier disputes could not quickly be erased from the memory. Even Lenin was exhausted. Yet this last question required some answers: how close could social-democrats draw to the political parties of the middle class? Potresov's proposal allowed for temporary alliances, so long as they did not harm 'the interests of the working class'. The Plekhanov-Lenin axis found this phrasing too bland. Plekhanov's counter-proposal, while permitting 'support' for other anti-autocratic groups, required the party nevertheless to 'unmask before the proletariat the limited and inadequate nature of the bourgeois liberation movement'.[119] Plekhanov desired a campaign against Struve. Martov, Akselrod and Trotski stood by Potresov. Lenin stood by Plekhanov. The Congress had already lasted over three weeks, and time and funds and patience were running out. Discussion was terminated. The Congress opted to approve both projects and to turn a blind eye to the discrepancies between them.[120] It was the peace-making of fatigue. Disagreements about attitudes to the liberals would soon in fact acquire even greater importance than those about organisation. Potresov and his fellow 'softs' were developing a sturdier belief in the possibilities of co-operation with Struve's adherents; the 'hards' offered an ever more dismal judgement upon the liberals as allied. The embryonic growth of two separate Marxist parties for Russia had begun.

6   From this Accursed Distance

POST-CONGRESS IMBROGLIO

Organisational cohesion does not come easily to an oppositional political party in emigration. A governing party experiences a myriad of impulses conducive to minimising internal fractiousness; and this is of assistance to any cabinet wishing to adopt policies as circumstances seem to require. The political will for unity is not universally secure in such situations. But a party in government possesses a further asset in the shape of its capacity to dispense patronage: it can move its favoured members to posts associated with authority and material comfort. Parties in opposition confront difficulties by comparison. Opportunities for the disbursement of office and affluence are restricted (although the German Social-Democratic Party's record before 1914 shows that they can still be substantial). Political frustrations are enormous. Fissiparous debates about strategy continually threaten to replace constructive practical operations. Collective support for unification has to be cultivated. This task is beset by problems all the more severe in organisations which are not only oppositional but also illegal, clandestine and partly based abroad; the technical as well as the political strains are immense. Their need for concerted action is in many ways more pressing than for legal, domestic groupings. And yet every attempt to bring about organised unity runs the risk of raising even higher the temperature in the political greenhouse of emigration.

Intemperate discourse and behaviour had made Russian expatriate revolutionaries notorious in the rest of Europe long before the birth of Russian Marxism. The reputation was beginning to attach itself to Russian Marxists too by the turn of the century. Emigré disputatiousness contrasted with the more restrained modes of disagreement characteristic of debates among the Marxists in Russia in the 1890s; and the susceptibility of the Swiss-centred groups to disruptiveness was made acute by the presence of theorists like Lenin and Plekhanov who had become so averse to compromise in party discussions.

Lenin was after the total exploitation of his triumph in the elections to the central party apparatus. His group called itself the *Bolsheviki* (or 'Majoritarians'), hoping to enhance its status as the legitimate leadership. Martov's group took the name of *Mensheviki* (or 'Minoritarians'). Martov himself re-opened hostilities. He wanted to win back Plekhanov. The opportunity arose at a gathering of the Foreign League Of Revolutionary Russian Social-Democracy in Geneva in October 1903. The Party Congress had established the League as the party's sole organisation abroad. Martov led the assault upon Lenin's position. Lenin learned that he had placed a gun in Martov's hands in early summer by making him privy to *Iskra*'s pre-Congress manoeuvres. Martov told of Lenin's plan to reduce the size of the editorial board to three persons. The intended victims included not only Akselrod, Potresov and Zasulich but even Plekhanov himself. 'Don't you see,' Lenin had purred to Martov, 'that if we stick by each other, we'll keep Plekhanov constantly in a minority and he'll be able to do nothing about it?'[1] The revelation shattered Lenin's composure. He made no defence. Having calculated the balance of forces at the League's gathering, he knew that he would be outvoted. He stormed out, slamming the door. Martov's allegations disturbed Plekhanov too. The 'state of siege' in the party had anyway been depressing him, to the point that he stated that 'suicide would be preferable to schism'.[2] Factional reconciliation was now his professed objective. To effect a truce he was ready to step down from *Iskra*. If Plekhanov resigned, many would take it as proof that Lenin truly was the party's tyrant. Lenin suddenly seemed to be facing defeat. On 3 November he announced his resignation from *Iskra* and the Party Council.[3]

Lenin soon cursed himself for having panicked.[4] Plekhanov revealed his alienation from Lenin; his scheme to reconcile the two warring groups would not be undertaken evenhandedly. Privately he called Lenin the party's Robespierre. And the removal of Lenin from *Iskra* by painless surgery induced the Mensheviks to think that their problems had disappeared forever. Not so. In abandoning *Iskra*, Lenin had not forgotten 'to keep a stone in his sling'. He asked to be co-opted to the Central Committee. The Central Committee consisted of Bolsheviks. And when, in mid-November 1903, Krzhizhanovski arrived in Switzerland from Russia it was an easy formality for Lenin to obtain membership. Lenin and fellow Bolshevik L. E. Galperin were appointed Central Committee representatives on the Party Council.[5] Plekhanov had to act with dispatch. *Iskra* presently had no Council representative apart from Plekhanov himself. Lenin could seize back control of the newspaper through his dominance inside the Central Committee. Plekhanov's responded by co-opting Mensheviks to the *Iskra* board.[6]

Stalemate resulted, and the Mensheviks anticipated that Lenin would be constrained to restore amicable working relations with them. Lenin, however, felt cheated by Plekhanov, and fought on for unconditional victory. But he reckoned without Krzhizhanovski. On 17 November 1903 there was a session of the Party Council and Krzhizhanovski, fearful of a party split, guaranteed to have Galperin withdrawn from Council membership; Krzhizhanovski also agreed to press the Central Committee to co-opt Mensheviks into its membership. Few Bolsheviks craved the exclusion of all Mensheviks from leading positions; and Krzhizhanovski asked Lenin whether he really could be right when so impressive a majority thought him wrong.[7] Krzhizhanovski's concessions were expected to initiate a new era in party relations. Lenin had other plans. He demanded the convocation of a Third Party Congress so that the party as a whole might adjudicate the Bolshevik-Menshevik dispute. In December, he bombarded groups and activists in Russia with letters of self-justification. In January 1904 he attended the Party Council, repeating his call for a Congress; he denounced the Mensheviks as opportunists and disorganisers. Martov in retort castigated Lenin as a power-crazed egomaniac; and he treated the idea of a Congress as financially insupportable and organisationally productive only of schism. Lenin's hopes of prising Plekhanov away from Martov faded. The Council turned down Lenin's proposals. Plekhanov was so infuriated by Lenin's belligerence that he denounced him in *Iskra* as a 'Bonapartist'.[8]

The Central Committee too was annoyed with Lenin. Krzhizhanovski, Noskov and the recently-co-opted L. B. Krasin were all Bolsheviks appalled by the possibility of an organisational rupture; they spurned Lenin's request that his supporter P. A. Krasikov be seconded to the Central Committee. In February 1904 they wrote: 'We all implore the Old Man to give up his quarrel and start work. We await leaflets, pamphlets and advice of all kinds – the best way of soothing the nerves and answering slander.'[9] Lenin replied that he was not a machine; and that he could not obliterate Martov's and Plekhanov's criticisms from his mind.[10] Krzhizhanovski thought him to have lost touch with Russian reality. The Central Committee invited him to leave Switzerland and join them in the underground. Lenin was unmoved and unmoving.[11]

In spring 1904 it became the conviction of other Bolsheviks in the Central Committee that Lenin was the greatest obstacle to the re-unification of the central party apparatus. Lenin had overstretched himself. In February, his friend R. S. Zemlyachka clashed with L. E. Galperin in the Central Committee. Galperin too had ceased to support Lenin. Zemlyachka in the heat of the moment announced her resignation from the Central Committee; and, to her horror, the other members were unwilling to allow her to retract.[12] Lenin blustered on. He endeavoured to browbeat the Central Committee firstly by resigning from the Party Council and then by threatening to withdraw from the Central Committee too. His bluff called, he resumed his positions before he lost them permanently.[13] Accordingly the all-Bolshevik Central Committee now had eight members: V. A. Noskov and G. M. Krzhizhanovski (who had been elected by Congress) together with M. M. Essen, L. E. Galperin, N. V. Gusarov, L. B. Krasin, F. V. Lengnik and Lenin himself (all of whom had been co-opted). Of these, only Essen and Lengnik were firmly with Lenin; and they wrote to Russia in hope of winning over the rest. They still considered that, if only the Russia-based leaders could see how the Mensheviks were behaving, the Central Committee would drop its peace-making proposals.[14] Noskov, however, took the initiative. He got the Central Committee members to issue him with a reprimand to deliver to Lenin. In May 1904 he reached Switzerland and, with the Central Committee's authority, forbade Lenin to campaign for the convocation of a Party Congress. Noskov objected to the savagery of Lenin's writings. He sought to halt publication of the anti-Menshevik tract *One Step Forward, Two Steps Back*. Again Lenin threatened to resign. Noskov compromised, feeling strong enough in the Central Committee in the contingency of further serious dispute. An agreement was made. Thenceforward Noskov and Lenin were to be joint representatives of the Central Committee abroad, and neither man would take any important decisions without the other's consent.[15]

'ONE STEP FORWARD, TWO STEPS BACK'

The same agreement permitted the continued distribution of *One Step Forward, Two Steps Back*. It had first appeared on 6 May 1904.[16]

Drafted and redrafted since February, its empirical basis was an extensive psephological analysis of the Second Party Congress. It was 'instant history'. The style was hectoring; *What Is To Be Done?*, in comparison, seems like exemplary disinterested research. No self-doubt, no self-criticism.

The work constituted the thrust of his counter-attack. It was an uncustomary operation for him. Always before, he had been the aggressor, the initiator of conflict. His earliest attackers after the Congress had been Akselrod and Plekhanov. Trotski then declared his support for them; and, when *One Step Forward* came out, he published his booklet *Our Political Tasks* in reply. Lenin's pronouncements had unexpectedly become an issue for European social-democracy as a whole. Rosa Luxemburg, the Polish Jew who was prominent in the German Social-Democratic Party, arraigned him in her *Organisational Questions in Russian Social-Democracy*. For a while, Kautsky thought of taking sides against Lenin; but he was deterred in the end by both fear of aggravating the dispute and recognition that his knowledge of the Russian Social-Democratic Labour Party was far from being comprehensive.[17] Akselrod, Plekhanov, Trotski and Luxemburg had been amazed and offended by Lenin's activity at the Second Party Congress; his polemical techniques struck them as mere abusiveness. They also challenged his doctrinal positions. They were picking up and extending arguments aimed against Lenin's *What Is To Be Done?* by Martynov and Akimov. Plekhanov openly acknowledged this; and Martov publicly regretted that he had not taken writers like Akimov seriously in the first instance.[18] Lenin's enemies, though making their forays independently of each other, drew upon a similar arsenal of ammunition.

Their assault upon Lenin's ideas was multi-directional. It was asserted that they were anti-worker; that they were the embodiment of bureaucratic centralism; and that they would, objectively, open the gates to precisely the political opportunism which they had been designed to disbar.

Akselrod maintained that Lenin expected factory workers to act as political cannon-fodder under the generalship of the radical middle-class intelligentsia.[19] Plekhanov concurred with Akselrod, and added that Russian socialism had been formed not by intellectuals in isolation but through a process of interaction between middle-class activists and discontented urban labourers.[20] This may possibly have been the gist of his original objection to *What Is To Be Done?* at the time of its publication. Be that as it may, Luxemburg expanded on Plekhanov's arguments. *What Is To Be Done?*, she maintained, eulogised the obedience and discipline instilled in the working class by the factory system. She, by contrast, saw rebelliousness against 'authority' as the primary desirable attribute of the true socialist. Lenin seemed to her to be crazed with regimentative pretensions and menace.[21] Plekhanov predicted that Bolshevik organisational theory, if taken to its logically consistent end, would establish not the dictatorship of the proletariat but 'a dictatorship over the proletariat'. Lenin would realise 'the ideal of the Persian Shah'.[22] Trotski agreed with Plekhanov and uttered the following prophecy: 'The organisation of the party takes the place of the party itself; the Central Committee takes the place of the party organisation; and finally "the dictator" takes the place of the Central Committee.'[23]

Such an internal regime, according to Lenin's adversaries, would be bureaucratic centralism. Akselrod accused Lenin of 'organisational fetishism': the Bolsheviks were politically so introspective that they risked overlooking opportunities for the advancement of the revolutionary cause in Russia.[24] Trotski went further. For him, *What Is To Be Done?* proposed a party structure which could not long endure.[25] Lenin's followers would become disillusioned with so strict an insistence upon their servility to him. The most talented activists would inevitably desert Bolshevism. It worried Trotski, though, that Lenin's prescriptions might become identified by Russian social-democrats as the only possible variant of centralism. The goal of centralisation would lose favour. And this would prepare the ground for 'socialist opportunists'. The discrediting of Lenin would lead to the discrediting of the entire programme of revolutionary social-democracy.[26] Trotski's fears were shared by Luxemburg. She stressed the tendency of party leaderships to take an increasingly conservative view of their duties. Her solution, as explained in her pamphlet, was for rank-and-file members to be encouraged to keep their committees on the path of revolution.[27]

Unrepentant, Lenin charged his critics with hypocrisy. He was helped in this by the fact that no social-democrat was yet fully convinced that epoch-making questions of principle underlay the Bolshevik-Menshevik dispute.[28] Even Plekhanov took months to complete his doctrinal case.[29] Lenin pounced on this. He claimed that the verbal violence of the Second Party Congress had occurred mainly because a minority of delegates had refused to accept majority decisions. The Bolsheviks had won by fair means. In order to justify the struggle after the Congress, the Mensheviks had been compelled to exaggerate the ideological importance of their differences with the Bolsheviks. Originally, according to Lenin, Menshevism was more a ploy than a doctrine. He despised its 'rhetoric'. When the Mensheviks called for guarantees of the right of freedom of speech for oppositions, he claimed, they did so from selfish motives. Underneath them lay no terrain of principle.[30] He was not alone in making this claim: Bogdanov and Lunacharski said equally forcefully that the Mensheviks were playing at politics and not articulating a doctrinal alternative. Neither Bogdanov nor Lunacharski had much time for émigrés in general. They considered that even Lenin was not entirely *au fait* with the Russian party's needs; but they treated the Menshevik leaders as the real villains of the piece in the disputes in Geneva.[31]

Yet the anti-Lenin phalanx had nevertheless made at least a few substantive theoretical points; and Lenin was obliged to offer his defence. He omitted to reply in detail to the charge that *What Is To Be Done?* drastically down-graded the functions of the working class in revolutionary struggle; he stuck to a curt, unelaborated denial that he regarded obedience as the greatest positive characteristic of factory labourers.[32] Bogdanov and Lunacharski were more forthcoming. They highlighted the sections of Lenin's book which emphasised the working class's 'vanguard' role; and themselves stressed the important strides made in political self-organisation by Russian workers.[33] It was only in later years that Bogdanov came to see Lenin's failure to provide a similarly strong pro-worker case as something sinister.[34]

At all events, Lenin in *One Step Forward* wished to focus on middle-class intellectuals rather than workers. His counter-charge against the Mensheviks was that they, with their abhorrence of Bolshevik discipline, were leaning towards 'anarchic individualism'. Menshevik ideas, if implemented, would give succour to desk-bound professors who would not work for the party and yet would quibble over the minutest aspects of party policy. 'Opportunists' would enter the party in an uncontrolled flood. Thus Lenin hoped to turn the tables on his opponents in debate: it was allegedly the Mensheviks who wanted to raise the power of middle-class intellectuals, not Lenin.[35] Yet his accusation does not entirely convince. The Menshevik criticisms had been directed at a different sort of intellectual: the full-time activist. Akselrod's main argument had been aimed against the emergence of an uncontrollable élite of professionals.[36] *One Step Forward*, judged as political theory rather than political invective, was consequently a disappointing work. In their own faltering way, his opponents had exposed the Achilles' heel of his organisational ideas.

What Is To Be Done? had indeed implied a certain condescension towards workers; its concrete recommendations were also potentially more injurious to the democratisation of party life in the years ahead than he supposed; and it assuredly did get centralisation and discipline a worse name than they would otherwise have attracted.[37]

ALPINE HOLIDAY

Lenin's wife and friends saw the strain telling on him. Even before the Second Party Congress he had been tired, and the ensuing winter of 1903–4 brought no relief. His physical condition was poor. While bicycling through Geneva, he had run into the rear of a tramcar and sustained gashes to the head. For some weeks he appeared at gatherings becowled in a white bandage.[38] He cut a somewhat terrifying figure.

The Bolshevik–Menshevik dispute, its rights and wrongs, pushed everything else to the back of his mind. Rarely has there been a more single-minded politician. At any one time it was his custom to elaborate a supreme immediate goal. Once defined, it had to be pursued at any expense. He doubted the efficaciousness of trying to follow a cluster of goals at once. He liked to keep his short-term politics uncomplicated (while yet being cognisant of the complexity of the continuing struggle for socialism in the years to come). This was both asset and draw-back for him. In 1917 it would be distinctly advantageous; from February to October, whereas his enemies were pondering the complications of policy, he had one main prodding thought: to seize power. But in 1904 monocentrism was less fruitful. Since the late 1890s he had believed that the party should cleanse its ranks of ideological impurity, should centralise its operations, should cleave to the strictest disciplinary code. It did not matter to him that many Mensheviks agreed with him about other aspects of revolutionary strategy. He conceived of political activity as being best undertaken in stages. And the current stage, he reasoned, should be taken up with the organisational formation of the party. Hence this otherwise flexible leader (and indeed his flexibility would become more and more notorious in many social-democratic milieux) saw no room for compromise.

But the pressure increased. The rift with Plekhanov and Martov affected his health. P. N. Lepeshinski described the change: 'I witnessed him in such a depressed condition of spirit as it was never my lot to see him in either before or after that period.' Despite his prodigious capacity for rapid writing, he had toiled like a novice over *One Step Forward, Two Steps Back*. 'It looks as though I shan't finish the booklet,' he had complained, 'I'll throw up everything and go off to the mountains!'[39]

The remark is doubly interesting. Unusual as it was for Vladimir Ilich Ulyanov-Lenin to lose his panache, it was still more extraordinary for him to communicate such a loss to his comrades. Among émigrés, his name was a by-word for optimism. His self-belief was crucial to the maintenance of a trusting group of activists around him. He sensed that a political party in autocratic Russia needed a leadership with more than intellectual self-assurance and organisational cohesion. Leaders had to supply emotional strength. At the slightest expression of doubts by his followers, Lenin would state and re-state the articles of faith: 'But look here: I myself, let me be allowed to inform you, am most profoundly convinced that I shall survive until the socialist revolution in Russia.'[40] Lenin treated it as his duty to offer the maximum of psychological support. If a Bolshevik fell into police custody, he and Krupskaya would dispatch a comforting letter. Lenin also tried to be the first to make personal contact with Russian social-democrats newly arriving in Switzerland. Martov, though well-meaning, lacked the self-application to compete with Lenin as an organiser. Lenin was the good shepherd to his flock.[41] Nikolai Valentinov, later a prominent anti-Bolshevik, never forgot the down-to-earth assistance rendered him on one particular day in Geneva. Lacking a private income, Valentinov had to work as a barrow-pusher. On an occasion when he was given a particularly heavy consignment for removal, he could find many comrades sympathetic with his plight; but no one's sympathy, except Lenin's, stretched as far as an offer of active help. Valentinov and Lenin pushed the load across the city to its destination; and Valentinov received his vital wage.[42]

In early 1904, however, this attractive component of Lenin's personality was slipping its gear. Lenin diagnosed the symptoms. He needed a break from the routine of politics. Since coming to Western Europe, he had not had much time for the sportive sort of relaxation he enjoyed. His regular afternoon strolls were too undemanding.[43]

He decided to take a couple of months' holiday in the Swiss Alps. Such a project did not then require plutocratic funding. Lenin was anyway not stinted for finances. He received an allowance from the party as Central Committee member; he was sent royalties on his legally-published books. And his mother supplemented his account when he felt hard-pressed.[44] Lenin and Krupskaya set off in the first fortnight of June 1904. They threw up their rented Geneva house; and Lenin drafted a note devolving his authority as foreign representative of the Central Committee to close supporters.[45] They limited the number of books in their baggage and, to their own astonishment, succeeded in avoiding reading most of what they took. Baedeker's *Switzerland* took pride of place in their knapsacks. They promised not to talk about political business, nor even, 'insofar as it was possible', to think about it.[46] They drew up no itinerary programme. By steamer they travelled to Montreux and visited the castle of Chillon. Mountain-walking was their principal recreation. They were not always alone, being accompanied for some days by Mariya Essen. Vladimir set them a fast pace. He chuckled at their discomfiture; in play as in work, he believed that personal satisfaction rose in proportion to effort expended. Postcards depicting Mount Jungfrau were sent by the self-styled 'vagabonds'.[47] Lenin's health and mood steadily improved. Towards late July they settled temporarily in a pension overlooking Lac de Bré, near Lausanne. There they stayed until the start of September (when they returned to Geneva).[48] They had partaken of the pleasures of contemporary tourism with the same zeal which, in the test of 1904, they devoted to the overthrow of the European bourgois political order. Lenin's spirit was restored.[49]

THE BUREAU OF COMMITTEES OF THE MAJORITY

Yet his game in the Central Committee in early summer had been played with weak cards. Noskov held trumps. Lenin knew Noskov could mobilise a Central Committee majority in favour of reconciliation with the Mensheviks. Before going off on vacation, Lenin had warned sympathisers in Russia that a *coup d'état* was possible; and privately he took a more dismal view, reckoning that an offensive by Noskov was not just a possibility but a likelihood.[50] Noskov asked for discussions with Lenin. Lenin refused. Noskov had already dragged him to the limits of what he regarded as conscionable compromise. But Noskov was determined to re-unify the factions. He proposed to co-opt two Mensheviks into the Central Committee in return for the co-opting of Lenin on to the *Iskra* board.[51] Neither Noskov nor his friends withdrew their admiration for *What Is To Be Done?*; and they still felt that the Second Party Congress had given the Bolsheviks the right to greater influence at the apex of the party than the Mensheviks.

But Lenin's policy, they feared, would split the Russian Social-Democratic Labour Party needlessly and destructively into two separate organisations.[52] Lenin in fact was not yet calling for a schism. Rather he demanded a reduction in Menshevik influence in the central party apparatus, and he had left for his holiday in a mood of angry self-righteousness.

Noskov, meanwhile, visited Russia. He contacted Galerin and Krasin. The three of them considered themselves entitled to act as the Central Committee. Zemlyachka had resigned. Lengnik had just been arrested. Gusarov and Krzhizhanovski were so dispirited by the in-fighting that they too had resigned. Mariya Essen was incarcerated upon return to Russia in midsummer.[53] Noskov, Galperin and Krasin could easily now outvote Lenin. They co-opted three more like-minded Bolshevik 'Conciliators' to the Central Committee: I. F. Dubrovinski, L. Y. Karpov and A. I. Lyubimov. A statement of regret and reproof was made that Lenin had recently written so few pamphlets; and Noskov was enjoined to communicate their so-called July Declaration to Lenin. They wanted a rapprochement between Bolsheviks and Mensheviks in the central party apparatus, and they hoped that Lenin would bow before the *fait accompli*.[54]

All along, Lenin had set his face against this. He had radiated the determination that his sterner version of Bolshevism would win the day in the party as a whole; and he had sworn to abandon the Central Committee and conduct 'a desperate struggle' if Noskov went through with a coup.[55] Receiving the Declaration in August, he was ready with his counter-stroke. He summoned a meeting outside Geneva. Twenty two Bolsheviks signed a letter of protest, *To The Party*. The place of the meeting was not mentioned; Lenin wanted to give the impression that the protesting voices had originated in Russia rather than Switzerland. *To The Party* demanded that a Congress be convoked immediately.[56] Among the signatories was M. S. Olminski. He had previously been based in Paris; he and his confederates in France had taken Lenin's side in the Bolshevik–Menshevik controversy. They were talented writers and organisers and had contacts with party groups in Russia. They had also welcomed Lenin's invitation to join him by Lac de Bré. Their leading lights were Aleksandr Bogdanov and Anatoli Vasilevich Lunacharski. Lenin and Bogdanov got on well personally; and, with appropriate interludes of mountain-walking and swimming, they formulated tactics to regroup the forces inside the party supporting the pro-Lenin Bolshevik cause. The Central Committee and *Iskra* were in the hands of the enemy. The two men concluded that the time had come to construct new organisational and publishing institutions.[57]

In autumn 1904, their emissaries hastened to Russia to arrange three regional conferences of Bolsheviks. The regions were northern Russia, southern Russia and the Transcaucasus. Each conference selected representatives to serve on a body which, on Lenin's suggestion, was dubbed the Bureau Of Committees Of The Majority.[58]

The Bureau was to stimulate the convocation of a Party Congress. It had no fewer than eight members, including Bogdanov. It also contained several leading organisers such as P. P. Rumyantsev, A. I. Rykov and R. S. Zemlyachka.[59] The Bureau's creation was complemented by a Bolshevik literary venture which was initiated by Lenin even before Bogdanov's arrival. This was the 'publishing house of social-democratic party literature of V. Bonch-Bruevich and N. Lenin'. Pamphlets and leaflets were issued.[60] Noskov's Central Committee obstructed progress by prohibiting access to the official party printing facilities. Funds too were running short. But to the rescue came Bogdanov. He knew of potential providers of subsidy in Russia and sped off to trace them. Lenin raged at him for not writing back regularly. Cursed by Lenin for his 'swinish' behaviour, Bogdanov went his own way.[61] By 27 November 1904 Lenin was changing his attitude. He wrote glowingly to M. M. Litvinov about Bogdanov's prospective success in attracting literary contributors and making approaches to a sympathetic millionaire.[62] Lenin's further aim was to set up a newspaper to compete with *Iskra*, now under Menshevik control. The name would be *Vpered* (or *Forward*). He expected to rely heavily upon the newcomers from Paris. Discussions led to agreement on an editorial board of Lenin, Bogdanov, Lunacharski, Olminski and V. V. Vorovski. Arrangements went well and *Vpered*'s publication commenced on 22 December; and, in a short while, Lenin was producing the newspaper on a weekly basis.[63]

Lenin's position inside his faction was now seemingly impregnable. He had worked for the creation of a factional Bureau and a factional newspaper; and, far from being swept overboard by Noskov, he had sailed on to achieve both objectives. The Central Committee, headed by Bolshevik Conciliators, was shocked by his group's ease in consolidating its network of agents in Russia. A. I. Lyubimov fell into despondency. He urged Noskov to face up to the fact that nearly all social-democratic organisations in Russia proper, except those in the south, were held by supporters of the Bureau.[64] This turnabout appeared to many as Lenin's personal victory. Yet his authority inside his faction was by no means dictatorial; and, within weeks, he was destined to lose his leading position to Aleksandr Bogdanov.

RUSSIAN TURMOIL AND THE CALL FOR A SPLIT

The urgent practical purpose of *What Is To Be Done?* had been to prepare Russian social-democrats to take advantage of a political situation likely to explode into revolution at any moment. The year 1904 was the most disturbing yet in Nikolai II's reign. Bolshevik leaders in Russia were keen to treat the crisis of the autocracy as the principal focus of social-democratic activity.

War had started in January between Japan and Russia. V. K. von Pleve, Minister of Internal Affairs, warned that military conflict might detonate ungovernable turbulence at home. Nikolai II ignored his counsel. For years there had been rivalry between the Russian empire and Japan over territory, trade and influence in the Far East. Russian armies were transported eastward by the Trans-Siberian railway, while the Baltic fleet set out on its voyage of twenty six thousand miles to the Pacific. But disasters occurred immediately. Japan's industrial growth made her a redoubtable adversary in her own sphere of operations in the Far East. In April, Japanese troops overwhelmed the Russians in the land battle of the Yalu river. Russia's Far-Eastern fleet was beseiged in Port Arthur.[65] The war had never been welcomed by the Russian empire's national minorities. Poles and Finns hoped for a Russian defeat. Anti-tsarist demonstrations occurred in Warsaw. As the set-backs in the Far East were reported, hostility to the government spread to Russia proper. Pleve clamped down. Already in 1903 he had dismissed Zubatov from his police post and thus terminated the experimental development of trade unions. The slightest weakening of state power was anathema to him. In spring 1904 he obstructed the activity of liberal-dominated zemstva.[66] Throughout the empire there were reports of unrest among workers and peasants. Strikes increased in number. The socialist-revolutionaries initiated a terrorist campaign. In July 1904 they struck. Sazonov, leader of their Combat Organisation, assassinated Pleve in St. Petersburg.

The emperor, convinced that appeasement of popular opinion was unavoidable, appointed P. D. Svyatopolk-Mirski as Pleve's successor. Mirski sought to attract the liberal activists' support by affording greater freedom to the zemstva; he even tried, unsuccessfully, to persuade the emperor to allow a handful of elected public representatives to take office in the central state administration. He relaxed the censorship somewhat. He withdrew the government's covert support for the programs against the Jews. The emperor, worried for the loyalty of the peasants, abolished the discriminatory legal provision whereby they could be subjected to corporal punishment for misdemeanours.[67] Yet the concessions were correctly interpreted as evidence of weakness. In August, Russian warships were sunk in an engagement off Vladivostok. Public disorder intensified at home. Demonstrations were organised in Warsaw, Baku and Riga. The boldness of the liberals, who had formed their Union Of Liberation in 1903, steadily increased. A conference of oppositionist groupings convened in Paris in autumn. Alongside Milyukov from the Union Of Liberation sat Chernov from the Party of Socialist-Revolutionaries, and these were joined by delegates from clandestine parties operating in the ethnically non-Russian areas of the empire. A concordat was produced to unite in an assault upon tsardom. It was commonly hoped that a democratic structure of state would be introduced in very short order.[68]

The liberals spread their ideas through speeches delivered in banquets held to commemorate dates of historical significance (such as the fortieth anniversary of the legal reforms of 1864). Execration showered down upon the autocratic regime. News from the Far East increased the monarchy's unpopularity: the Japanese took Port Arthur on 20 December 1904.

Social-democratic activists, in Russia and in emigration, were surprised at the government's failure to quell the liberals in the *zemstva* and in the Union Of Liberation. Absorbed for a year in internal wrangles, the Russian Social-Democratic Labour Party was being overtaken by events in the country. There were still only around 10 000 party members.[69] Their committees and propaganda circles existed in every major industrial town; and yet they recognised that they were losing their hegemony over the movement of political opposition to the autocracy. Social-democratic committees had not everywhere managed to attract the sympathy of the urban working class. There had been 550 strikes in 1903. Even so, contact between the factory workers and the party was not satisfactorily close. This was true even in Petersburg. At the Putilov Works, the largest armaments plant in the empire, the labour force struck for higher wages and better conditions in December 1904. Social-democratic activists had no part in the strike's organisation. Leadership was in fact provided by the Assembly Of Russian Factory And Mill Workers Of The City Of St.

Petersburg; and this Assembly was an off-shoot of the police-controlled unions formed by S. V. Zubatov. The Assembly's inspirer was an Orthodox priest, Father Georgi Gapon. It was not guided by St. Petersburg social-democrats of either Menshevik or Bolshevik inclination. Circumstances now compelled the Russian Social-Democratic Labour Party to abandon its organisational distractions.

On the eve of 1905, its leaders asked how they could exploit the social tumult in Russia; and, in particular, they pondered the policy to be adopted towards the oppositional movement of middle-class liberals and striking workers.[70]

The Mensheviks were first into the field with their answers. Martov perceived the situation's dangers. It was distinctly possible, he warned, that liberal groupings might set up their own labour organisations. Social-democrats could not afford to stand aside from the liberals' campaign against the government; abstention would edge the working class towards support for the Union Of Liberation. He was exaggerating; and he did so in order to press home the argument that social-democrats and liberals should form an anti-monarchical alliance. This would involve a combination of legal and illegal activity; and it would contradict Lenin's prescription for exclusively underground party organisations.[71] *Iskra* followed this up with a special leaflet. The purpose was to explain that, while fighting alongside the liberals, social-democrats should nonetheless make workers aware of the half-heartedness of the Union Of Liberation's democratic intentions. An alliance would give a chance to put pressure upon the liberals. The Union Of Liberation had to be prevented from accepting a constitutional settlement restricting the electoral rights of the working class and peasantry.[72] Such a policy required tact. Akselrod affirmed that social-democrats should discourage public disorders necessitating the intervention of the police and army. Violent street clashes would scare the liberals back into political passivity.[73] Many social-democratic committees in Russia, even some of those dominated by Bolsheviks, saw sense in *Iskra*'s plan.[74]

Lenin was outraged by it. Immediately, in November 1904, he wrote a piece castigating *Iskra*'s proposed pact with the liberals. The party could not rule out violence against the state authorities. In Lenin's view, social-democrats should therefore concentrate not on being tactful but on savagely criticising Russian liberalism. In essence this was a call to snub any alliance with the Union Of Liberation.[75]

Lenin's altercations with the Mensheviks had never been gentle, not least on his side; he had intended to shove them out of leading positions in the party. The new articles by Akselrod and Martov impelled him further. Now, for the first time, Lenin demanded a total split.[76] The Bolsheviks should have their political party and the Mensheviks theirs. It was a summons of epochal importance. He had been prepared to tolerate the Menshevik presence, however discontentedly, so long as their theorists did not act unequivocally against what he regarded as 'orthodoxy'. Their present policies were fundamentally unacceptable to him. They implied that the middle class would lead the revolution against the absolute monarchy. This robbed the working class of its 'vanguard' role.[77] *Iskra* replied that Lenin's fulminations exhibited a lack of acquaintance with developments in Russia; and that chances of political advance would be lost unless liberal groupings were handled with care.[78] Both sides of the argument had cogent aspects. The Mensheviks were indeed starting to defer to liberal political leadership; the Bolsheviks, however, were largely abandoning the old social-democratic commitment to seeking out the liberals as political allies. Indubitably it was vital for Russian Marxists to decide what forms of political struggle were in the interests of industrial workers in the winter of 1904–5. Yet the whole debate had a surrealistic quality. Neither *Iskra* nor *Vpered* addressed itself in a timely fashion to the burning question: what is the Russian Social-Democratic Labour Party going to do about the Assembly Of Factory And Mill Workers Of The City of St. Petersburg? The year 1905 was to jolt social-democratic activists and theorists into taking such questions seriously.

7 *Sturm und Drang*

BLOODY SUNDAY

Yet it was not only expatriate social-democrats like Lenin who were caught unprepared by the political storms of 1905. All parties in Russia and in the emigration were astounded. Nor did the government itself, despite its hundreds of police informants, show any greater prescience. The events in Paris in 1968 prove that unanticipated general conturbations may shake even countries enjoying universal adult suffrage. But the problem of unpredictability is greater in undemocratic states. The suppression of civil liberties makes popular opinion difficult to gauge; and the absence of other outlets of political activity renders it likely that opposition, when it eventually reaches the streets, will take the most violent forms.

So it was in Russia on 9 January 1905. Georgi Gapon had arranged for an unarmed procession of workers to make its way to the Winter Palace in St. Petersburg. The marchers carried a petition calling for the transfer of agricultural land to the people, for the instant cancellation of redemption payments and for the legalisation of independent trade unions. They wanted the emperor to grant popular representation in government. Nikolai II disdained to receive the petition. Despite fears about a forcible dispersal of the march, Gapon refused to alter his plans.[1] The Putilov strike had not been settled and, by early January, the work-force of other factories also were engaging in industrial conflict. 125 000 employees were striking. The demonstration itself attracted a crowd of 200 000 men and women. Cossack troops were ordered to charge into them. Still Gapon urged his followers onward. Disorder ensued. Upon arrival at the Winter Palace, the demonstrators were fired upon. Hundreds of unarmed civilians, gathered under the banners of Tsar and Church, fell killed or grievously wounded.[2] Thus ended Bloody Sunday. The brutality of the authorities was notorious in the Russian empire; and yet until 9 January 1905 the population had generally absolved the monarchy of direct responsibility. The killings dispelled illusion. Emperor Nikolai II had rejected his people's loyal petition.[3]

122

Military violence neither broke the Putilov strike nor restored calm to the capital. Nikolai II met a delegation of St. Petersburg workers; and on 29 January he appointed a commission under N. V. Shidlovski to determine the causes of unrest.[4] A concession was made to workers. They were permitted to elect representatives to contribute to the commission's investigation. Social-democrats competed in the elections with reluctance: they felt that the commission would steer the workers away from making political demands. Nonetheless compete they did. And, though securing only a fifth of the votes, they were beginning to make up the lost ground of 1904.[5] Throughout the empire there were strikes in sympathy with the victims of Bloody Sunday. Moscow and other cities in central Russia witnessed demonstrations; and clashes between urban crowds and the authorities took place in Poland and Latvia.[6] The growing turbulence stiffened the resolve of the Petersburg workers to elicit wage rises and the freedom to organise unions. More strikes broke out. This intransigence made Shidlovski's strictly-circumscribed job impossible; the commission was aborted. On 18 February, the emperor instructed his new Minister of Internal Affairs, A. D. Bulygin, to announce the intention of calling 'worthy representatives of the people to participate in the preliminary consideration and elaboration of proposed laws'. Simultaneously the emperor asked for support for the autocracy.[7]

Events in Russia had their own momentum; the situation changed so fast that no émigré leader, not even an epistolary zealot such as Lenin, could provide detailed advice to committees at home. The strikes tailed off in March. But the Russian army had suffered another defeat in late February at Mukden; and it was the navy's turn three months later: the Baltic fleet was annihilated in the Tsushima Straits. As before, military reverses increased the government's unpopularity.

In May 1905, 200 000 industrial workers were involved in strikes. Labour unrest was severe in Ivanovo-Voznesensk. 70 000 textile workers downed tools on 12 May and formed their own Assembly of Plenipotentiaries. Their expressed grievances were mainly economic. They wanted an eight-hour working day and a guaranteed minimum wage. The Assembly demanded the right to negotiate on behalf of all workers in Ivanovo's factories; it called upon the authorities to legalise strikes. But the Assembly was not only a strike committee. It assumed responsibility for keeping civil order on the streets. Thus it marked a stage on the road towards the elective, administrative bodies created by St. Petersburg workers in autumn 1905 and given the name of 'soviets' (or 'councils').[8] Social-democrats, mostly Bolsheviks, led the

Ivanovo Assembly. Elsewhere they were often unenthusiastic about
leading strikes, on the grounds that workers should be dissuaded from
'economistic' ambitions. But industrial conflict was pulling an increasing number of social-democrats, both Mensheviks and Bolsheviks, into
the fray despite such inhibitions. The summer of 1905 witnessed
further strikes and demonstrations in Tver, Lodz and Nizhni Novgorod. Cossacks re-imposed control; the employers made only slight
concessions. Yet the government was deeply worried by the persistent
challenges to the status quo.[9]

Lenin had for years been preaching a fire sermon against tsarism;
and his cursing of the government had been equalled in ferocity only by
his blackguarding of those revolutionaries who seemed to him to lack
the fullness of his own resolve to pull down the entire autocratic order.
It surprised no one in the first half of 1905 that his pronouncements in
these months were shot through with *Sturm und Drang*.

The rebellious mood of the industrial worker was shared by the
peasant. Seventeen rural disturbances were reported in January 1905;
the number rose to 492 by June.[10] Illegal felling of timber and illegal
use of pastures occurred widely. Rent strikes were frequent; and
peasants working as wage labourers on the latifundia struck for better
pay and conditions. The socialist-revolutionaries struggled to consolidate their network of party groups in the rural areas; but, as in the
towns, the population required little goading from political parties
before taking action in each locality. Liberals and socialist-
revolutionaries vied to put the peasant movement on a national basis.
The result was the founding Congress of the All-Russian Peasant
Union, held in July and attended by elected delegates from most
provinces in European Russia. The Congress called for the transfer of
all agricultural land to the peasantry.[11] The liberals were also active in
the formation of unions inside the middle-class professions; and in
May 1905 they combined them in a Union Of Unions.[12] Whatever
proposals came out of Bulygin's constitutional enquiries, the liberals
intended to exert continued pressure upon the government. Even in
the armed forces, discontent grew; ministers distrusted the loyalty of
Russian soldiers in the Far East. Trouble erupted in the Black Sea
Fleet. The crew of the battleship *Prince Potemkin* went to the full
length of a mutiny.[13]

The autocracy was in crisis. Those sections of the population which
called for the overthrow of the monarchy still constituted a minority;
yet the emperor perceived that this phenomenon might not be
long-lasting. Revolution seemed imminent.

LENIN IS THWARTED

The salient facts of Russia's tumult were quickly transmitted to revolutionaries in Switzerland. Lunacharski learnt of the Winter Palace massacre on 10 January. He and his wife hurried off to inform Lenin and Krupskaya. All then hastened to the centre of social-democratic life in the city, Lepeshinski's eating-house.[14]

The tables were crowded, the mood exultant. To many in that restaurant it appeared that the party's bickerings were a bizarre episode now best forgotten. But not to Lenin. From the last fortnight of 1904 he had been calling for a complete organisational split between supporters and opponents of the Bureau Of The Committees Of the Majority; and, to widespread consternation, Bloody Sunday induced no change in his position. Krupskaya, writing on his behalf to Bogdanov on 17 December, had mentioned 'the total split' as if it were a *fait accompli*.[15] This reflected Lenin's wishes, not organisational actuality. His *Vpered* first-issue editorial on 22 December demanded a severance of 'all relations' with the Mensheviks; and, in case his message might not have been clear enough, six days later he dispatched a staccatoed summons to Bogdanov: 'Now a complete split, for we have exhausted all means. A Third Congress against the will of the Central Committee and the Council and without them. A complete break with the Central Committee. A direct declaration that we have our own Bureau. The complete removal of Mensheviks and supporters of the new *Iskra* from all places.'[16] The Central Committee and *Iskra*, he announced to Bolshevik comrades in Zurich on 5 January 1905, had forfeited their claim to legitimate authority; by their own actions they had 'placed themselves outside the party'. The recurrent images had a medical quality. 'We also felt ourselves far better,' he affirmed, 'when we broke with the Minority.'[17]

The recipients of his correspondence found no detailed explanation of his switching of tactics; he apparently assumed that *Iskra*'s recent articles left the Bolsheviks no choice. It was a reckless assumption.

Even before December 1904, when he first demanded scission, he had encountered resistance inside the Bureau Of Committees Of The Majority to his tactical proposals. He had pushed for the breaking of the regulations governing the calling of a Party Congress. He simply wanted a Congress called, and did not care how it was done.[18] Zemlyachka opposed him. She had always contended that such an infringement would bring the Bolsheviks into unnecessarily bad odour; and the Bureau agreed with her. The Bureau would not convoke the Congress until the Central Committee had definitely refused to do so. Lenin pooh-poohed such feelings as formalism. Zemlyachka accused Lenin of having lost touch with Bolshevik opinion in Russia.[19] Lenin was enraged. His mood was not improved in November 1904 when he heard rumours that the Central Committee might indeed agree to a Congress. The thought of Noskov was quite odious to him. Convinced that he had been improperly treated in summer 1904, Lenin had broken off personal relations with Noskov.[20] It would be difficult for Lenin to dominate the central party apparatus if Noskov returned to the scene. Noskov's Bolshevik Conciliators would insist that Mensheviks be allowed to be elected as Congress delegates.In late 1904 the Mensheviks were increasing their strength in many committees in Russia.[21] To Lenin's way of thinking, Menshevism was a cancer in the body of the party: it had to be cut out immediately.

Lenin's one-man proclamation of the parting of the ways was saluted by a number of Bolsheviks in Geneva and Zurich.[22] It obtained paltry favour in Russia. Zemlyachka stuck to the tactic of presenting an ultimatum to the Central Committee; and Bogdanov pointed to the ever firmer evidence that the Central Committee would indeed convoke a Congress. Even Gusev, who until then had mirrored Lenin's ideas, thought it wise to make an agreement with the Central Committee about joint actions in St. Petersburg in December 1904.[23] The Winter Palace massacre reinforced this mood. The Bureau instructed Gusev to explain to Lenin that the policy of following the constitutional procedures for calling a Congress must stand.[24] Lenin replied on 29 January 1905. It horrified him that the *Iskra* group would be invited to the Party Congress. He now despised his own associates. Nine tenths of them, he raged, were 'pitiful formalists'; and he added: 'I'd hand the lot of them over to Martov.'[25] Second thoughts prevailed. He cut out the more offensive phrases before Krupskaya encoded the letter. Yet his essential position was unchanged: 'Either by truly iron discipline, we bind together all who want to wage war, and through this small but strong party we will smash the crumbling monster of the ill-assorted elements of the new *Iskra*; or else we will prove by our behaviour that we deserve to perish as contemptible formalists.'[26] This was wartime, Lenin declared. Half-heartedness and pessimism were dangerous to the party's interest; Lenin urged that social-democrats spreading despondency should be 'shot on the spot'.[27] The war referred to by Lenin was not the military conflict in the Far East but rather the struggle among social-democrats; and the Bureau members repudiated his metaphors as counter-productive rhetoric.

On 9 February, furthermore, the Central Committee finally met to discuss the proposal for a Third Party Congress. The police had been alerted. They burst indoors to arrest the seven members of the Central Committee who were present. Among them was Noskov. But two members evaded capture: L. B. Krasin and A. I. Lyubimov. These by now eagerly desired a Congress.[28] Negotiations between the Bureau and themselves produced an agreement, on 12 March, to form a joint Organisational Committee. The request for a Congress was to be relayed to the Party Council. If the Party Council rejected it, the Organisational Committee was to proceed independently.[29] Lenin would at last get his Congress. And yet he scarcely derived satisfaction from these events: he resented the Bureau's rejection of his tactics; and he can hardly have been pleased not to be asked to join the Organisational Committee. His editorials continued to be less than conciliatory to the Central Committee.[30]

But he accepted the agreement; the alternative was political suicide. Not for the last time, his colleagues wrongly inferred that they had put an end to Lenin's disruptions. No good word was offered for his organisational divisiveness. And yet we cannot leave the matter at that. It must also be noted that he did not regard his machinations as an end in themselves. He genuinely believed, in so far as his inner calculations may be assessed, that Menshevik strategy as it was evolving in the winter of 1904–5 constituted a menace to the prospects of successful revolution; he was therefore equally intent upon breaking with any Bolsheviks like Noskov who refused to engage in unconditional struggle with the Menshevik leaders. The point to be made is not that Lenin was being fundamentally insincere. Rather it is that his judgement, affected as it was by the prickles and jabs of a year's polemics, had played him false. He failed to perceive the harm he might be doing to the chances of amicable co-operation among Bolsheviks of all shades; and this was all the more regrettable a failure since he himself recognised that revolution was impossible without a large corps of experienced, militant activists.[31] He also made it harder for Mensheviks to come over to the Bolshevik side.[32] Factional adherences were always fluid. Lenin's intemperate mode of behaviour harmed his own cause. His activity had made him a less effective pursuer of his faction's strategic goals than he could have been. Only much later in the year, towards autumn, would he show that he eventually made a similar assessment.[33]

'TWO TACTICS OF SOCIAL-DEMOCRACY IN THE
DEMOCRATIC REVOLUTION'

Evidence for the authenticity of his belief in the imminence of
revolutionary upheaval is found in his theoretical writings. He
composed a series of articles for *Vpered* from February to May 1905,
and by June he was ready to sum up his considerations in a treatise.
Two months' further work led to the completion of *Two Tactics of
Social-Democracy in the Democratic Revolution*. It was his most
important book since *What Is To Be Done?* He had it quickly published
and transported clandestinely to Russia; and the rapid approval of its
strategical outline by virtually every Bolshevik demonstrates his
continuing popularity as a theorist even at a time when his prestige as a
practical leader was entering a partial eclipse.[34]

In his *Vpered* editorials and in *Two Tactics*, he announced it as the
party's supreme, urgent task to organise armed insurrection. Since
1902 he had called for the preparation of measures to bring about the
autocracy's demise. Bloody Sunday, he argued, marked the finish of
the preparatory stage. The moment for revolt was approaching. He
acknowledged that Martov, Plekhanov and Akselrod accepted the
need for violence after Bloody Sunday; but he objected to the
assumption, which surfaced from time to time in *Iskra*, that the
revolution could simply be 'unleashed'.[35] No, said Lenin: the uprising
had to be planned and co-ordinated from above by the social-
democratic party central leadership. Revolutions required organisation. Naturally too, he maintained, success could not be achieved
unless the insurrection had the support and participation of industrial
workers. In addition, agitators should be sent into the army and the
countryside. Soldiers and peasants should be dissuaded from allowing
themselves to be used as counterrevolutionary forces; the party should
aim to create a ubiquitous condition of insurgency. Tsardom should be
confronted by 'the people in arms'.[36] No matter what concessions
might be introduced by Nikolai II's government, popular uprising
should remain the objective. Social-democrats should co-operate with
all political parties seeking a democratic revolution; but it had to be
anticipated that the liberals, as untrustworthy as ever, would grasp at
any chance to cobble together a settlement with the monarchy.[37]
Nothing short of revolt would therefore suffice.

As soon as published, Lenin's words attracted a familiar accusation:
populism! His scenario appeared to Mensheviks as further indication
of his fondness for a conspiratorial élite acting in the name of the

people and yet not caring about the people's own aspirations.[38] Lenin's reply was caustic. He enquired whether the *Iskra* editors thought that a revolution could happen by spontaneous self-generation.[39]

The *Vpered* and *Iskra* standpoints on the organisation of insurrection came closer together in the rest of 1905.[40] As this gap narrowed, another widened. Social-democrats, feeling that the regime's last days might be at hand, started to deliberate about their policies towards the post-autocratic government. Lev Trotski quickly formulated his proposal. We should lead the uprising, he said, and we ourselves should constitute the new central administration. The party should establish a 'workers' government'.[41] The idea had been suggested to Trotski by Alexander Parvus. It was Parvus who composed the preface to Trotski's pamphlet on Bloody Sunday (which was published in February). Parvus contended that Russia's socio-political history diverged from the route already taken by 'Western' countries such as Britain and Germany. He regarded Russian industrialisation as primarily the product of the state's military exigencies; and, like the nineteenth-century narodniki, Parvus viewed Russian capitalism as almost completely a governmentally-directed development. This consideration led Parvus and Trotski to a striking conclusion. The Russian bourgeoisie lacked not only the political will to destroy the autocracy but also the social and economic power necessary for the governance of Russian society once the popular insurrection had occurred. It would therefore fall to the Russian working class to carry out the democratic reforms vital to the reconstruction of state and society: workers would carry through the democratic revolution.[42]

Parvus and Trotski touched a raw nerve. Did not their plans contradict the Russian Marxist prognostication that a socialist revolution could occur in any country only after a lengthy epoch of government by the bourgeoisie? Had not Engels warned against premature seizure of power? Was it not true that Russia's cultural and economic level of development was too primitive to permit the immediate transition to socialism? Parvus's answer was ready. He did not expect his 'workers' government' to rule forever. Its task would be to lay the fundaments of a democratic state structure in Russia; and it would eventually be pushed aside, through the ballot box, by the political parties of the bourgeoisie. Thus Parvus attempted to avoid the charge of populism.[43] Trotski's ideas veered away from his friend's at this point. Instead he called for 'permanent revolution'.[44] He scrapped the timetable which prescribed separate epochs for the democratic and socialist revolutions. Immediately he was accused of offering a disguised version of populism. His retort was twofold. Firstly, his government would not try to introduce socialism overnight. It would preside over a period of capitalist economic development. Secondly, he predicted that social-democrats would swiftly be ejected from power unless fraternal socialist revolutions occurred in the more mature industrial societies of Europe. His revolution would need political and economic support from abroad, or else it would perish.[45]

The webs spun by Parvus and Trotski momentarily encoiled Lenin. Admittedly, he made occasional criticisms. Yet he mounted no sustained barrage; he fired many more salvoes in 1905 at *Iskra* than at Trotski.[46] Sometimes he seemed to borrow Trotski's lexicon, using phrases such as 'uninterrupted revolution'.[47] Lenin assured his followers: 'We shall not stop halfway.'[48] But such comments occurred only fitfully in his *Vpered* output. He drafted two articles, entitled *The Picture of the Provisional Revolutionary Government* and *Conditions, Direction and Prospects of Revolution*, which offered his own version of Trotski's perspective.[49] Both lay unpublished. Intellectual scruples conquered intuitive inclination.

In fact, Marx himself in 1850 had used terminology remarkably like Trotski's; and he too had spoken against treating the bourgeois and socialist revolutions as distinct phases.[50] Lenin exhibited no knowledge of this. Yet it is inconceivable that he could not have found some support in Marx's writings if he had really planned to draw still nearer to Trotski's position. *Two Tactics* remained his doctrinal summary in mid-1905. This fact alone shows how simplistic it is to represent him as a mere maximalistic opportunist. The Russian Marxist notion of the two-stage transition to socialism was not yet jettisoned. Lenin nonetheless argued that socialists should constitute the first temporary government after the absolute monarchy's removal. But he rebutted the call for a 'workers' government'. Russia's population was still overwhelmingly rural. Lenin maintained that, if the revolutionary potentiality of the peasants was to be realised, their political representatives had to obtain a share in power. Social-democrats might not necessarily gain a monopoly of authority. Allying with the Party Of Socialist-Revolutionaries, they should aim to form a 'provisional revolutionary government'. Such a coalition, even with social-democrats in the minority, would reconstruct the Russian state. It would achieve the reforms demanded by the Russian Social Democratic Labour Party. Opposition by the former ruling groups would be ruthlessly smashed. Initially the middle and upper classes would be subjected to a 'revolutionary democratic dictatorship of the proletariat and the peasantry'; they would be deprived of political rights until such time as the provisional government's democratic reforms seemed durable enough to permit it to proceed with elections based on principles of universal adult suffrage.[51]

Lenin emphasised that his provisional revolutionary government would not be introducing socialism. In his opinion, indeed, the reforms would foster the maturation of a capitalist economy. Russia was not yet ripe for socialist revolution; and the socialist coalition presumably would eventually lose power to other political parties as economic modernisation was realised.[52] The monarchy's destruction could not be immediately followed by 'the dominion of the proletariat'.[53]

Lenin's disclaimers, like Parvus's and Trotski's before him, did not convince the *Iskra* group. Martynov was now his principal adversary. He and the Mensheviks referred Lenin to the decision of the Second International, taken in 1904, forbidding socialist parties to enter coalition governments.[54] Lenin had his reply to hand. The Second International's intention had been to prohibit socialists from forming coalitions which would prop up a capitalist order in advanced industrial countries. The Russian provisional revolutionary government's task would be entirely different. It would involve the destruction of feudalism. Lenin's enterprise had nothing in common with the entry of the French socialist leader Alexandre Millerand into a coalitional ministry with 'bourgeois' politicians.[55] Less easy to brush aside was Martynov's further point. To the Mensheviks it mattered little that Lenin did not intend to decree instant socialism: Lenin's subjective aims did not greatly bother them.[56] They were concerned rather by the practical consequences likely to arise. Lenin's revolutionary dictatorship, unbridled by legal constraints, would quickly become oppressive. It would simply amplify the authoritarian characteristics of tsarism. According to Martynov, massive violence would have to be meted out not only to the bourgeoisie but to the peasantry too. The rural population would not voluntarily accept Bolshevik agrarian policy; and immense discontent would occur if the socialist coalition was determined to carry out its policies. Civil war would result.[57]

Lenin had hoped to pre-empt such criticisms by enlarging the enticements to the peasantry in the party programme. In 1903, the Second Party Congress had called for the return of the 'cut-off strips' to peasant households. In 1905, Lenin observed the countryside's ferment. He recognised that his party's policy was unlikely to gather rural support when that of the socialist-revolutionaries demanded so much more: the socialisation of the land. He urged his party to raise its bid.

He demanded that all agricultural soil owned by the gentry, the aristocracy, the church and the royal family be expropriated. Property in land should be nationalised.[58] And yet, far from reassuring the Mensheviks, Lenin's proposals alarmed them. P. P. Maslov argued that land nationalisation, even if undertaken originally by a socialist coalition, would provide the upper classes with limitless latitude to augment even tsarist dimensions of oppression and exploitation if a counterrevolution should take place.[59] Lenin argued that he had been misunderstood. Although he wanted the state to have rights of ownership, he explained, it would be left to elected committees of the peasantry to distribute the land among those wishing to work on it and make private profit from it. His further reasoning was not yet stated in detail. But the broad intention was evident by implication: the rent payable to the state would be fixed at a low level; and sub-letting of land would be forbidden so as to prevent rent-racketeering. The peasant farmer would flourish as never before. No longer would he pay cripplingly high rents to the local landlord. The profitability of peasant agriculture would soar. Under such a regime, asked Lenin, where would counterrevolutionaries get the necessary backing to form an army to destroy the democratic institutions created by the provisional revolutionary government?[60]

As with so many other discussions inside the Russian Social-Democratic Labour Party, the argument ultimately returned to the agrarian question. It is difficult to judge who was more right, Lenin or Maslov. The problem is beset by hypothetical considerations. The political framework envisaged by Lenin in 1905 was destined never to come into existence in precisely the shape described by him. The October Revolution of 1917 gave rise to policies which differed importantly from Lenin's earlier projections. But Soviet rural history still offers clues for the adjudication of the Lenin-Maslov controversy. The Bolshevik government encountered stiff resistance when it intervened directly and heavily in the operations of the peasant economy: the New Economic Policy of 1921 was a recognition by the government that the peasants were intent upon ordering their economic life as they saw fit. Lenin's writings in 1905 overestimated the Russian peasantry's predisposition to welcome policies designed to effect rapid modernisation of agriculture. Maslov, moreover, was correct in saying that a government insistent on steeply increasing the pace would have to resort to force. On the other hand, Lenin's performance as Soviet premier demonstrated his acumen in adjusting policy to circumstances. Probably his proposals of 1905, if modified so as to avoid peasant revolts, provided greater chance of success in stimulating change than Maslov's. Central governmental intervention, as the experience of countries in Africa and Asia as well as the European Economic Community shows, lends important assistance to agricultural development.[61]

THE THIRD PARTY CONGRESS

The disputes of 1905 covered vast canvasses, and the projects of the theorists were still rudimentary sketches. The war against the monarchy was yet to be won. Obviously the Third Party Congress would lack the time to give a ruling on every single question in the air; but it would at least be able to adumbrate plans of immediate practical moment. The arrangements for the Congress were out of Lenin's hands.[62] As things turned out, the composition of the delegations was closer to his wishes than he had expected. Suitably unobtrusive premises were rented in London. Apart from a scare when customs officers showed interest in the trunk holding Central Committee material, there was little bother. The Central Committee's participation encouraged several pro-Menshevik organisations to send representatives from Russia; but these, on arrival, found that little effort at reconciliation with *Iskra* had been made. They departed to a Menshevik Conference hurriedly organised in Geneva.[63] Krasin was disappointed. He had made the Central Committee's participation conditional upon three-quarters of the local committees sending delegates. He used his disappointment as a bargaining counter. He steered the Congress away from allowing representation to Bolshevik splinter groups in cities where the legitimately-constituted committees favoured the Mensheviks. Bogdanov gave ground, worried lest the proceedings should lose all approximation to status as the Third Party Congress. 'It is not our business,' he affirmed, 'to form another party.'[64]

Proceedings started on 12 April 1905. Disagreements proliferated. Krasin's conciliationism attracted many delegates; and Bogdanov won favour from others on questions which found him at odds with Lenin. Such set-backs were predictable. So that perhaps the most intriguing fact made manifest by the Congress was that he could not safely rely even upon those 'Leninists' who had supported him staunchly in the past.

Lenin's mood, however, was buoyed up by the early broadly-based support he obtained for his call for a strategic offensive. Insurrection was his vital concern. Lunacharski and Bogdanov took his side, arguing that uprisings could not be 'unleashed' but had to be 'organised'. This was universally approved.[65] Yet Krasin was not the only delegate to express doubt that Russian workers acknowledged the necessity of political revolution.[66] D. S. Postolovski warned pointedly against the menace of 'revolutionary adventurism'.[67] Preparatory propaganda was needed. Lenin found this acceptable: he and his associates agreed to modify the motion. The finally-agreed clauses obliged the party not only to prepare for insurrection but also to conduct a vigorous, preliminary campaign for the idea among the working class.[68] Lenin was content. Concurrence on the need for revolt had been his towering goal, and he had achieved it. His speeches were almost light-hearted, quite different (as he delighted to remark) from his reputation as 'an irreconcilable'.[69] Ensuing debates reinforced his claim to have been the victim of political caricaturists. P. P. Rumyantsev, an associate of Bogdanov's, proposed a motion deploring the maintenance of purely clandestine modes of party activity. Bloody Sunday had caught the party unawares. The lesson to be learned was that, at a time of street demonstrations, social-democrats had to offer leadership of a more overt kind.[70] Lenin sided with Rumyantsev.[71]

On the connected issue of participation in trade unions, Lenin went even further than Rumyantsev. Lenin wanted the party to start forming trade unions. Rumyantsev was unpersuaded; he retained that widespread Bolshevik distaste for activity that appeared directed towards non-political ends. He wished party activists to work inside trade unions but not to dedicate their energies to forming them.[72] The Congress's drafting commission overruled Lenin.[73] And, when the commission's motion came before the Congress itself, many delegates still regarded even Rumyantsev's formulations as an unpardonable departure from Bolshevism. M. Tskhakaya, in particular, contended that the Russia of mid-1905 differed little from the Russia of 1902.[74] Eventually only minor amendments were passed, and the resolution offered by Rumyantsev became official policy.[75] At all events the discussion had shown how far removed was Lenin from seeking the eternal application of *What Is To Be Done?*'s organisational prescriptions.

Lenin's first report to the Congress dealt with entrance into a 'provisional revolutionary government'. Plekhanov was the butt of his remarks. Marx, according to Plekhanov, would never have espoused

Lenin's proposals; and the corroborative evidence was supposedly to be found in articles inveighing against those socialist 'opportunists' who were ready to do a deal with the middle class.[76] Lenin rehearsed the case already mounted in reply to Martynov. Bolshevik policy was designed to prevent, not to engineer a Millerandist sell-out. In addition Lenin urged the Congress not to be browbeaten by *Iskra*'s taunts about Jacobinism. The founders of Marxism, he maintained, had despised those who despised the Jacobins. Lenin went further. He claimed that Marx had generally enthused about mass terror as a means of consolidating revolutions; his evidence was a remark in 1848 that Robespierre's guillotine in 1793–4 had been 'the plebeian method' of eradicating the old order.[77] This particular citation was accurate. But it was also selective; for Marx, while sometimes condoning the French terror unequivocally, on other occasions condemned it severely. In *The Holy Family* in 1844 he had stated that Robespierre had inadvertently and against his own designs created the conditions for his regime's overthrow.[78] Lenin drew a veil, presumably consciously, over Marx's changeability. And indeed there was something akin to anticipatory relish in Lenin's further statement that the revolutionary dictatorship of the workers and the peasantry in Russia should organise its own terror.[79] The narodnik element in his thought was strong in 1905. He recommended populists like Petr Tkachev as essential reading matter for his close associates.[80] His advocacy of terror did not reach the pages of *Vpered*. Lenin must have sensed the need not to supply the Mensheviks with additional literary gunpowder to fire against him. But Congress speeches were never so carefully planned as newspaper articles. It may well be that Lenin was carried away in the heat of the moment, and that he revealed a policy which he otherwise preferred to cosset with euphemisms.[81]

Bolsheviks of all complexions anyway warmed to his speech; not a single delegate rose to oppose him. Krasin was euphoric. He put forward an amendment to Lenin's motion, but it was an amendment readily accepted by Lenin. Krasin argued that the revolutionary government should be installed in the process of the insurrection. This would guarantee the social-democrats a toe-hold in the new administration. The Lenin–Krasin resolution won a massive majority.[82] A few delegates were confused by the debate. P. A. Krasikov confessed to being unable to see how such a government, with all its power and with all its radical reforms, could be said to be initiating 'the dominion of the bourgeoisie'.[83] But his objections were rejected.[84] Thus encouraged, Lenin opened the discussion on the agrarian question. He omitted mention of land nationalisation. The drafting commission had apparently insisted upon a vaguer formulation invoking the party to support all revolutionary measures to improve the peasantry's lot; and these measures were not to stop short of 'the expropriation of gentry land'. Lenin defended the formulation loyally at the Congress.[85] It at least gave him a huge extension of peasant-oriented concessions, and he postponed consideration of his specific arguments for nationalisation. Again a delegate asked the question about historical stages. M. K. Vladimirov enquired where the party should in fact stop with its agrarian reforms. 'Never stop!' was Lenin's response.[86] Not for the only time in 1905 the urge to move towards Trotski's 'permanent revolution' showed itself in Lenin's reflex reactions.

Next on the agenda came Bogdanov's motion to induce more workers to join the party. Postolovski recounted how easier it was for a student than for a worker to obtain the acquaintance with Marxism often demanded as an entrance qualification.[87] To many delegates (such as V. S. Desnitski, L. B. Kamenev and A. I. Rykov) this appeared demagogical.[88] Lenin, however, sided with Bogdanov. He also backed Bogdanov's suggestion that a greater 'dose of democratism' would facilitate the entrance of workers to the party. He was dismayed by the narrow focus of the Bolshevism of the Kamenevs and the Rykovs.[89] True, Lenin and Bogdanov obtained the scrapping of Martov's definition of the terms of party membership in favour of Lenin's;[90] but their other recommendations encouraged a relaxation of hierarchical arrangements. Lenin also voted to accord greater freedom to local committees to run their own newspapers.[91] And this reflected the opinion of most delegates.[92]

Lenin and Bogdanov, however, disagreed about the structure of the central party apparatus. Both wished to abolish the unwieldy Party Council. But Lenin wanted to retain a bipartite arrangement whereby the Central Committee was situated in Russia and the party newspaper in Switzerland; Bogdanov held that both should be based on Russian soil. Delegates from Russia sided with Bogdanov.[93] They had had their fill of the émigré disputes of 1903–4; many hinted that Lenin had been among the most offenders. M. G. Tskhakaya went the nearest to outright attack. He objected to the growth of a cult around Lenin, declaring: 'I am not a Leninist, I'm a party activist, a revolutionary social-democrat, a Marxist.'[94] Engels had not talked of Engelsism. And Lenin's admirers, insisted Tskhakaya, should desist from elevating Lenin to a higher pedestal than that of Marxism's co-founder.[95] Nobody rose to repudiate Tskhakaya. In addition, the vote on the central party apparatus was a triumph for Bogdanov. Only V. V. Vorovski, himself an émigré, supported Lenin's proposal to keep the party newspaper abroad.[96] So as to prevent Lenin's total humiliation, Desnitski proposed a vote of thanks for *Vpered's* services to the party. A substantial minority of delegates abstained.[97] Lenin's contribution to party life was highly esteemed, but not regarded as being indispensable. His behaviour at the Congress itself was perfectly proper. But this was an all-Bolshevik affair. Lenin still exhibited fractiousness towards those social-democrats not espousing Bolshevism. Before the Congress he had proposed a motion denouncing Plekhanov.[98] The Congress drafting commission rejected it. Equal impatience was shown to Lenin's motion to excoriate the Mensheviks as 'disorganisers' who should be treated as 'standing outside the party'.[99] A more schismatic suggestion was hardly conceivable. Bogdanov sought the re-unification of the party, albeit a party united under Bolshevik leadership. He forced compromise upon Lenin. They agreed upon a motion criticising the Mensheviks for their 'partial deviation from the principles of revolutionary social-democracy'.[100] The Mensheviks were not to be expelled. They need not even recant their general opinions so long as they were willing to obey party policies in practice.[101]

Lenin had the sense to retreat with composure. He defended the compromise in debate.[102] And he secured himself a position in the new Central Committee. There were four other members of this all-Bolshevik body: Bogdanov, Krasin, Postolovski and Rykov.[103] Each was independently-minded and had a record of standing up to Lenin. There was little possibility of Lenin's railroading his policies through the new central party apparatus in the months to come.

AUTOCRACY IN RETREAT

Third Congress delegates, when proceedings ended on 27 April 1905, felt sure that political unrest in Russia was about to increase in severity; the debates had put Lenin in closer touch with his native land, if only through the medium of activists who had journeyed thence to London. The Bolsheviks wanted insurrection. Until midsummer they had reason to feel that their optimism was justified, and their leaflets underlined the autocracy's growing incapacity to govern autocratically.

Returning to Geneva, Lenin still shared this optimistic ebullience.

But gradually the news began to make him reconsider. Russian factory workers found it difficult to sustain the strike movement. It is true that certain cities such as Odessa witnessed fierce street confrontations in midsummer; but there were many more places where order was maintained with ease.[104] Industrialists were facing down wage demands. The government was cheered by the entrance of organised groupings of landowners into politics. The most influential was the Union Of The United Gentry. The war with Japan was coming to a close. The Japanese government refrained from imposing humiliating terms. A treaty was signed on 23 August. A rise in confidence in Russian stocks and shares was registered abroad. In February 1905 the government had undertaken to convoke a representative assembly; but the gathering lull of midsummer induced Nikolai II to make the barest political concessions. A manifesto was issued on 6 August. The assembly was to be called the State Duma and its powers would be exclusively consultative. The method of election would be socially-discriminatory. Voters were to be divided into their respective social estates and to choose representatives to serve in electoral curiae. These representatives would meet to elect the Duma's members. The unfairness of the system consisted in the allocation of 34 per cent of Duma places to the landowning gentry. Property qualifications were mandatory for urban inhabitants. The effect was to deny the franchise to factory workers and to many low-ranking members of the professions and the civil service.[105]

But the public mood was still hostile. Printing workers struck in September, their demands being political as well as economic. Industrial disputes occurred across central Russia. In October, a strike of railwaymen began.[106] Liberals, moreover, felt cheated by the August Manifesto. Inside the Union Of Unions, P. N. Milyukov led a moderate group inclined to participate in the forthcoming Duma elections. The government ill-advisedly arrested him. All liberals became hell-bent upon extracting more substantial concessions; and they lent expression to their resolve by holding the founding congress of the Constitutional-Democratic Party on 12 October.[107]

As Lenin and the other émigrés pondered the struggle from afar, their doubts began to be balanced again by more sanguine feelings. The cause for their joy was the activity of the workers of St. Petersburg. On 13 October they formed a Soviet. The Russian word means Council; and the Petersburg Soviet's original purpose was to provide leadership of the current wave of strikes in the capital. There were about forty delegates at the Soviet's opening meeting. By 15 October, the number had risen to 226; and these delegates represented the workforce of 96 factories and five trade unions.[108] The original chairman was G. S. Khrustalev-Nosar, a left-wing liberal. But Lev Trotski with his tactical and oratorical skills quickly came to the fore. The Mensheviks, the Bolsheviks and the Socialist-Revolutionaries were invited to send activists to work in an advisory capacity inside the Executive Committee. The Soviet declined to advocate the pro- gramme of any single political party or group; it aimed, as a 'non-party organisation', to unite the capital's workers. On the other hand it still pursued political goals. The strikes were intended to achieve civic freedoms as well as higher wages; the Petersburg Soviet's slogans called for the formation of a democratic republic.[109] The Soviet introduced its own administration, including a workers' militia. Trotski regretted that the Soviet could not manage to re-unite the social- democratic factions in the capital. The Mensheviks collaborated with him willingly, but the Bolsheviks baulked for a time at the Soviet's insistence upon its 'non-party' status. Nevertheless the government was deep in trouble. Nikolai II made concessions. On 17 October 1905 he issued a further Manifesto. It guaranteed the freedoms of opinion, assembly and association. It abolished the censorship. It promised to extend the franchise for the State Duma. It granted not only consultative but also legislative authority to the Duma.[110] On 19 October, an amnesty for political offences was granted.[111]

Lenin had to read all about this in the Swiss press. It was not yet obvious how he would react to such events; he had rampaged inside his party for the past year, and few were aware that he was at that very moment having second thoughts about policy. The last months of 1905 were to reveal how drastically he had altered his mind.

8 Predicting the Tide

ST. PETERSBURG

Voices were raised at court, as well as in monarchist organisations in the country, urging Nikolai II to retract his Manifesto. They recommended a harsher regime. By this they did not simply mean that undisguised revolutionaries like Lenin should be caught and hanged. They demanded a yet more pervasive repression; and they suggested that the political tumult had occurred precisely because the autocracy had conceded too much to its liberal and socialist critics. Yet such recommendations overestimated the power available to the tsarist government. Nikolai II never in fact envisaged introducing the methods which were later to characterise the rule of Stalin in the USSR and Hitler in Germany; but, even if he had so inclined, the results would not have brought him advantage. Tsarism lacked a mass movement of support; there was no social class, save for the gentry, which it could reliably mobilise. Its ideology, such as it was, was associated with a past held in contempt by the population at large. Its rituals no longer secured social cohesion. Its police lacked the large-scale technology of control developed in subsequent years. Its army's ranks were filled with peasants who were a dubious instrument of the monarchical will in times of crisis. Consequently the semi-constitutional manoeuvres of 1905–6 were probably the nearest that the imperial government could prudently move towards the maintenance of its centuries-old prerogatives. Any more aggressive posture would have invited further revolutionary upheavals.

In any case, the Constitutional Democrats (or Kadets, as they were abbreviated) agreed to participate in the elections.[1] November and December were testing months for the regime. Soviets were springing up in towns and cities; as many as fifty had established themselves by the end of 1905.[2] Strikes dislocated industrial production. Mutinies broke out in regiments in the Far East. The countryside seethed with discontent. 792 rural disturbances were recorded for the month of November alone.[3]

Until the Manifesto's promulgation, few leading émigré revolutionaries would countenance returning to Russia. Safety still mattered. Plekhanov, Lenin, Martov and Akselrod were career politicians; they viewed the possibility of arrest as an unacceptable risk: the party's loss would be irredeemable. Not all the 'lords' of the party, as they were dubbed,[4] felt this way. Bogdanov hastened back into Russia in 1904.[5] Trotski followed in 1905.[6] Lenin refused all invitations to emulate their action.[7] Nonetheless the frustrations of Switzerland mounted; he bemoaned 'the accursed distance' separating him from St. Petersburg.[8] After the Third Party Congress, the Central Committee had appointed him as its representative abroad and as editor of *Proletari* (or *Proletarian*). *Proletari* was the new mast-head for *Vpered*, claiming status as the entire party's central newspaper. The editorial routine was onerous. And Lenin felt that the Central Committee, with its anti-émigré animus, deliberately kept him short of assistants and financial support.[9] This was painful enough. But in July 1905 he also learned that Central Committee members were taking important decisions without consulting him. A meeting had taken place between the Central Committee and the Menshevik Organisational Commission. It appears that agreement was reached to reconstitute the Central Committee with representatives from both factions.[10] Lenin was irate that no one had even asked his opinion. His plea for a Central Committee meeting to be held abroad was greeted with the suggestion of Finland as the venue.[11] This too displeased him. The Finnish border was only a few miles from St. Petersburg; the possibility of his imprisonment could not be discounted. He wrote back proposing Stockholm.[12] Thus the Manifesto came to his rescue in October: he would return, he would tackle his colleagues face to face at last.

They had plans, well before the Manifesto, to start a legal Bolshevik newspaper based in Russia (and perhaps its creation would have compelled Lenin to go back to St. Petersburg even if no Manifesto had been issued). The newspaper's name was to be *Novaya Zhizn* (or *New Life*). He looked forward to joining the editorial board.[13] He also aimed to introduce practicality to the Central Committee's affairs. Valuable time was being lost on trivia. In Lenin's opinion, the Central Committee should concentrate upon the regular production of bulletins; it should sketch general plans, leaving it to lower party committees to flesh out the details.[14]

Those acquainted only with the Lenin of *Two Tactics* knew solely a prophet of all-out strategical offensive. But there was another Lenin (and many more besides). Right from his alliance with Struve's coterie in the mid-1890s he had been adept at tactical manoeuvres and adjustments in policy. In the second half of 1905 it was this Lenin who came to the fore. He now claimed, to Bogdanov's bemusement, to be quite unbothered by the prospect of joining up again with the Mensheviks; he even chided those Bolsheviks who 'exaggerated' the points of dispute between the two factions.[15] Bogdanov too wanted to secure Bolshevik dominance inside a re-unified social-democratic party; but many local groups of Bolsheviks were destroying his bargaining position by recombining with Menshevik groups without the Central Committee's permission. He continuingly made acerbic anti-Menshevik remarks. He was to warn, too, against a 'unificatory orgy'.[16] Lenin by contrast was almost benign. He conceded that the Bolshevik Central Committee (as if he himself had played no role in the matter) had in the past unfairly cashiered social-democratic committees led by Mensheviks.[17] His magnanimity was a prudential calculation. He sensed, along with the Mensheviks, that Bogdanov and Krasin might be contemplating a hasty attempt at insurrection. Lenin wanted to delay it until spring 1906; but he again noted ruefully that the Central Committee had not invited his advice.[18] He worried even more about the attitude of many Bolsheviks to non-party working-class organisations. The reluctance to participate in trade unions persisted. The Mensheviks took part with zest. Lenin did not endorse their general viewpoint any more than previously; but he shared the priority given by Martov and Akselrod to ensuring that social-democrats did not let other political parties dominate the organisations of the Russian labour movement.[19] Lenin now welcomed the Mensheviks in the party as a means of putting pressure on his own Bolsheviks to bend more readily in his own direction of policy.[20]

Winding up *Proletari*'s affairs, he packed his case for St. Petersburg. He travelled across Germany, stopping over in Stockholm (to pick up a false passport) and arriving in Russia around 8 November 1905.[21] He already knew of the Petersburg Soviet. He brought with him a draft article advocating Bolshevik participation, expecting to get it published in *Novaya Zhizn*.[22]

He had read the newspaper's early issues and was shocked by the editorials expressing suspicion and even antipathy towards the Soviet.[23] He steeled himself for a struggle. He was allotted rooms in P. P. Rumyantsev's apartment. Lenin now learnt, for the first time, the details of the Central Committee's recent activity. Bogdanov's policy had been that the Central Committee should involve itself in the

Petersburg Soviet only on condition that the Soviet accepted the social-democratic programme. The Soviet had predictably repudiated this demand. The Central Committee had thereupon urged all Bolsheviks to withdraw from the Soviet.[24] It took weeks for Lenin to soften this intransigence. Indeed his article remained unpublished.[25] The day-to-day grind of the *Novaya Zhizn* editorship lay claim to his energies.[26] The Central Committee's posture gradually changed. It could hardly have been otherwise; the Bolsheviks, if ever they were going to organise an insurrection, were bound to have to enter mass working-class organisations. Nevertheless the diffidence remained. Lenin himself, possibly under Central Committee pressure, attended the Soviet only infrequently. He seldom spoke. For so eloquent a leader, it must have been intensely irritating to attend mainly as a spectator. But, according to his colleague B. Gorev, he 'sat and kept silent'.[27] There was still no answer to the question whether he could adjust himself to an era of 'mass politics'. Trotski's name, not Lenin's, was on Petersburg workers' lips.

ON PHILOSOPHY AND ON THE SOVIETS

Lenin and Bogdanov announced their differences over soviets and trade unions as being of secondary importance in the winter of 1905–6; the overriding task was to prepare an uprising to instal a provisional revolutionary government. This consensus fortified Lenin's factional loyalty. But outward allegiance was accompanied by the conviction that he was right about the soviets and Bogdanov wrong; and he attempted to put his thoughts into coherent order. His determination was reinforced by chagrin. He, the founder of Bolshevism, knew scarcely any Bolshevik leader in St. Petersburg not claiming to interpret Bolshevism better than he.

Lenin objected to Bogdanov's essential conception of Marxism.[28] Philosophy divided them. In epistemology, Lenin sided with Plekhanov. In the 1890s he had rejected the suggestions of Struve and others that Marx's philosophical standpoint was unsatisfactory.[29] And, while in exile in Shushenskoe, he had warned fellow social-democrats against adopting the neo-Kantian notions then becoming popular among Austrian Marxists.[30] Kant's 'categorical imperative', together with its political moralism, was unattractive to Lenin. So far, Bogdanov and Lenin were in agreement.[31] But Bogdanov, unlike Lenin, felt that writings by contemporary non-Marxists could nevertheless be useful in refining Marxist philosophy. He had in mind not Immanuel Kant but Ernst Mach and Richard Avenarius. He liked their work on human perception; they seemed to him to have demonstrated the fallacy of the psychological model which drew a sharp distinction between subject and object, between the observer and the thing that is observed. Bogdanov linked their outlook with Marxism. For him, Mach had inadvertently supplied an epistemological basis for Marxist social theory.[32] The interfusion of subject and object meant that absolute truth was unattainable; and this, in Bogdanov's opinion, entirely accorded with Marx's arguments that every society's ideas are historically-conditioned and amenable to change in response to changing circumstances. Bogdanov made particular study of Marx's *Theses on Feuerbach.* He was very far from being a slavish admirer of Mach, Avenarius and the other 'Empiriocritics'; indeed he tried to show that they treated problems of perception in too individualist a mode and neglected the effects of collective social experience. He referred to his own doctrine as Empiriomonism.[33]

Lenin dismissed all this as mumbo jumbo.[34] He, in contrast with Bogdanov, believed in the independent objective reality of the external world; in the ontological primacy of matter over mind; and in the attainability of incontrovertible truth.[35] He felt that Marx and Engels could be shown to have supported Plekhanov's basic position.[36] As early as 1904 he communicated his criticisms to Bogdanov.[37] Nevertheless Lenin and Bogdanov concurred that philosophical disagreements need not affect their political alliance. They made epistemology a truce zone.[38] Lenin expressed outrage when Plekhanov declared that a causal link existed between Bogdanov's 'subjectivist' philosophy and his 'voluntarist' pursuit of a revolutionary dictatorship.[39]

Lenin was of the opinion, all the same, that Bogdanov lacked the intellectual flexibility appropriate to the politician. The charge was not without foundation. Free-ranging in philosophy, Bogdanov in 1905 was dogmatic about the concept of the 'vanguard party'. If the soviets would not accept leadership from the Russian Social-Democratic Labour Party, he implied, then too bad for the soviets.[40] And too bad also for the workers who elected delegates to those same soviets. He was as doctrinaire about this as any Bolshevik hardliner (even though such an attitude was not in fact a logically unavoidable conclusion to be drawn from *What Is To Be Done?*). Lenin's view, as sketched in November 1905 and elaborated in his 1906 pamphlet *Victory of the*

Kadets, was different: he wanted the soviets to act as 'the embryos of the new revolutionary power'.[41] He warned against fussing about the procedural niceties. The Petersburg Soviet should initiate the process by selecting representatives to announce themselves as 'the provisional revolutionary government of all Russia'.[42] His views were not yet phrased definitively. He was not entirely clear about the task to be fulfilled by the soviets. Nevertheless he did not envisage them as an enduring institutional network for the country's governance. The soviet, he declared, was a 'fighting organisation for the attainment of specific goals'. And seemingly the principal goal in his mind was armed uprising to overthrow the monarchy and construct a democratic structure of state.[43]

But how could there be certainty that the soviets would be adequate to their task? Lenin's reactions tugged him in opposing directions. At times he wrote exultantly about popular creativity;[44] he attacked those who doubted that the people could perform 'miracles'.[45] He even characterised workers as being 'instinctively social-democratic'.[46] It was almost as if his pronouncements of 1902, with their denial that the working class could spontaneously evolve socialist ideas, had never been made. He scourged the party's 'committee-men'. In his view they were obsessed by hierarchy and insufficiently attuned to the need to encourage popular initiative. The party required renovation. Lenin, who had once sung the praises of the 'professional revolutionary', wanted to fling open the gates of the party to ordinary, inexperienced workers without a smattering of Marxist doctrine: all to prod the committees out of their 'inertia'.[47] Workers should be given leading positions in local organisations; they should be promoted to committee membership to put intellectuals in a minority in places of authority.[48] Thus revitalised, the party should encourage workers outside the party on to further stages of self-liberation. Bomb-making instructions should be distributed and workers be allowed to get on with the business. Let them blow up a police station.[49] Let them organise raids to steal money for funds, let them conduct military training for street-fighting.[50]

Yet Lenin simultaneously repeated that the party alone was the repository of revolutionary wisdom. Ideological education, he averred, remained indispensable. The party was needed to transmute the social-democratic instincts of workers into true 'social-democratic consciousness'.[51] The party's tutelary duties were not to be forsaken. Organisational discipline too had to be preserved; and party committees should ensure that their activists in the soviets toed the party line.[52] Lenin occasionally spoke as if it was a pity that Bolsheviks had to join the soviets at all. But circumstances, he noted, 'can compel us'.[53]

Consequently Lenin, however far he swam out towards the notion that the working class was Marxist by instinct, did not toss away his lifebelt of traditional Bolshevism; and, though he had pragmatic reasons for continuing with his overtures to the Mensheviks, he still also conceived of Menshevism itself as an impractical strategy. He censured Akselrod, Dan and Martov even though they were the party's only theorists who produced articles which prefigured the emergence of the soviets in late 1905. Akselrod's dream of a 'workers' congress' now seems a not uneffective work of prophecy.[54] Even before the government's announcement of the highly restrictive franchise for the State Duma in August, he had proposed that workers should take politics into their own hands by electing their own delegates and demanding the convocation of a Constituent Assembly. The delegates to each workers' congress would automatically arrange local 'revolutionary self-government'. Social-democrats should work to ensure their own election to the congress-cum-soviet.[55] Whenever he read of such plans, Lenin returned to his centralist premises. Revolutionaries should not aim merely to prevent the government from ruling the localities. They should also, as a first measure indeed, establish their own central state authority. Like Trotski, Lenin thought that the 'democratic dictatorship' could be installed only by simultaneous processes of central direction and local self-organisation.[56]

FAILURE OF INSURRECTION

If Lenin's thinking in 1905 was more tension-laden than was customary even for him, it must be appreciated that Russian politics changed with bewildering rapidity inside a few months. But there is a further difficulty. Lenin was an active politician, not an armchair commentator. He wrote to achieve impact over his party and through his party. Rhetorical flourish and exaggeration were fair play. Since Lenin was concerned lest the Bolsheviks might float adrift of working-class opinion, it was natural for him to make a strong case for the instinctive virtues of the factory labourer. No statement of theory made by him was unaffected by his immediate political goals. His 'political thought' is therefore mishandled when, as was done in his day and is still done today, it is treated as a thing unto itself. The parts lack ultimate definition; they are constantly in motion. The system of his ideas is an interplay of tendencies: it is not a static, particularised code.

Before 1905 he had experienced small difficulty in communicating policies to his Bolsheviks; but his editorial job in *Novaya Zhizn*, upon his return to Russia, was in the gift of a Central Committee suspicious of his pro-soviet enthusiasms. His articles were often therefore cautious in their phrasing.[57] His departure from Switzerland had a second untoward result from his angle of view. He no longer presided over correspondence with committees throughout Russia; by coming back to Petersburg he had placed a greater distance, organisationally speaking, between himself and the rest of the country. Semen Shvarts was then a Bolshevik agitator in the capital. He read and contributed to *Novaya Zhizn*. Yet he knew nothing of Lenin's idiosyncratic stance in the Central Committee (even though Shvarts himself much approved of participation in the soviets).[58] Many Bolshevik committee-men at lower levels shared the Central Committee's distrust of non-party organisations. On 21 November 1905 there began a conference of party committees in the Moscow region. The delegates accepted the soviets' right to existence, but only where the party 'cannot direct the proletariat's mass action in any other way'. Soviets should be treated merely as 'the technical apparatus' for carrying the party's leadership to the working class.[59] Yet circumstances indeed obliged. The months from October to December witnessed the entrance of Bolsheviks into more mass organisations such as the trade unions and the soviets. Their purpose was always the same. They sought to use the soviets as a base for propaganda in favour of armed insurrection. They helped in strengthening the Moscow Soviet in December (which contrasted with their behaviour in St. Petersburg, where they were half-hearted participants).[60]

Events spurred them on. In November 1905 a sailor's mutiny broke out on the island of Kronstadt, a few miles from the capital. The Petersburg Soviet called upon the people to withhold tax payments. Workers in Nizhni Novgorod and Ekaterinoslav took to the streets. In the Transcaucasus, Georgia was already under a revolutionary admini- stration of Mensheviks. But the Ministry of Internal Affairs under its new head P. N. Durnovo went on the offensive. On 3 December, Durnovo ordered the arrest of the Soviet. No resistance was offered. The Petersburg Soviet's life was ended as suddenly as it had begun.[61]

Lenin's influence over events in St. Petersburg was slight. It was no greater elsewhere. The Moscow Bolsheviks, who held the party's city committee, decided to mount an insurrection before the authorities repeated their attempt at suppressing revolutionary activity. The Moscow Committee consulted with representatives from the Central Committee, but the armed initiative seems to have been local.[62] The Moscow Soviet sanctioned the uprising.[63] The insurgents lacked sophistication; they had no plan to seize the telegraph offices or cut the rail link with the capital. The Soviet possessed only a poorly-armed militia. Efforts were made to secure sympathy from garrison soldiers, but the main hope was reposed in the workers in Moscow's industrial quarters. The violence lasted several days. Neither party nor soviet exerted great impact over operational details. Troops were hurried by the government from St. Petersburg and, by 17 December, the fighting was over. At least a thousand persons perished, most of them civilians.[64] The workers had not risen in the manner necessary to give any chance of success. Social-democrats tried to assess the reasons for failure; and it was agreed that the venture had been undertaken without the necessary consultation and preparation of opinion outside the party. Lenin's doubts, expressed in early autumn, had proved well-founded. Paradoxically it was the incautious policy which he and others had urged on the party in spring 1905 that led to the disaster.

TAMPERE AND THE DUMA

While insurrection took place in Moscow, a Conference of Bolsheviks was being held to the north. The venue was Tampere (or Tammerfors). This was a Finnish town, just over the border from St. Petersburg. The original intention was to hold the Fourth Party Congress there; but the detainment of the Moscow Committee by the street-fighting induced the other delegates to declare their meeting, less weightily, a Conference. Forty-one representatives were present.[65] Sessions were held in the house of an indulgent police chief. A musical concert was arranged to celebrate the Conference's commencement. A Red Guard patrolled outside. Lenin was elected as Conference chairman; his deputies were B. I. Gorev and M. M. Borodin.[66] The crisis in Moscow led to a breakdown of communications between Russia and Finland. Krasin, travelling back and forth to Petersburg to keep abreast of events,[67] brought unexpected news: on the 11 December the government had published its electoral law for the State Duma. Representatives were to be elected by each social estate separately. The government wished to keep working-class representation to a low level. The gentry would receive a deputy for every two thousand voters whereas the workers would for every ninety thousand. Nikolai II, expecting the peasants to show faith in the monarchy, approved regulations designed to provide them with a majority of the seats in the Duma.[68]

The Tampere Conference's reaction was almost monolithic: the electoral law was a travesty of parliamentarism, it was a 'police Duma'. The elections should be boycotted. The urgent task was to dissuade the people from casting votes. Insurrection remained the Bolshevik priority.[69] Initially there were two dissenters: Gorev and Lenin. They viewed a policy of boycott as yet another sign of the Bolsheviks' naive inflexibility. Lenin had dreaded this since summer. In a note to Lunacharski, he had stated that social-democrats might have to ally with liberals in order to constrain the emperor to grant democratic methods of election.[70] Evidently his anti-liberal vehemence was temporarily in suspension; he refused to hold to unvarying tactics. By contrast, nothing would have induced Bogdanov to proffer a hand to Milyukov. Bogdanov was equally hostile to the law of 11 December. Lenin's attitude was less rigid. Like all Bolsheviks, he denounced the law's provisions as a mockery of constitutionalism. But he believed that the electoral rules could be cleverly exploited. The law called for workers from each factory employing over 150 persons to send a representative to a town assembly. The representatives were then to choose a number of electors; and the electors from all towns in each province would come together to select their Duma deputy. Under the cover of this process, Lenin argued, it would be possible for workers to re-establish the soviets.[71] Gorev, agreeing with Lenin, offered to present the case to the Conference. Lenin continued to discuss the matter with other delegates. Intense hostility to his plan caused him abruptly to abandon it, and he fell back into line with the call for insurrection.[72] But Gorev knew nothing of this. His speech on the Duma met extreme disfavour. He turned to Lenin for backing. Lenin said he had changed his mind. His 'confession' earned stormy applause, and he evoked the Conference's sympathy with the quip that he was 'retreating in full military order'.[73]

The debate sheds light on politics inside the Bolshevik faction. Mensheviks often remarked that Lenin could not abide to work alongside leaders of intellectual prowess equal to his own. The secret of his alleged domination over all things Bolshevik, it was asserted, lay partly with his ability to beguile committee-men of inadequate formal education. Undoubtedly Lenin deployed his erudition to advantage. But he was not always successful. Among the boycottist leaders at the Conference was Iosif Vissarionovich Stalin, whose lack of a university degree in no way inhibited him from expressing himself forcefully. Men of humble social origin were legion in the Bolshevik faction. Their speeches exuded confident judgement; the Stalins and Nogins felt that their own experiences in life gave them a proper and full understanding of the socialist movement's needs. Throughout his career as a party boss, Lenin had to take their feelings into account.[74]

In its other debates, between 12 and 17 December, the Conference agreed on the need to re-unite the Russian Social-Democratic Labour Party. A Fourth Party Congress should be arranged.[75] Preliminary measures could be taken forthwith: the central bodies of the two factions should coalesce on terms of parity. Local committees should also recombine activity. The principle of democratic centralism should be established. Committees should everywhere be elected from below and should be accountable before the party's lower echelons. Centralism was not to be abandoned. Once elected, committees should be accorded 'the entire fullness of power in the matter of ideological and practical leadership'.[76] The Conference also discussed the agrarian question. The reporter was Lenin. The record of his speech is not available; it is not known whether he tried to present the case for land nationalisation. In any event, the Conference avoided so precise a declaration of policy. The Tampere delegates, following the line of the Third Party Congress, called simply for the expropriation of territory held by the crown, the church and the gentry; they left open the problem as to who would hold the property rights, the peasantry or the state.[77] Negotiations between Bolsheviks and Mensheviks followed hard on the Conference. Lenin and Martov were present. Organisational re-unification was agreed.[78] Lenin also loyally pressed the Bolshevik argument for boycotting the Duma. Martov demurred. Ironically, he made a case not dissimilar from Lenin's earlier one: that the Duma elections should be exploited as an instrument for revolutionary self-organisation by the working class. Bolshevik opposition, however, was strong; and the Mensheviks, being themselves suspicious about the Duma, bowed to their arguments.[79]

Over the winter of 1905–6, however, the political situation in the country became clearer. Tsarism was not on the verge of collapse. And the Mensheviks warmed further towards the elections. Akselrod urged unconditional participation. It became the Menshevik position that the chances of a insurrection were waning; and the priority, according to Akselrod, was the acquisition of seats in the Duma.[80] But the conversion of policy came too late for the mounting of a full-scale electoral campaign. Furthermore, Menshevik enthusiasm was checked by the government's announcements in early 1906 restricting the Duma's authority. The tsar aimed to counterweight the Duma with an Imperial Council, whose members would be chosen by himself and various public institutions. The emperor retained control over the army and foreign policy. He could veto any legislation passed by the Duma. He could disperse the Duma at will; and, under article 87, he could promulgate laws without hindrance until the next Duma was elected. Important aspects of the state budget were to remain 'iron-clad': no parliamentary pressure was to hold Nikolai II to ransom.[81]

THE FOURTH PARTY CONGRESS

The elections to the First Duma were not yet completed when the Fourth Party Congress began on 10 April 1906. The United Central Committee, formed from an equal number of Bolsheviks and Mensheviks, chose Stockholm as the location. Fifty seven party organisations were represented by 112 delegates with voting rights.[82] A bureau was elected to manage Congress business. The successful candidates, in order of popularity, were Plekhanov, Dan and Lenin.[83] This order revealed the balance of forces at the Congress. The Mensheviks were going to have a majority. Lenin accepted imminent defeat calmly, and to Stalin he confided his motto in such situations: 'Don't whine!'[84]

Party Congresses nearly always revealed dissensions which would otherwise been barely visible. Initially the Fourth Congress seemed to be an exception. Agrarian policy was its first agenda item.[85] The discussion occupied nearly a third of the time of the entire proceedings. Lenin's report proposed land nationalisation. Apparently he expatiated on his pamphlet *Review of the Workers' Party's Agrarian Programme*, which had been written specially for the Congress.[86] He denied that he aimed at immediate socialist revolution. He described his scheme as essentially 'a bourgeois measure'; he underlined and repeated that the peasant who rented his land from the state would be producing for an economy dominated by capitalist relations. *The Development of Capitalism in Russia* had suggested that the peasantry, if left to itself, would shortly develop an agricultural system as modern as any known in the world at that time. Without fully abandoning this position, Lenin now also contended that intervention and control by government would powerfully increase the rate of economic change.[87] He knew to expect criticism from the Mensheviks, and was quite happy to be provocative. He attacked Plekhanov, who supported Maslov on the peasant question, for inconsistency; he noted that the Emancipation Of Labour Group, back in the 1880s, had called for a 'radical revision of agrarian relations'.[88] Lenin's remark implied that Plekhanov had originally not opposed nationalisation. This was both devious and incorrect. In any case Lenin himself could hardly claim complete consistency in policy. Even he admitted that his 'cut-off strips' scheme of 1902 had been too small a concession to peasant aspirations.[89]

The Menshevik project, drafted by Petr Maslov, remained just as insistent that the land should be taken away from the monarchy, the church and the gentry. But Maslov, in accord with his ideas of 1902, wanted ownership to pass to local urban authorities. In this fashion he hoped to curtail central bureaucratic interference.[90]

The disagreement between Maslov and Lenin over agrarian policy reflected differing expectations about the post-tsarist Russian state. As a Menshevik, Maslov anticipated the immediate installation of a 'bourgeois' government'. Nor did he discount the possibility of a monarchical counterrevolution.[91] Lenin, as a Bolshevik, envisaged a different scenario. The Romanov dynasty's overthrow was to be followed by a temporary dictatorship which would initiate socio-economic reforms that might render the chances of counterrevolution infinitely remote.[92] The cut-and-thrust of Congress debate compelled the protagonists to broaden their arguments still further. Discussion covered the entirety of Russian history. Feudalism became the principal issue. Maslov, Plekhanov and Martynov maintained that, whereas in western Europe it had been social conflicts and technological discoveries which had caused the emergence of the feudal state, in Russia it had been the state itself which transformed society. Russian feudalism was a bastard variant. Martynov called it 'state feudalism'.[93] Plekhanov maintained that the country's agrarian history had affinities to oriental despotism as well as to the feudalism of France and England.[94] Lenin had challenged this view in the 1890s. Suddenly, a decade later, his historiographical differences with Plekhanov were seen to underpin a question of enormous immediate relevance: what was the nature of this tsarist state and how best could social-democrats dismantle it?[95]

The dispute continued for years. But it was already obvious from the Congress's composition that Maslov would carry the majority with him on this occasion. Another fact had been less self-evident. This was that

Lenin, for all his agro-economic expertise, was unable to keep most Bolsheviks with him.

S. A. Suvorov, a Bolshevik who was politically and philosophically close to Bogdanov, baulked at land nationalisation; instead he proposed a scheme which would designate all agricultural land as the property of the peasantry.[96] Peasant committees could distribute it as they saw fit. Suvorov made a single exception in his planning: the large-scale capitalist farms were not to be broken up but to be turned over to 'organs of local self-government'.[97] Suvorov obtained backing from delegates like Stalin who, while unruffled by Menshevik warnings about oriental despotism, predicted that nationalisation would be unattractive to peasants. Such Bolsheviks considered it impossible to prevent the peasantry from appropriating whatever they wanted in the countryside once the revolutionary conflagration had begun.[98] Lenin came some way to accommodating Suvorov's objection. Abandoning reference to nationalisation, he called for the land to become 'the common property of the entire people'.[99] But most Bolsheviks stayed with Suvorov. And Lenin, thinking Suvorov's ideas to be incorrect but not fundamentally damaging to Bolshevik strategy, voted in his support and against Maslov.[100] It is an illuminating episode. Not only does it show us Lenin the practical politician under pressure to back policies which were not entirely to his liking. It also reveals how, even on a major question of policy such as land tenure, Lenin was not the master of the Bolshevik faction. And it also demonstrates, if we look forward a few years from 1906, that the Bolshevik disavowal of land nationalisation as governmental policy in October 1917 by no means represented an abrupt reversal of Bolshevik traditions.

The Congress accepted Maslov's motion by fifty two votes to forty four.[101] Bolshevik attitudes remained under fire. Already in the Congress, Lenin had been accused by Plekhanov of talking like a socialist-revolutionary.[102] The charge was repeated by Martynov in the debate on 'the contemporary moment and the class tasks of the proletariat'. Lenin's insurrectionism was said to have blinded him to other political opportunities.[103] This made painful listening for Lenin; it had been the Central Committee, not he, which had been reluctant to participate in the soviets in 1905. But Martynov's mistake also brought advantages to Lenin. The Mensheviks, by publicly over-estimating his influence, helped to increase it in reality.

As the debate was descending into a desultory slanging-match, the Mensheviks moved to proceed to next business. This was Akselrod's report on the Duma. Akselrod recalled that most Menshevik activists in Russia had originally opposed the entrance of social-democrats into the Duma; and that the tardiness of their change of position had left a clear field for rival parties.[104] Lenin led off for the Bolsheviks in reply. He spoke to a draft resolution, written by himself in collaboration with Lunacharski and I. I. Skvortsov-Stepanov, which defended the boycottist line of the December 1905 Conference. He ridiculed Akselrod's expectations about the Duma's role. Yet he himself did not expressly mention the boycott. He retained reservations about Bolshevik policy; but factional ties prevented him from stating them openly.[105] It fell to Krasin to put the boycottist case. He impugned Akselrod for implying that pro-boycott workers were guilty of 'political indifferentism'.[106] Akselrod jabbed back: 'I was talking not about the proletariat but about you, the leaders.'[107] Then Rykov took another swing at Akselrod, claiming that there was 'a scent of Alpine air' about his speech.[108] Momentarily the Fourth Party Congress looked like turning into a repetition of the Second. This was the last thing Akselrod wanted. He stated that he did not hold comrade Lenin exclusively to blame for the party's past troubles.[109] Conflict faded. The Mensheviks went on to ratify their proposal to sanction the party's participation in the State Duma.[110]

Lenin accepted the result with equanimity. At times he had displayed considerable graciousness, even agreeing to Akselrod's being given greater time for his Duma report than himself.[111] He also announced that he did not believe that Bolsheviks and Mensheviks could not work together in the same party.[112] The Mensheviks, for their part, refrained from stirring up controversy about the party rules.[113] But they were not uniformly placatory. They spoke against the armed robberies that the Bolsheviks had undertaken to increase their faction's treasury.[114] Lenin's support for such 'expropriations' was well-known. And the resolution passed by the Fourth Congress, at Menshevik instigation, was an embarrassment for him.[115] Yet Lenin's generally low-key performance does not demonstrate that he was intimidated. It was surely politically-motivated. He knew very well that the Mensheviks wanted to enter the Duma and to avoid further premature attempts at insurgency; he needed them still to countervail against Bogdanov's insurrectionary impatience. Only once at the Congress did Lenin break cover about such calculations. This happened when the Mensheviks made a previously-untabled proposal to participate in the Duma electoral campaign still in progress in the

Caucasus. Unlike the majority of Bolsheviks present, Lenin sided with the Mensheviks.[116]

The Party Congress then chose officials for the central party apparatus. Negotiations evinced an accord to include seven Mensheviks and three Bolsheviks in the Central Committee. Lenin was not among them. The Bolsheviks chosen were Desnitski, Krasin and Rykov (who was to be replaced by Bogdanov upon his release from prison).[117] Lenin's non-inclusion cannot have been a random occurrence. It was possibly a signal from his factional associates that he and his close supporters had moved too far away from their line of policy; but they cannot have felt extremely strongly about this since he continued for the rest of 1906 to assume a leading position, alongside Bogdanov and Krasin, in Bolshevik discussions.[118] Conceivably the main intention was to keep administrative decision-making out of his grasp. His energies were to be reserved for his widely-acknowledged specialism: editing Bolshevik newspapers and other publications.[119] At any rate, the entire Bolshevik leadership was at least agreed on the need to maintain an autonomous factional central apparatus inside the formally re-united party. A Bolshevik Centre was secretly established. Plekhanov closed the Congress with a speech of thanks for the ending of the organisational schism.[120] He knew of course that the wrangles were unresolved; but he had at least some grounds for thankfulness. Lenin found the Congress less gratifying. He had lost a faction and not yet gained a party.

9 For the Good of the Cause

ON THE RETREAT

If political reactionaries in Russia exaggerated the efficaciousness of repression, it is equally true that the country's liberals (as well as many socialists) underestimated the difficulties that would be posed by the inception of a fully democratic order. Their aspirations were understandable and worthy of emulation. But the events of 1917 were to show how many, how potent and how mutually antagonistic were the social forces held down by the autocracy. Parliamentary compromises would have been extremely hard to achieve in any event. The later experiences of other countries offers further food for thought. It is by no means self-evident that India's political democracy has aided economic modernisation; or that the absence of such a democracy in China in the post-war years retarded the advance from a backward, feudal economy.

Be that as it may, the clamour of Russian oppositional groups for elective, representative government had never been stronger than in 1906. The Duma duly convened on 27 April. No single political party held a majority, and the emperor's expectation of a right-wing victory was not fulfilled. Out of 499 deputies, over a hundred were of the peasant estate; but few of these supported the government. Most peasants in the Duma affiliated themselves to a quickly-improvised grouping which called itself the Trudoviki. The largest Duma fraction was constituted by 161 Kadets.[1] The government offered no full-scale legislative programme, and not surprisingly attracted vehement criticism from Kadet and other deputies.[2] There were only seventeen representatives from the Russian Social-Democratic Labour Party, and only two from the Party of Socialist-Revolutionaries. The social-democratic fraction, consisting entirely of Mensheviks, sought to co-operate with the Kadets. The tactic was approved by the Central Committee. It was disliked by Bolsheviks, including those like Lenin who had been unhappy about boycotting the Duma elections in the first instance.[3] For a while, in May 1906, the emperor altered his stance. Confronted by a Kadet-led alliance inside the Duma, he empowered his new premier Petr Stolypin to parley with the Kadets with a view towards their entry into ministerial office. But Milyukov refused to attenuate the demands of the Kadet programme. Nikolai II, resuming his earlier posture, dissolved the First Duma on 9 July.[4]

The Kadets appealed to the population to withhold taxes and conscripts.[5] Milyukov endorsed peaceful methods of resistance. But it appeared that his bargaining position with the government was only strengthened when many socialist activists took to the streets again. Mutinies broke out in the naval garrisons of Sveaborg and Kronstadt.[6]

As Lenin had feared, Stolypin's reaction was fierce and effective. The mutineers were swiftly crushed. The government had been dispatching punitive expeditions into the countryside throughout the year; rebel peasants had been arrested in their thousands. Police and army were active in the towns. In the months after the October Manifesto, tens of thousands of persons were sent into prison or exile inside the country.[7] Stolypin now strengthened the attack. In August 1906 he invoked article 87 of the Fundamental Laws to create field courts-martial to mete out summary punishments. He also continued to harass the legally operating political parties.[8] But Stolypin perceived that courts-martial would not intimidate the peasantry forever. He introduced a series of agrarian reforms. He had extensive royal domains handed over for sale by the Peasant Land Bank. He issued ordinances to undermine the peasant commune, believing that the collective ties of contemporary village life fostered mass pauperisation and thereby encouraged anti-governmental discontent. Stolypin wanted to put an end to strip-field methods and repartitional practices. His legislation was meant to facilitate voluntary exodus from the commune and to supply each household elder with ownership rights to the land he cultivated; he wanted also to help those leaving the commune to receive their land in the form of a single, consolidated holding.[9]

Meanwhile the Bolshevik Centre's activity was focused on the towns. It set up a factional newspaper, *Proletari*. The Centre's leading figures were Bogdanov, Krasin and Lenin.[10] The Fourth Congress, with its Menshevik majority, had enjoined committees to desist from raising funds through bank raids. The Congress had been equally keen to discourage the formation of armed 'partisan' squads.[11] The Bolshevik Centre flouted both injunctions. But Lenin, unlike Bogdanov and Krasin, was unhappy that the Centre should remain involved in the organisation of military training;[12] he knew too that his two colleagues retained objections to official party policy on participation in the Second State Duma.[13] Even so, a spirit of compromise pervaded the Centre's internal relationships. It was strengthened by an external factor. So long as the three leaders concurred that the Menshevism constituted the most pernicious trend inside the party it would remain their common goal to maintain the offensive against Martov, Dan and their associates.[14]

On the other hand it was not in his interest to drive the Mensheviks to break with the Bolsheviks. The electoral campaign to the Second State Duma was set to occur in the coming winter; the Duma itself would convene in February 1907. Bogdanov and Krasin demanded an electoral boycott. Lenin called for participation. The Party Central Committee called a Conference, in Tampere again, from 3 to 7 November 1906. The Mensheviks did Lenin's job for him. Leading a majority of delegates, they flatly rejected any reconsideration of the principle of electoral participation. The question for debate was different. Martov wanted party committees to·be permitted to form electoral alliances with the Kadets. Lenin's reaction was the same as that of Bogdanov and Krasin. His momentary thoughts of agreements with representatives of liberalism were a thing of the past; he joined all the other Bolsheviks in an anti-Menshevik front. But the Menshevik proposal won by eighteen votes to fourteen.[15] Bolsheviks, though by no means all of them, then campaigned to get social-democrats elected to the Duma. Police intensified harassment of oppositional parties. Social-democratic rank-and-file membership remained numerically buoyant; there was a rise from 10 000 to nearly 150 000 between Bloody Sunday and early 1907.[16] Party work was conducted cautiously; and the environment of repression began to tip the balance of social-democratic opinion in the Bolsheviks' favour, however marginally, after the closure of the First State Duma.[17] Bolshevik doubts about the Central Committee's higher hopes about parliamentarism seemed justified. Nevertheless the electoral battle for the Second Duma had yet to be fought. In the event the party fared not too badly. It obtained sixty five seats. And Bolsheviks were among them for the first time; eighteen of the faction's candidates secured election.[18]

The Second State Duma, meeting in February 1907, was somewhat dissimilar from its predecessor. The Kadets lost ground, having won only ninety eight seats. They also lost nerve. Afraid lest the emperor should again dissolve the proceedings, they avoided assault upon governmental policy. They hoped by persuasion to bring an end to the policy of field courts-martial; and to persuade Stolypin to extend his agrarian reform with a scheme for the compulsory expropriation, with compensation, of the gentry's agricultural land.[19] Their trepidation was despised by the Duma's social-democratic and socialist-revolutionary fractions. The Trudoviks too found the Kadets too deferential to the throne, and their peasant deputies called for the expropriation of gentry-held land without compensation.[20] Administrative repression was another vexed issue (and even the Kadets demanded the realisation of the civic freedoms promised in the October Manifesto). The Second Duma, while witnessing a strengthened influx of socialist deputies, was a very divided assembly. The monarchist political parties had increased their representation. Right-wing deputies pointed out that terrorist activity, undertaken mainly by socialist-revolutionaries, had led to the deaths of over three thousand government officials in 1906. And monarchist organisations in the country urged the emperor to dismiss the Duma forthwith.[21]

PARLIAMENTARISM, THE STATE AND AGRICULTURE

The articles produced by Lenin to interpret the developing trends in the Russian empire in 1906–7 make a mixed impression. None attains his usual level of confident, comprehensive generalisation. His analytical framework has to be carpentered together from scattered materials;[22] his ideas were more probative than definitive. The result is a structure forever threatening to collapse through internal strains and incompletenesses. And yet this relative looseness of thought yields penetrating insights. The range of his considerations is remarkable. In addition, his writings immediately after 1905 are pervaded by modes of discussion closely identifiable with Marx and Engels. So much so that both friends and enemies in the party were to accuse him of an uncritical willingness to perceive the Russian historical experience as the mere repetition of a German model. The charge that he was a crypto-populist faded somewhat, if not completely; and it is difficult to accept many later scholars' judgement that the entirety of his work was essentially traditional Russian revolutionism without connection with Marxism.

His themes were the current concerns of Russian social-democratic debate. He wrote about parliamentarism as a revolutionary tactic, about the nature of the Russian imperial state and about the Stolypinian agrarian reform. His standpoint was idiosyncratic. He was unmoved by Trotski's *Results and Prospects*, which was published in

1906;[23] he objected equally to the multi-volume studies on contemporary Russia produced by the Menshevik leadership from 1909
onwards.[24] He also rejected the general political scenario painted in
Bogdanov's various works (although it was not until the latter half of
1907 that Lenin engaged his rival in open disagreement at a Party
Conference).[25] His views were at their most direct on the parliamentary question. For him it was axiomatic that Marxists should not
ignore opportunities to have their deputies in Houses of Commons,
Reichstags and Dumas. Such neglect would constitute a drift into
anarchism.[26] Marxism held that tactics and methods had to be adjusted
to circumstances. It offered no invariable operational schema; it
adjured its proponents to accept 'compromises' as the necessary
accompaniment to the onward march of history.[27] At times a boycott of
parliamentary elections would be appropriate. Lenin still defended the
Bolshevik refusal to participate in the First State Duma. That boycott,
he argued, had been of the 'active' kind. It had been conducted in a
period of 'revolutionary upsurge'. The chance had existed to overthrow the monarchy. At such a moment there was no sense in entering
a parliamentary institution whose powers had already been so tightly
restricted by the monarch himself.[28]

As the old regime re-asserted itself, however, the prospect of
successful insurrection faded. Consequently Lenin now found a
boycott quite unjustifiable. It would only rob the party of a means,
however limited, of undertaking nationwide agitation and propaganda. The Duma should be used as an instrument for 'enlightenment, education and organisation'.[29] Lenin's position was 'centrist'
inside Russian social-democracy on the parliamentary question; he
disagreed with both Bogdanov to his 'left' and Martov to his 'right'.
Bogdanov was accused of unconditional anti-parliamentarism. Lenin
correctly noted that the German Reichstag was elected on principles
which were far from wholly democratic, and that the German
Social-Democratic Party nevertheless did not boycott it.[30]

In fact Bogdanov's views were distorted in Lenin's presentation.[31]
Bogdanov fully expected Bolsheviks to enter a Constituent Assembly
in Russia once a democratic republic has been established; but he
argued that the Duma was an utterly paltry constitutional body when
compared with such a future Assembly or even with the existing
Reichstag. The Russian political situation, moreover, was inherently
unstable. The explosion of 1905 might recur at any moment. By
participating in the Duma, Russian social-democrats would help to

legitimate the existing political order and fail to concentrate upon mobilising the workers and the peasantry into armed action against the monarchy.[32] In reply, Lenin agreed that politics in Russia were susceptible of sudden transformation; he, no less than Bogdanov, expected violent political 'breaks' and 'leaps' to take place.[33] The current task, as Lenin saw it, was to design tactics which would permit the party to consolidate itself nationally in advance of the recrudescence of a revolutionary situation. Bogdanov, in his turn, declared that Lenin's tactical shimmyings amounted to a sell-out of Bolshevik programmatic goals to Menshevism.[34] Lenin retorted that he was no Menshevik. He stressed repeatedly that he was urging the Duma fraction never to trim the demands of the party programme or collude with the Kadets in parliamentary dealings.[35]

The discussion on parliamentarism was tied to considerations on the nature of the Russian state. Along with other social-democratic theorists, Lenin had written little specifically about the autocracy. Society, rather than the state, had attracted their attention. Until 1905 their main aim had been to demonstrate that, however unmodern its general appearance, the Russian economy had decisively embarked upon a course of capitalist development.

On the whole, they had assumed that the Romanov monarchy was a relic from Russia's past which inhibited further economic modernisation.[36] Lenin's own *Development of Capitalism in Russia* implied agreement with this. Feudal 'vestiges' had to be destroyed if capitalism was to mature. Yet the party's theorists, including Plekhanov, had also pointed out that the state's role was not uniformly retardatory in the economic sphere. They recognised the powerful impetus imparted to Russian industrial growth by Peter the Great at the beginning of the eighteenth century and by the government's ministers at the end of the nineteenth.[37] Such references to the ambivalent impact of the government had not yet been proposed in book-length form. Trotski's *Results and Prospects* filled the gap. Its central supposition was that Russia had followed an idiosyncratic course of historical development, combining features characteristic of 'backward' and 'Asiatic' countries with features associated with the 'modern' industrial countries such as Britain or Germany. Russia was a hybrid. Economically speaking, her condition expressed itself in technologically up to date, vast factory complexes existing cheek by jowl with small-scale, out-moded peasant agricultural communities. Trotski, like most other social-democratic writers (ranging from Bogdanov on one side through to Martynov and

Maslov on the other), emphasised how little the position of the monarchy had been changed by the post-1905 'constitutional' reforms; the political edifice was basically unaltered.[38]

Lenin had often in the past referred to the 'Asiatism' of Russian political life, nor did he cease to do so; but he also maintained that the Russian state had been greatly altered by 1905. It was now directed, he proposed, by a 'bourgeois monarchy'.[39] This phrase was unacceptable to his opponents, Bolshevik and Menshevik.[40] Was he not thereby claiming an excessively 'progressive' function for tsarism? In terms of the long-standing consensus in Russian Marxism, was his standpoint not heresy? Lenin's response drew attention to two matters: German history and 'Bonapartism'.[41] The German state under Bismarck's leadership rested upon support by the traditional Junker landlords and the rising industrial bourgeoisie. Bismarck, according to Lenin, had manoeuvred between these two groups. He had played them off against each other. At the same time he had ensured that the balance of state policy fell increasingly in favour of industrial capitalism. The German monarchy's mediaeval trappings were therefore a superficial phenomenon. Lenin added that Bismarckian politics were not a novelty. He noted that Marx himself had described how Napoleon III, in mid-nineteenth century France, had established his power by attracting support from influential social groups (including above all, in this instance, the peasantry) which yet had clashing economic interests. Thus both Germany and France had effected economic modernisation through a 'Bonapartist' programme.[42] Premier Stolypin, in Lenin's judgement, was introducing such Bonapartism to Russia. His government promoted the interests of the landed gentry and industrial bourgeoisie; it also allowed both groups, with their mutually antagonistic claims, to influence policy informally while it reduced the Duma to the status of a talking-shop.[43]

Lenin's approach shows him not to have been strait-jacketed by the prejudices of his colleagues. His thought here has a freshness about it. He understood that capitalist development was achievable through a variety of class coalitions; and his perception of the possibilities open to the autocracy continues to offer valuable guidance to historians (even though that guidance has been largely overlooked outside the USSR).

But Lenin did not trumpet his conclusions as early as was usual for him; occasionally he undermined his own 'Bonapartist' interpretation by suggesting that the gentry alone did indeed still govern Russia.[44] This uncustomary tentativeness may well have stemmed from problems of reconciling his view of the post-1905 Russian state with his observations on trends in the peasant economy. Like all social-democrats, Lenin regarded Stolypin's agrarian reforms as a project to feather-bed the landed gentry. Russian agriculture was thus being pushed down 'the Prussian road'. Social-democrats noted that land reform in Germany in the nineteenth century had not curtailed the gentry's political and economic power in the countryside. Stolypin too, in their estimation, had set his face against such curtailment. While fostering the emergence of a group of small-holding farmers from the ranks of the peasantry, he simultaneously protected the landed gentry by refusing to expropriate their land and by consequently ensuring that many peasant households still had to buy or rent land to subsist. All the social-democratic alternatives involved expropriation. Virtually all Mensheviks wanted to do this through the 'municipalisation' of property in land, most Bolsheviks through letting the peasants seize it for themselves; and Lenin had his own policy of 'nationalisation'.[45] Expropriation would terminate the government's attempt at a Prussian solution to the agrarian question. Lenin made a striking contrast between the 'Prussian' and 'American' roads of development;[46] he was in agreement with his entire party that capitalism would fully flourish in the rural areas of Russia only when the retarding influence of the average landed nobleman had been removed, and he suggested that the peasants would then be able to compete among themselves just as small-holders had done in the USA when the prairies had been thrown open to agricultural exploitation.[47]

Disagreement, however, remained about the impact of the Stolypin land reform. Maslov still felt that *The Development of Capitalism in Russia* had massively over-stated the possibilities for capital accumulation inside the contemporary peasant economy.[48] He himself emphasised the adverse effects of the rural population explosion.[49] Above all, he tried to show that tsarist taxation and absentee landlordism were bound to keep even the better-off sections of the peasantry at a permanently low economic level.[50] Few Marxists after 1905 were inclined to challenge Maslov's argumentation, especially as it accorded with notions of the regime's reactionary, feudalistic aspirations; and his studies gained increasing popularity in the party in the years before the First World War.[51]

If there was going to be such a challenge, Lenin was the likeliest person to make it. He had indeed always underlined the Russian peasant economy's inherent dynamism; and now he lost no opportunity to castigate Maslov's stress upon population statistics as being non-Marxist.[52] Starting from his own usual premises, Lenin would hardly want to affirm that the Stolypin reform did other than facilitate the further embourgeoisement of the richer households in the village. Once he did in fact ascribe 'progressive' characteristics to it as an economic policy.[53] But his remarks were patchy. Moreover, he did not believe that Stolypin's gambit would work out satisfactorily for the government. At the very best it would require 'decades and decades'; and Lenin remained convinced that a revolutionary political crisis could re-emerge at any time.[54] Beyond that, he ventured the thought that the amount of economic progress achieved under Stolypin was 'negligible'.[55] But he made no fresh attempt to tackle the Menshevik assertion that the better-off peasants were not really turning into rural capitalists. Indeed it was in 1907 that he at last conceded that his early writings had exaggerated the level of Russian capitalist development; and that feudalistic practices were stronger than he had once imagined.[56] Little attention was adverted to this statement at the time. Perhaps his opponents were more interested in the fact that he still maintained that the general direction of change as described in *The Development of Capitalism* was correct.[57] So there was no total recantation.[58] But there was no characteristically militant self-defence either. This was not without irony. On the whole, later research has shown that the years immediately before the First World War, like the last two decades of the nineteenth century, were a period when both capital accumulation and agricultural output by the Russian peasantry increased substantially.[59]

But if Lenin could have protected his empirical case more vigorously than he did, he was completely uninhibited in attacking Maslov on the level of general economic theory. Maslov contended that the analysis of capitalist development offered by writers like Tugan-Baranovski was fundamentally flawed. He acknowledged virtues in narodnik economic thought. In particular, he held that a mass consumer-oriented market was essential for capitalism's maturation. He claimed that textiles and other consumer products had been the springboard for the USA's economic modernisation;[60] and he criticised those Marxists who saw producer's goods as more important.[61] Lenin held fast to his original position. And his logic was not unimpressive. In the first place he, unlike Tugan, had never prescribed that industrialisation was achievable exclusively through the producer's goods sector. He had constantly recognised the need for products of mass consumption.[62] Of course, he had nevertheless argued that producer's goods would inevitably require by far the greater share of investment. And here we come upon a controversy as unresolved today as it was in the lifetime of Lenin and Maslov. Some economists would perceive Lenin's accent upon heavy industrial production as realistic; others would attribute practicality rather to Maslov's insistence upon mass social welfare.[63]

THE FIFTH PARTY CONGRESS

The Fifth Party Congress opened in London on 30 April 1907. Over three hundred delegates with voting rights were present. It was announced that the Party had increased the number of its members to 150 000.[64] The Bund, the Social-Democracy Of Poland And Lithuania and the Social-Democracy Of The Latvian Region had made formal arrangements about entrance to the party, and a delegation of Armenian social-democrats did the same at the Congress.[65] All organised Marxists in the Russian empire were, for the first time, represented at a Party Congress. Speakers from Britain appeared. Harry Quelch and Ramsay MacDonald greeted the Congress.[66] This warm reception was not offered by everyone in East Ham. Several delegates were beaten up by hooligans.[67] Finances too were a problem. Dozens of delegates were workers whose money ran out when the Congress moved into its third week. Appeals for donations were made to wealthy supporters of the party.[68] Monetary stringency, however, impeded discussions less than political division. Factionalism was rife. Fedor Dan's first sally was directed against Lenin. He wanted him excluded from the Congress's presidium for having written that the Mensheviks had prostituted their Marxism.[69] It took three whole days for the Congress to finalise its agenda. The Mensheviks objected to the delay. The Bolsheviks detected questions of principle in every item proposed by their opponents; and they charged them with disregard for the importance of 'theory'.[70] This Congress would patently be more disputatious than its predecessor.

All but three days of the remainder of the proceedings were given over to discussions which in one way or another centred upon the State Duma; and Lenin's speeches and behind-the-scenes activity showed how deft he was at extracting the maximum political advantage available. Bargaining was necessary. No faction or group could obtain everything it wanted. Lenin, through tactical astuteness, got as much as he could reasonably have hoped for.

Martov reported on the Central Committee.[71] Bogdanov too

volunteered a report, prompting Martov to surmise that his adversary's task would be to comment on the work of 'another secret institution'.[72] This was a reference to the Bolshevik Centre. As evidence of Bolshevik duplicity, Martov noted that Bogdanov, Krasin and Lenin had refused to hand over to the Central Committee the sum of 60 000 roubles left to the party in the will of the industrialist Savva Morozov.[73] On they argued, each side claiming that the other had a Duma policy which damaged the prospects of revolution. The Menshevik Martynov jibed that, while he stood for 'permanent revolution', the Bolsheviks preferred 'permanent chatter'.[74] But the Mensheviks were no less chattersome. The Polish, Latvian and Bundist delegations found the Bolshevik–Menshevik altercations tiresome. Their impatience could not be neglected. The Bolsheviks, having won only a handful of places at the Congress more than the Mensheviks, did not command an absolute majority. Consequently Bogdanov (who had kicked up yet another furore by denouncing Martynov as 'a desperate opportunist')[75] was unable to resist the motion to pass on to the next item of business. This was the Menshevik Tsereteli's report on the Duma fraction[76] G. A. Aleksinski, a deputy in the Duma and also a Bolshevik, delivered a hostile co-report;[77] and Lenin dismissed Tsereteli's words as 'the purest revisionism'.[78] Trotski stepped between the two factions.[79] But his pleas had no effect. Plekhanov stirred up further wrangling when he suggested that the philosophical standpoint of Mach and Avenarius, so beloved of many Bolsheviks, was irreconcilable with Marxism; he also asserted that syndicalist ideas might soon take hold inside the Bolshevik faction.[80]

Again the Poles and other non-Russian delegates intervened and the Congress was hauled forward to its third item: Lenin's report on the party's 'relation to the bourgois parties'.[81] He argued that social-democrats in the Duma should ally themselves with the Trudoviki and the Socialist-Revolutionaries and not with the Kadets. He based this upon his optimism about the peasantry's democratic leanings.[82] Mensheviks opposed him. They agreed with him that the owners of the larger industrial and commercial enterprises had turned their face against revolution; but they claimed that the 'middle bourgeoisie', especially the members of the various professions, constituted a powerful anti-monarchical force. Martynov tried to ridicule Lenin's *Development of Capitalism*, comparing it unfavourably with Maslov's economic studies.[83] Lenin was accused of using the slogans of the narodniki.[84]

But the Bolsheviks obtained strong support from the Congress floor.

Trotski and Luxemburg spoke out against the Menshevik view on the middle class.[85] So too did Leo Jogiches, of the Polish delegation.[86] Trotski, Luxemburg and Jogiches thought Lenin over-optimistic about the scale of potential assistance from the peasantry; but the Bolsheviks this time stood their ground and, after some vacillation, most Poles voted for the Bolshevik motion.[87] Thus the Bolsheviks recorded their first unqualified victory at the Congress. They continued their offensive in the following debate on Akselrod's proposal that the party approve the organisation of a 'workers' congress'. Akselrod stated that the party was dominated by 'petit-bourgeois' intellectuals; he also declared that ways should urgently be found to promote the direct involvement of workers outside the party in the revolutionary cause. A 'workers' congress' remained his recommendation.[88] Speaking for the Bolsheviks, G. D. Leitezen branded Akselrod's policy as syndicalist.[89] The Mensheviks knew that the Bolsheviks would win the resultant vote. Nevertheless they made some rebarbarative criticisms. Why was it, they asked, that the Bolsheviks looked upon workers' soviets as nothing better than a 'necessary evil'? Should not socialists welcome independent activity by the mass of the working class?[90] Neither Bogdanov nor Lenin responded. Bolshevik opposition to Akselrod's scheme earned the Congress's approval.[91] Lenin also won the day on the Duma question. Because of Polish pressure, the Congress had so far desisted from framing a resolution lest factional bitterness be aggravated. Yet some policy declaration was plainly a necessity. On 18 May the Bolsheviks finally won most of the Latvians and the Poles to their side. They paid a price. The Latvians insisted that the Bolsheviks make excisions from their motion, especially the clause justifying the boycott of the First Duma. Thus modified, the Bolshevik motion was passed by Congress.[92]

Dan assailed the Bolshevik leaders as wheeler-dealers: 'And it is impossible by your words to paint over the fact that you were against participation in the State Duma, and now you're sitting in it'.[93] On all sides he saw signs of Bolshevik trickery. He opposed Lenin's effort to put off the Congress's discussion on armed robberies.[94] The Bolsheviks had ignored the Fourth Congress's prohibition on bank-raids; and the Fifth Congress reprimanded them for it. Robberies were repudiated as symptoms of 'anarchist tendencies'. They were said to discredit the party in society's eyes and to invite the government to become even more repressive.[95]

The sessions came to their end on 19 May 1907. It had been in near-panic that the delegates attended to three final crucial items of business before returning to Russia. They were presented with a joint motion on the trade unions by the Bolsheviks, the Poles and the Latvians. Its chief point was a call to get unions to acknowledge the 'ideological leadership of the party'; it also demanded closer links between the party and the unions.[96] The motion was passed. The Congress then, very quickly, debated the Party Rules. Membership qualifications remained unchanged.[97] The Congress also re-asserted the authority of the Central Committee. It had already specified that the Duma fraction should operate 'under the Central Committee's leadership'; it now affirmed also that the Central Committee should have full control over the central party newspaper.[98] Finally the Congress turned to elect the Central Committee. There were to be fifteen members. Five were Bolsheviks: I. P. Goldenberg, N. A. Rozhkov, I. F. Dubrovinski, I. A. Teodorovich and V. P. Nogin.[99] There were four Mensheviks. The six other places were divided equally among the Poles, the Latvians and the Bund.[100] The Poles would be useful allies for the Bolsheviks on many issues. But the Bund would be hostile. It was already crystal-clear that the Bolshevik faction would not be able to do just as it liked in the Central Committee, no more than it had in the stormy proceedings of the Congress.

STOLYPIN'S COUP

No Fifth Congress delegate, not even highly circumspect ones like Lenin, had elaborated a policy for the contingency that the emperor might again dissolve the Duma. On 3 June 1907 this possibility became reality. Stolypin had been complaining about Marxist propaganda in the armed forces, and his police had been working to establish that social-democratic deputies to the Duma were implicated. The flat of deputy I. P. Ozol was raided. Stolypin asked the Duma to waive Ozol's immunity from arrest. The Duma's non-compliance led Stolypin to disperse it.[101] He also announced that the government, would convoke a Third State Duma only after altering the electoral rules. He wished to increase the representation of the landed gentry at the expense of the peasantry. His new regulations cut back still further the electoral force of the urban workers. And the ethnically Russian sections of the population were to be accorded a disproportionately large number of Duma seats; the rebellious non-Russian nationalities were to be under-represented.[102] Stolypin aimed to acquire a Duma more to his political liking, even if this required measures which amounted to a *coup d'état*. The Third State Duma convened on 1 November 1907. By and large, Stolypin had got his way: by far the largest fraction in the Duma were the conservative Octobrists, with 150 members and with a leader in A. I. Guchko who was ready to work in harness with the government. The Russian Social-Democratic Labour Party mustered only nineteen places.[103]

Most Bolshevik leaders had called for a boycott, pressing their case at an emergency Party Conference in the Finnish town of Kotka on 21 July. Bogdanov believed that participation in the Duma amounted to collaboration with class enemies.[104] The Mensheviks still felt otherwise; and they were able, with Lenin and his associates, to block the passage of Bogdanov's motion. They themselves, however, had insufficient backing for their scheme for a parliamentary alliance with the Kadets. Lenin therefore held the ring between Bogdanov and Dan. He announced that he considered boycottist plans to be against the party's interest.[105] He spoke openly against Bogdanov for the first time. He trimmed his own motion a little. He agreed to include a sentence which stated that many factory workers were indifferent to the results of the Third Duma elections; and he incorporated a call for anti-government meetings and demonstrations.[106] This made his proposal somewhat more attractive to Bogdanov's group. Bogdanov had his reservations about Lenin's motion recorded for dissemination to the party at large, but in the end he voted for it as a lesser evil than the project of the Mensheviks.[107]

Lenin's 'centrist' resolution was victorious at the Party Conference. Nonetheless the time had passed since the Ministry of Internal Affairs worried about the party's official decisions. Repression increased after June 1907. The entire labour movement, with its trade unions and its welfare-scheme organisations, was affected. The prison population more than doubled in the four years after Bloody Sunday.[108] About five hundred trade unions were closed down from 1906 to 1910; and the number of union members declined from 250 000 in 1907 to 13 000 in 1909.[109] The police hunted down revolutionary parties. According to Trotski's estimate, the Russian Social Democratic Labour Party's membership dropped from 150 000 in 1907 to 10 000 in 1910.[110] A harassed labour movement was unable to maintain its previous level of opposition to the state and to the employers. Millions of workers had gone on strike in 1905. By 1910 the situation had so changed that only 222 cases of industrial stoppage, involving merely 46 000 workers, were reported; and, of those 222, only 8 were linked to political demands.[111] State coercion was not the only reason.

Unemployment increased. Under Stolypin's premiership, the industrial sectors of the economy were gripped by a recession caused by world trade problems as well as by the disruptions of 1905 at home. Average real wages did not rise. In addition the government, laden by its immense foreign debt and deprived of peasant redemption payments as a source of revenue, felt itself in no position to lower indirect taxes. Workers were paying more for their food and other consumer products.[112]

But Stolypin's legislative energies were directed towards agrarian reform. By late 1907, repression had pacified the countryside and he anticipated years when the 'sober and strong' among the peasants would quit the commune and become solid, prosperous supporters of the social order.

The results were disappointing. Between November 1906 and May 1915 only fourteen per cent of allotment land in European Russia was decommunalised.[113] There was a further difficulty. Stolypin desired that peasants abandoning the commune should consolidate their allotments into a single, enclosed holding. Such enclosures were thought important for agricultural progress. In fact only 1 260 000 households achieved this by 1916, and they constituted a mere tenth of all the households in European Russia.[114] Stolypin's aims were not approved by the mass of the peasantry. After 1909 the spate of applications to leave the commune subsided. Stolypin introduced laws restricting the rights of commune members to refuse to allow others to leave; it also loffered free land in Siberia for cultivation.[115] But social relationships in the first half-decade after 1905 remained remarkably unaffected. On the other hand, the government could also report successes. There was a sharp rise in the empire's grain production. Output increased by thirty seven per cent in the period 1909–13 as compared with 1900.[116] The gentry-owned latifundia werc not alone in contributing to this. The richer peasants too, whether or not they had left the commune, were marketing steadily larger quantities of grain; and it is calculated that four fifths of the modern equipment in use in Russian agriculture in 1917 belonged to the peasantry.[117]

While fostering this economic improvement (as Lenin, almost alone among Russian social-democrats, had predicted to be possible),[118] Stolypin endeavoured to keep the majority of the Third State Duma with him. At times his own respect for the monarch was cast into doubt. The Octobrists in 1908 prevailed upon Stolypin to concede power to the Duma to vet affairs in the imperial navy. Nikolai II overruled him.[11] The Octobrists too found cause to distrust Stolypin. They went into outright opposition to him when, in March 1911, he temporarily suspended the Duma in order to introduce legislation on the empire's western provinces.[120] Isolated from tsar and Duma, Stolypin was in trouble. Even among industrialists he had enemies.[121] By 1911, the difficulties facing him were enormous: he had not built up the peasantry as a bastion of the imperial state; he was losing the affections of the middle class. The working class was cowed, but its quiescence was unlikely to be permanent. Stolypin did not live to tackle these problems. On 1 September 1911 he was assassinated.[122]

THE FINNISH BASE

Stolypin's government had constrained all Russian revolutionaries to re-polish all their underground skills. Throughout 1906, Lenin had avoided exposing himself to the danger of arrest;[123] and his caution was strengthened when the Second Duma was suspended in June 1907. Police agents infiltrated the party's ranks. Lenin knew that among the various *caches* of literature frequently confiscated by the authorities were copies of his own pamphlets.[124] He was high on the government's list of politicians to be apprehended.

Yet he could cope with the situation. Rejecting thoughts of emigration, he accused Plekhanov of presuming to pontificate on the Russian revolution from the safety of the Alps.[125] The Bolshevik Centre recognised, even in 1906, the importance of acquiring a safe, secret base. Proximity to St. Petersburg was desirable. And the decision had been taken to move headquarters to G. D. Leitezen's dacha, outside the Finnish town of Kuokkala.[126] There Lenin lived with Bogdanov and Krasin, and the troika had Krupskaya as their secretary. The working atmosphere grew stickier in the aftermath of Stolypin's coup. The fact that Bogdanov and Krasin fought all the way against the party's taking part in the Third Duma elections steadily soured relations. Nevertheless joint activity continued. Contact with the Central Committee was maintained. Both Bogdanov and Lenin had been elected as its candidate members at the Fifth Party Congress, and they encouraged their colleagues to come out to their hideaway on frequent visits.[127] The Petersburg party organisation too held meetings nearby in Terioki.[128] Lenin and Bogdanov also managed to find time to write lengthy theoretical pieces.[129] While in Finland, Lenin lived under the pseudonym of Ervin Veikov. He also revived his ambition to get his books published legally in Russia through his old pen-name of V. Ilin.

A contract was signed for a multi-volume edition of his works, to be entitled *Over the Past Twelve Years*.[130] And on one of his trips to St. Petersburg, back in 1906, he addressed a covertly-organised gathering of over two thousand persons. He was nervous in advance about his oratorical abilities, never having spoken to so large an audience before. But on the night he was well received.[131] There is even a story that he contemplated standing as social-democratic candidate for the State Duma.[132]

The tale cannot be corroborated in its own terms. But it is suggestive in another sense. It strengthens the impression that Lenin now thought of himself as a permanent body in the Russian political firmament. At times he delivered statements of 'statesmanlike' soronity and patriarchal serenity. He called grandly upon activists to work together 'more amicably',[133] and once even asserted that social-democracy was of a single mind about political policy.[134]

Such pronouncements, however, were not evidence of a change of heart or even style. He was still the bilious commentator, the spiky and cantankerous in-fighter. Useful as the Mensheviks were to him, he disapproved of their ideas and did not refrain from inveighing against them. He wondered, provocatively, whether Maslov could continue to be regarded as a 'comrade'.[135] He fostered divisiveness in the Petersburg party organisation, so much so that in spring 1907 the Central Committee established a 'trial' to investigate his behaviour.[136] He was impenitent. Indeed he advised his co-factionalists to intensify 'military operations against the opportunists'.[137] His intransigence was not unique among Bolsheviks. Mensheviks frequently complained about the rival faction's breaches of etiquette. But this only encouraged the Bolshevik Centre to persist in its kind of behaviour. Martov, Maslov, Martynov and their like were not cowards; they knew how to trade punch for punch. But they did not like to hit below the belt. The Bolshevik leaders by contrast revelled in a machismo of personal insensitivity in debate. Several followers enjoyed the spectacle. 'I heard Lenin', wrote a girl about a conference of St. Petersburg activists held in Terioki, 'and I was enraptured.'[138] But her adoring attitude was not universal. Party Congresses always witnessed speeches by Russia-based delegates who resented the disputatiousness of party chiefs.[139]

What sustained Lenin was his total conviction that his policies were totally right. He seemed to have inexhaustible energy. He kept up this appearance right through 1906 and until the end of the Fifth Party Congress in May 1907. The Congress was an emotional turning-point. The chance of an alliance with the Poles in order to defeat the

Mensheviks was a chance not to be missed; but it required the long, tedious back-room sessions of cajolement and concession. Such manoeuvring wore him down. He fretted about the Central Committee and the Bolshevik Centre's far from secure grasp on it. Even sharper was his concern about Bogdanov's influence in the Bolshevik Centre. Bogdanov's ally Krasin held the Centre's purse strings; and Lenin, without Krasin, would lack the finances to run a newspaper.[140] In 1907 Lenin minimised personal reference to Bogdanov both in his writings and, apparently, in his speeches; he attacked policies, not personalities.[141] But his patience was becoming wafer-thin. A Party Conference, attended by twenty seven delegates, was held between 5 and 12 November in Helsinki to discuss how the social-democratic deputies should operate in the Third State Duma. Lenin's anti-Kadet motion won the day.[142] Yet it did not reflect the attitude of all Bolsheviks; and many boycottists, having failed to prevent the party's electoral participation, soon began to think of ways to stop the Bolshevik Duma deputies from attending the Duma. A split between Lenin and Bogdanov was in the making.

That Lenin should contemplate such a break is used by his critics as proof of his schismatomania. The Bolsheviks were a mere faction. How could Lenin justify cleaving them into two mini-factions? It would be fruitless to deny that Lenin had a factitious trait in his character; or that he was not unattracted by the notion of being king-pin in the organisations to which he belonged. But it also must be appreciated that the State Duma, for him, posed the central immediate question for Russian social-democracy. In addition, there was an underlying intellectual rationale for his behaviour. He believed that a political group's numerical weakness in a period of political repression had only limited significance for the future. A revolutionary explosion was to be expected. And political parties would be made great not by virtue of having built up a large organisation before the revolution.[143] Greatness would accrue rather to those which, in the course of the revolution itself, had programmes and policies which corresponded with the interests of particular social classes. Lenin declared: 'Individual parties can hide in the underground, give no sign of themselves, disappear from the political centre-stage; but, at the slightest revivification, the basic political forces will again reveal themselves, perhaps in altered form but with the same character and direction of activity, until the objective problems of a revolution which has suffered this or that defeat have been resolved.'[144]

Such thoughts yielded the conclusion that revolutionary leadership in times of unfreedom was better undertaken by a few men with correct theory than by many who united around a hotchpotch of incorrect ideas. In 1907 Lenin was not ready to break with Bogdanov. He must have been tempted. For he had before him the prospect of gaining financial independence from Krasin when V. K. Taratuta, Lenin's supporter in the Central Committee, inherited a vast sum of money.[145]

In any case, other practical considerations interposed themselves in the second half of 1907. Stolypin's coup led to increased anti-revolutionary vigilance. The St. Petersburg authorities were given clues about Lenin's whereabouts by police agents in Paris.[146] But nothing untoward followed. Lenin may unconsciously have thrown his pursuers off the scent by departing for Stuttgart in Germany on 1 August as his party's representative on the International Socialist Bureau and at the ensuing congress of the Socialist International.[147] He also gave up the Kuokkala house in favour of another deeper in the Finnish countryside.[148] But the police continued to close in. A watch was placed on Lenin's movements on 14 November. Official orders were given to suspend publication of his collected works, and it looked most unlikely that the Bolsheviks would succeed in putting out a party newspaper legally.[149] Reluctantly the Central Committee decided to send most of its members abroad. Lenin became a fugitive. His daily physical exercises stood him in good stead. With the help of Finnish social-democrats he eluded chase by moving, under cover of darkness, from island to island in the archipelago of the Gulf of Bothnia. His plan was to catch the Finland–Sweden passenger steamer which started from Abo. But police officers were scanning the Abo boarding area. He therefore had to make a dash, this time by walking and climbing over the icefloes, to the steamer's next port of call in the bay of Nagu island. The ice gave way. Lenin was nearly cast down into the Gulf's bitterly cold waters. But he had both the agility and the luck to jump on to a solid icefloe and to reach Nagu. On 12 December 1907 Lenin joined the steamer bound for Stockholm; on 21 December, joined at last by Krupskaya, he left Sweden for his second period of emigration in Western Europe.[150]

10   Doubts and Certainties

TOWARDS THE BREAK

The desire of Russia's political intelligentsia for an integral view on the universe grew strongly in the nineteenth century. The country's Marxists inherited a commitment to science and rationalism. The same may be said about their counterparts in Germany; but in Russia the intensity of the search for comprehensiveness was greater. It is striking how eagerly Russian Marxists read the latest research in physics, psychology and philosophy. And practical tactics, they assumed, were undecidable without reference to general premises. Lenin stoutly defended this tradition. The failure of the 1905 revolution did not depress him: victory could be delayed but not postponed forever. His high morale was unusual. The defeats of 1906–7 had a widely demoralising effect upon revolutionaries. Political disarray was accompanied by a mushrooming interest in religion and metaphysics, and poets and artists sought solace in outlandish imagery and techniques. The intellectual's usefulness to Russian society came under question. The Pole Jan Machaisky declared that the intelligentsia, though proclaiming its democratic motivations, would contrive to dominate the mass of the population after a revolution no less heavily than the tsarist regime had done. This attack from the left was followed by another from the right. A group of liberal conservatives, former Marxists and religious mystics combined in 1909 to produce *Landmarks*, a book which urged intellectuals to abstain from politics and concentrate upon their individual moral self-perfection.[1]

Lenin reinforced his emphasis upon organisational control and ideological 'purity'; he discerned no other antidote to the dissolute and dissolving conditions he diagnosed. The autocracy's counterrevolutionary offensive, he guessed, might be effective for a further three or four years.[2] His tactical aggressiveness to opponents inside the party increased in 1908. The Mensheviks, now that the Third Duma elections were over and Bolshevik deputies were taking their seats, were less use to him than before. Lenin's campaign against them in the Central Committee was relentless.

175

The involuntary emigration of leaders like himself called for some institutional re-organisation. The Central Committee left some members behind to handle party affairs in Russia. Four Bolsheviks were particularly active: Dubrovinski, Goldenberg, Nogin and Rozhkov. Meanwhile, the Menshevik presence in the Central Committee was depleted by arrests.[3] Bolsheviks exploited their advantage. They ensured that their factional newspaper *Proletari* appeared frequently from autumn 1907.[4] By contrast *Social-Democrat*, which was intended to serve the party as a whole, was reduced by the Bolshevik-Menshevik strife to only fitful publication both then and in the following year.[5] The Menshevik N. V. Ramishvili demonstratively resigned from the Central Committee in February 1908; and Polish members like A. Warski expressed growing distaste for the virulence of Bolshevik assaults upon adversaries.[6] The Central Committee met abroad on 21 August. A bipartite sub-structure was created. A five-man team would direct the party in Russia while a new troika would handle affairs in Western Europe. The Bolsheviks' influence was diminished. Goldenberg was to be their single representative in the team for Russia. He was to be balanced by the Menshevik M. I. Broido.[7] The other three members were to be a Pole, a Latvian and a Bundist; it was expected that their influence would keep the factional rivalries to a minimum. This was not to Lenin's liking. But it should not be assumed that Bolshevik opinion in general took his attitude. There was much, in any event, for the Bolsheviks to be pleased about. By late 1908 they were doing well in local party committees in Russia proper (even though their record against the Mensheviks in the Ukraine and the Caucasus remained less satisfactory).[8]

But such committees often had little contact with rank-and-file members; Dan and Martov challenged the Bolsheviks to put their position to the test of a Party Congress. The Bolshevik Centre ignored them, and instructed its representatives in the Central Committee to repudiate the Menshevik request.[9]

Yet the Russian social-democrats incurring Lenin's fiercest wrath were found among his own Bolsheviks. To his consternation, he heard in spring 1908 that the idea of 'recalling' social-democratic deputies from the Duma was gathering a strong following in Russia. The Duma social-democratic fractions behaviour exacerbated the problem. A number of instances were reported showing that the party's deputies had disregarded the Central Committee's instructions.[10] The stronghold of 'Recallism' was the Moscow region.[11] But the hostility to having party members in the Duma also found favour with committees

elsewhere in the empire.[12] Maksim Gorki strove to effect a reconciliation between Lenin and Bogdanov. He invited them to stay with him in
his house on the island of Capri off the Italian mainland.[13] Unlike
Bogdanov, Lenin for some time refused. But a minimal level of
co-operation was unavoidable. Lenin and Bogdanov, with Dubrovinski, were *Proletari*'s editors. The newspaper had to be attended
to. Lenin persuaded Dubrovinski to remain in the anti-Bogdanov
camp. *Proletari* must not go Recallist. Ignoring Gorki's peace-making
gestures, Lenin made clear that he would shortly engage in an attack
upon Bogdanov's philosophical writings. The intra-Bolshevik truce
about philosophy was to be terminated. Coaxed out to Capri in April
1908, Lenin rejected any compromise with his former partner; he was
also worried lest all Bolsheviks should become branded by Plekhanov
as renegades from Marxist philosphical 'orthodoxy' by virtue of being
in the same faction as Bogdanov. Lenin's political views might be seen
as 'heretical' by the guilt of association with Bogdanov.[14]

Lenin spent several weeks in the British Museum beginning the
preparation of his onslaught. In May 1908, he equipped Dubrovinski
with criticisms of Bogdanov's epistemology to be delivered by
Dubrovinski when Bogdanov lectured in Paris.[15] Bogdanov objected
to Dubrovinski's vituperative comments. When Lenin rallied to
Dubrovinski's side, Bogdanov resigned from *Proletari* (though not
from the Bolshevik Centre) rather than submit to further editorial
humiliation.[16] First blood to Lenin.

Yet the Bolshevik Centre declined to appoint any of Lenin's
confederates in Bogdanov's stead. Its nominee was V. L. Shantser.[17]
He and G. A. Aleksinski from August 1908 were initiators of a
modified version of Recallism which became known as Ultimatumism.[18] It was simply not in the party's power, they pointed out, to recall
deputies from the Duma, Shantser and Aleksinski also argued that the
eighteen social-democrats, after a poor start, had done much to
discomfit governmental ministers and to help in the Duma's preparation of useful legislative projects on labour reforms. Rather than make
a futile attempt to prise them out of their Duma seats, the party should
'allow' them to remain on condition that they obeyed the Central
Committee's instructions. The Ultimatumists wanted to give a formal
warning to the Duma fraction: either you do as you are bid, or you will
be expelled from the party.[19] This was too strong for Lenin's taste, but
not to the extent that he could not work with Shantser. Recallism was
another matter. He resolved to quit the Bolshevik faction altogether
should Recallism win a majority in the Centre.[20] Meanwhile he plotted

strategy for the Fifth Party Conference, due to meet in Paris on 21 December 1908. Recallists and Ultimatumists could muster only a handful of votes; and again it was Lenin's 'centrist' motion that willy-nilly won their support as being at least better than that of the Mensheviks.[21] But Lenin was by no means contented. Ultimatumism involved a down-grading of the significance of legal political activity. Bogdanov himself endorsed a policy similar to Ultimatumism; and it seems that he combined this, even in late 1908, with a belief in the need for immediate steps to be taken to organise armed insurrection.[22] Lenin would move heaven and earth to get Bogdanov removed from the Bolshevik Centre.

'MATERIALISM AND EMPIRIOCRITICISM'

The product of Lenin's philosophical studies was *Materialism and Empiriocriticism*. Its subject was epistemology. Bogdanov had refined his ideas between 1904 and 1906 in his trilogy *Empiriomonism*. Lenin's assault took a year to prepare. It appeared in April 1909. He had always thought that his socio-economic analyses were fragile unless supported by sound philosophical struts. But he had shown only sporadic interest in theories of cognition. Now he made a virtue of his limited expertise. His purpose, he declared, was merely to re-state the 'orthodox' precepts of Marx and Engels; he described himself as a 'rank-and-file Marxist' in epistemology. He re-read Marx. But it was Engels, Plekhanov and Chernyshevski who seem to have claimed the lion's share of his attention.[23] He foresaw that he would be accused of being 'uncritical' towards his favoured authors; he defiantly proclaimed at the outset: 'And don't cry, Machist gentlemen, that I rely upon "authorities"!' He asserted that it was better to rely upon Marx and Engels than upon 'bourgeois' scholarship.[24] Stridency pervades the book. No stylistic means of deriding Bogdanov was neglected. Lenin's sister Anna, who handled the book's legal publication in Russia (under his old *nom de plume* of V. Ilin), urged him not to 'spoil' the contents by an excess of denigration; she liked his poking fun at people, but drew the line at his questioning of Bogdanov's honour. Brother Volodya was stubborn. He agreed to withdraw only such passages as might offend the censor.[25]

Many of the main positive propositions of *Materialism* repeat Plekhanov's work. Dispute already raged between Plekhanov and Bogdanov. In 1906 Plekhanov had gathered some early philosophical pieces into a book called *Critique of Our Critics*; in 1908 he issued the first instalments of *Materialismus Militans* with Bogdanov as his target. Plekhanov's old themes were reiterated. He made affirmations about the independent reality of the external world, about the primacy of matter over mind and about man's ability to have exact knowledge of the world.[26]

Bogdanov was accused of repudiating the independent reality of the external world. In fact this was not quite what he said. He made no such express repudiation; for him, such a proposition about reality was simply unamenable to verification. He began from different premises. Cognition in his estimation was not a process whereby an external entity, 'matter', imposed itself upon 'mind'.[27] The mind-matter dichotomy was untenable. Rather the universe was 'an endless web of complexes consisting of elements identical to elements of sensation'.[28] And all these elements, according to Bogdanov, existed in a permanent state of interaction and mutual alteration. Cognition was not a 'pure' act of contemplation. It was conditioned by sense-organ chemistry and by historically changing circumstances. 'Absolute' truth was therefore a chimera.[29] That which is true, he asserted, is that ideology or those ideas which 'most harmoniously and elegantly' organise society in the existing social environment. Thus Catholicism had a truthful function in mediaeval Europe inasmuch as it consolidated the contemporary socio-economic order. *Das Kapital* was analogously describable. Marx's treatise in Bogdanov's view was not of eternal validity but, rather, 'an objective truth' for the pre-socialist, industrial societies of the epoch.[30] For Bogdanov, ideas were a powerful organising 'force'. He, more than any other leading Marxist theorist after Marx, emphasised the impact of 'culture' (as distinct from 'economics') upon the course of history.

Plekhanov and Lenin regarded this as anti-Marxist. Bogdanov's phrasing gave them temporary advantage; he had stated, in 1904, that 'social being' and 'social consciousness' were the same.[31] Marx by contrast had said that social being gives rise to such consciousness.[32] Charged with confounding cause and effect, Bogdanov justifiably replied that his original intention had been to indicate that consciousness, though conditioned by 'being', also has an interactive relationship with it.[33] But Plekhanov and Lenin had other criticisms too (and in any case Lenin the polemicist refused to take any notice of Bogdanov's rejoinders). Lenin adduced Engels's remark that materialists, among whom Engels classified himself, believed in the ontological primacy of matter.[34] This led to a further assertion. Marxism, according to

Plekhanov and Lenin, held that the universe exists independently of human perception.[35] Engels's materialism lacked a definition of matter itself. Plekhanov, with Lenin's approval, obliged. He defined matter as 'nothing other than the totality of things in themselves inasmuch as these things are the origin of our sensations'.[36]

Bogdanov retorted that Plekhanov's definition, far from amplifying Engels's materialism, had reduced it to tautology.[37] Plekhanov's interpretation of Engels was equally unacceptable to Bogdanov. 'Things in themselves', according to Bogdanov, were used by Engels as a convenient terminological short-hand and were not part of his considered epistemological standpoint. This does not entirely convince. Nor, for that matter, did Bogdanov address himself to Lenin's quotation of Engels on the subject of materialists. Yet Engels was not lost to Bogdanov completely. *Anti-Dühring*, as Bogdanov delighted in repeating, insisted on the relativity of social knowledge. Engels deemed absolute truth about society to be unattainable.[38] Bogdanov derived even greater succour from Marx's own texts; and he took the view that Engels's occasional 'lapses' made him a less reliable interpreter of Marxism than Marx himself. Marx's *Theses on Feuerbach* explicitly attacked the eighteenth-century treatment of cognition as the passive contemplation of object by subject. His own conception was dynamic. It proposed that man not only was the product of material and social circumstances but also could act upon and change circumstances; and that the verisimilitude of his ideas is testable only by practical activity.[39] Admittedly, Marx often referred to 'laws' governing socio-economic behaviour;[40] and this lent some support to Lenin's declaration that Marx felt that human perception could be absolutely accurate. But Marx's work was not without its own contradictions. His more directly philosophical remarks, especially in his *Theses on Feuerbach*, jar against a great deal of *Materialism and Empiriocriticism*. There is justice in Bogdanov's claim to be closer than Lenin and Plekhanov to Marxian epistemological theory.[41]

The dispute, of course, was not merely about ·'orthodoxy' but equally about who was right. Discussions among philosophers in ensuing years have not produced agreement. Views on the question of the independent existence of the external world still differ; but Lenin's attitude undoubtedly has strong current backing. He would secure fewer sympathisers on other points. It is now more or less generally accepted that what knowledge we have is conditioned by the processing effects of our sense organs. And it is a rare philosopher who affirms the attainability of absolute truth.[42]

Lenin's epistemological optimism was extreme. Plekhanov, while characterising our mental impressions as 'signifying exactly' what existed in the external world, avoided the concept of absolute truth.[43] Moreover, he called these impressions 'hieroglyphs'.[44] Lenin thought Plekhanov to have introduced an unnecessarily indeterminate factor. He rejected all talk of intermediary hieroglyphic signs. Instead he conceived of the mind as a sort of camera; he thought that it could copy reality and produce photographically accurate pictures.[45] Lenin's more defiant opposition to Bogdanov was buttressed by points that were not strictly epistemological. He offered a sociological survey. Most contemporary natural scientists, he declared, were avowed 'materialists' like himself. Thus the viewpoint of Engels and Plekhanov could be represented as progressive and scientific.[46] This brought him to a second contention. Lenin, following Engels, asserted that there were essentially only two possible positions in epistemology: materialism and idealism. But rather than positions Lenin spoke of 'parties'.[47] His language had a political nuance. His 'party', he affirmed, was that of the materialists. On the other side stood the party of the idealists, and Bogdanov was to be regarded as among its newly paid-up members. Lenin proceeded to a third point. He claimed that philosophical idealism, traditionally and currently, was associated with religious faith (whereas Marxism endorsed atheism). Plekhanov and he noted the recent writings of Lunacharski on the subject of 'god-building'. They were horrified. Lunacharski proposed a humanist 'religion'; he wished to canalise society's existing religious feelings into a form of worship which rejected belief in a heavenly deity and directed all reverence to Man himself.[48] Bogdanov was criticised for having epistemological opinions remarkably like Lunacharski's.[49]

For his part, Lenin stated that *Kapital* was eternally true. It was an inalienable basis for all future knowledge. He concurred that not everything about the world was yet known. But absolute truth was still attainable. It would be gained through a cumulative process. Partial truths of an absolute nature would be piled up on one another and would eventually constitute the comprehensive science of the universe.[50]

Bogdanov made a scathing, though nowadays little-known, riposte in his book *Faith and Science*. He repeated his view on the relativity of knowledge; he again adduced Marx and Engels in support.[51] In his general offensive against Plekhanovite epistemology, he included particular attacks on Lenin. He took up Lenin's camera analogy. Without knowing it, Bogdanov teased, Lenin had adopted an Empiriomonist viewpoint through his references to chemically-based photographic processes.[52] He also tackled Lenin's points on the beliefs of scientists, on 'party-mindedness', on religion. Bogdanov suggested that his opponent had displayed a wholly unscientific, authoritarian spirit.[53] Allegedly, Lenin had not shown philosophical competence. His brandishing of lists of authors was, according to Bogdanov, merely a device to disguise ignorance; it did not even mean that he had genuinely read his supposed sources.[54] Lenin hoped to intimidate. His quotations of Engels, moreover, were so ritualistic as to testify to the same religious frame of mind that he claimed to oppose.[55] Bogdanov pursued the point. The essence of Lenin's position was that Marx's writings were unassailably true.[56] This was hardly science as conventionally understood. Furthermore, Lenin's description of the attainment of absolute truth was not only un-Marxist: it was also absurd. How, asked Bogdanov, was it logically possible to reach the infinite by a finite series of steps?[57]

Evidently these mutual criticisms by Lenin and Bogdanov were not merely about cognitive psychology. Lenin in a single instance discussed political implications. Reversing his earlier contention that Bogdanov's practical policies were uninfluenced by his epistemology, he stated that *Empiriomonism* was a recipe for 'voluntarism' in politics; and that Bogdanov, by assigning no credence to absolute truth, was in a position to dream up whatever mad-cap policies he liked.[58] Bogdanov had never disowned the connection between his philosophical and political opinions. He felt that the same was not true of Lenin. For Bogdanov, *Materialism and Empiriocriticism* was a piece of opportunistic posturing designed to win immediate factional advantage.[59]

In fact, both of the rival works were reflections of differing political attitudes. *Materialism and Empiriocriticism*, so far from being a monument of dissembling (or, as some would have it, an aberration), was an autobiographical fragment. It eulogised, by implication, the individual human mind's ability to understand the world. It was, indirectly, a paean to the intellectual. The veracity of an idea, asserted Lenin, was not increased in proportion to the rise in the number of persons believing it. *Materialism* was a philosophical counterpart to the politics of *What Is To Be Done?* Through the doctrines of Marx and Engels, according to Lenin, the party could explain reality to the masses and win them over to the revolutionary cause.[60] None of this was stated explicitly in *Materialism*; and indeed he refrained from comment on many sections of *Empiriomonism* regarded by Bogdanov as being crucial to his world-view. Bogdanov did not confine himself to analysing ideologies of the past and the present. He called for the creation of a 'proletarian ideology'.[61] Believing that the middle class held workers in thrall as much by the dissemination of capitalist ideology as by direct political and economic pressure, he wanted the party to establish working-class schools and organisations directed at the extirpation of the influence of 'bourgeois culture'. The socialist movement should begin by cleansing its own house. Revolutionary leaders were too wedded to 'bourgeois' modes of thought; they should cease to presume that the intelligentsia could anticipate all the answers to the problems of the introduction of socialism. The party's internal behaviour before the revolution should prefigure the collectivist, democratic forms of organisation to be encouraged when society as a whole was launched into the transition from capitalism.[62] It was up to the workers themselves to start to develop a 'proletarian' ideology, using Marxism as a broad guide, to carry the revolutionary process onward.[63]

Lenin saw Bogdanov's case as an unwarranted attack upon the intelligentsia (even though he himself had had harsh words about it in the past); he also had a higher regard for the scientific and cultural achievements of capitalism than Bogdanov.[64] Yet Lenin refused to be drawn further, limiting himself to the implicit argumentation of *Materialism*. His refusal is tantalising. He talked to no one about it. We can only hazard guesses as to the reasons; but one possibility must surely come into the reckoning: an attack upon Bogdanov's cultural programme would only have invited accusations of hostility to the notion of independently-minded workers; he would also be branded as a devotee of authoritarianism. Such charges would have been simplistic (though not without a large area of foundation). But mud sticks. Probably Lenin wished to avoid the pillorying he had received when he published *What Is To Be Done?*[65]

THE BOLSHEVIK CENTRE

Lenin's forays against groups inside the party did not signify that he yet aimed to abandon all co-operation with those social-democrats who were not his closest supporters. In fact his self-distancing from Bogdanov was complemented by moves towards a rapprochement with Plekhanov. Here Lenin was pushing his luck. *Materialism* contained several acidic statements about Plekhanov's works, and Plekhanov's friends unsurprisingly replied to Lenin in kind in their reviews.[66] In addition *Materialism*, though sincere, was not an exhaustive exposition of its author's attitudes to cognition. Exact knowledge and predictability were its reiterated theme. But in other writings, both before and after 1909, Lenin had emphasised the need for revolutionaries to take gambles. Already he had often strained to foreshorten the schedule of political change more than was warranted by the 'objective' socio-economic environment; and there were aspects of his policies in 1905 had risked horrendously adverse consequences should they have been tried in action. Lenin had his contradictions. This reverse side of his epistemological outlook implied that 'practice' was the test of 'theory'. It carried him close to Bogdanovist positions.

But he referred to his own 'experimèntalism' only in later writings; it may even be the case that he only became conscious of its existence when he resumed his philosophical studies in the First World War. Plekhanov was anyway not unresponsive to his overtures in 1909. The two leaders shared a growing concern about trends in the Bolshevik and Menshevik factions. Both men rejected Ultimatumism. They noted that many followers of Bogdanov wanted to boycott not only the Duma but also legally-permitted mass organisations such as the trade unions.[67] Lenin and Plekhanov had no intention of abandoning illegal party activity. The clandestine party apparatus was to be preserved. But they thought it naive to neglect opportunities of influencing the working class through whatever legal channels might be available. On the other hand, both were opposed to the trend of so-called Liquidationism in the Menshevik faction. Many Mensheviks, led by Potresov, argued that the underground party committees had atrophied in 1907–8 to an extent that made it inappropriate to make them the focal point of social-democratic energies. Work should be concentrated in the trade unions. Potresov did not specifically urge the liquidation of clandestine party activity. He simply said that such activity was already moribund and should not be revivified.[68] The niceties of this policy did not interest Lenin and Plekhanov. They called Potresov a Liquidator. To let the illegal party expire for want of care, in their opinion, was tantamount to killing it. Plekhanov urged Mensheviks to ostracise the Liquidators. Martov and Dan, while disagreeing with Potresov's indifference to the underground party, ignored Plekhanov's summons. Plekhanov thereupon abandoned the Menshevik faction.[69] His action meant that there were now three organised trends in Menshevism: Martov's Mensheviks, the Liquidators and Plekhanov's Party Mensheviks.

Neither Lenin nor Plekhanov ceased to object to each other's programmatic intentions in other areas. Theirs would be a conditional alliance.[70] They vied even about the matter which had brought them together in the first place: legal activity. Until 1907 it had been party policy to spread revolutionary ideas in the unions without insisting that the unions give formal allegiance to the party. Plekhanov continued to hold this view, as did Mensheviks of all types.[71]

Lenin, however, shifted his ground. Now he called on the party to seek to get trade unions to affiliate themselves to it.[72] He reportedly even toyed with the suggestion to accord voting rights to affiliated unions at Party Congresses on a parity with the normal underground committees;[73] But he had second thoughts, perhaps recoiling from a plan which would infringe the principle of the party's hegemony of the labour movement (or perhaps simply because he foresaw insuperable opposition from his own section of the Bolshevik faction). In any case the episode revealed how strongly committed he remained to consolidating the party's influence in the trade unions. This necessitated a settling of organisational accounts with Bogdanov. Lenin's objective was clear. He aimed to win the Bolshevik Centre to his side and force Bogdanov's exodus. His tactics were attributable to his political forcefulness. And they were facilitated to some extent by the financial independence he at last in 1908 enjoyed from Bogdanov and Krasin. A wealthy young man called N. P. Shmidt had died in 1907. He had left hundreds of thousands of roubles for disbursal to organisations supporting the cause of revolution in Russia; his two sisters were to supervise the distribution. The Bolsheviks V. K. Taratuta and A. M. Andrikanis paid court to the women in a successful attempt to get control of the monies. Taratuta handed over his fortune, or a goodly portion of it, to Lenin.[74]

Animosity between Lenin and Bogdanov increased. On 8 February 1909 Lenin broke off personal relations, ending a friendship begun in 1904.[75] The battle was on for the Bolshevik Centre. The scene was set for a final confrontation at a meeting of the editorial board of the Bolshevik newspaper *Proletari*; all members of the Bolshevik Centre were to be invited.[76]

The board meeting, lasting from 8 to 17 June, was basically a conference of the Bolshevik faction. Lenin proposed a resolution condemning Recallism and Ultimatumism. He grumbled that the Mensheviks were amused that members of his faction were accusing him of being a Menshevik; and that Bogdanov had refrained from defending him against the charge. The conclusion was obvious: differences of principle separated the two tendencies in Bolshevism.

Lenin declared: 'There is nothing worse than an absence of open struggle'.[77] Recallism and Ultimatumism were denounced as being un-Bolshevik; it was urged that a 'decisive fight' be begun with all such 'deviations from the path of revolutionary Marxism'.[78] The meeting denounced Lunacharski's 'god-building'. It also criticised Bogdanov for planning to set up a school for party workers on the island of Capri. Bogdanov protested that his views were being misrepresented. He claimed in particular that he was not hostile to the party's participating in legal mass organisations. M. P. Tomski, who had just left Russia, rounded on him. Bogdanov's claim did not alter the fact that few Recallists or Ultimatumists were entering trade unions. Still moving with Lenin, the meeting approved Dubrovinski's motion seeking an alliance with Plekhanov's Party Mensheviks.[79] The meeting's next step was to confirm the anti-Recallist policy organisationally. Bogdanov was to be driven out of the Bolshevik faction. Lenin had been charging him with aiming at a total 'split'; but, on Tomski's suggestion, the meeting reformulated the indictment: Bogdanov was said not to have divided the faction but to have broken away from it. Lenin approved.[80] He liked the implication that Bogdanov's real influence over party committees in Russia had never been great enough to threaten a split.

With the departure of Bogdanov on 12 June, Lenin had won his victory. The Bolshevik Centre could now quickly complete the remaining business. This was in fact a trying time for Lenin. In the moment of his triumph he was to witness the Bolshevik Centre taking decisions which made his organisational position weaker in many ways than it had been before the meeting. Trouble began with I. P. Goldenberg's report. Goldenberg supported the request of the Duma deputies to found their own newspaper in St. Petersburg. Lenin was far from keen. He hinted that such a newspaper would not necessarily pursue a consistently Bolshevik line.[8] But Goldenberg's proposal was carried.[82] The meeting then discussed the work of the Central Committee. Arrests in 1908 had again undermined activity. It was agreed that the situation would be improved if the émigré press were re-organised. *Proletari* was criticised. Delegates from Russia felt that Lenin's editorial policy had given too much space to theoretical disquisitions; they urged the creation of a popular workers' daily. A. I. Rykov proposed *Proletari*'s closure but in the end Goldenberg's compromise was accepted: *Proletari* was to be turned from a weekly into a monthly.[83] This was bad enough for Lenin. But worse ensued when it was decided to undertake negotiations with Trotski, who already ran a popular social-democratic newspaper called *Pravda* (or

Truth) in Vienna. The plan was to persuade Trotski to make *Pravda* a joint venture with the Bolsheviks.[84] Lenin's reservations were ignored. Most delegates, while approving Bogdanov's expulsion from the faction in order to exploit more fully the legal political opportunities in Russia, were reluctant to regard the Plekhanovite Party Mensheviks as their only allies.[85] A more general worry was also voiced. The meeting concurred that émigré factitiousness had got out of hand. A cure was proposed. Bolshevik Centre members operating in Russia were to be permitted to take decisions without constant reference to members abroad; the 'Russian' party was to be freed from 'foreign' entanglements.[86]

Not only was this an implicit indication to Lenin that certain of his basic tactical recommendations were unacceptable. It was also a practical limitation on his activity in the immediate future; he had disengaged himself from Bogdanov only to find himself even more closely controlled by his colleagues than before.

LENIN'S DEFEAT

Initially he accepted the position phlegmatically. But a great lassitude came over him (as it had in his previous time of trial in 1904). Wanting fresh air, he retreated to a rented villa in the countryside outside Paris.[87] Thoughts about his position gnawed at him. It annoyed him to consider what Rykov and Goldenberg might be getting up to in Russia. Matters were no better in France. The Bolshevik leadership chose A. I. Lyubimov to act as the Centre's secretary. Lyubimov had taken a constant stand against Lenin's divisive tactics.[88] He was a leading Bolshevik Conciliator. Lenin could have been forgiven for feeling nostalgic about his earlier years in Switzerland. Before 1905 he had not won every political battle inside the Bolshevik fold; but at least he had been in operational control of the faction's émigré team. In mid-1909 the sensation of organisational impotence bore heavily upon him. He complained about his 'nerves'.[89] He was not eating very well, and it was noticed how thin and pale he had become.[90] Not until mid-August did he feel recovered; and around the middle of September he returned to Paris.[91] He had formulated tactics. He aimed at the overturning of all the resolutions made in June 1909 which had displeased him. He had attempted, as early as August, to keep Lyubimov from negotiating too gently with Trotski. Apparently the Bolshevik Centre was finding it difficult to secure parity of editorial authority over the Viennese *Pravda*; Lenin urged Lyubimov to stand firm.[92] It was Lenin's hope that Trotski would be discouraged from further co-operation with the Bolsheviks. To Zinoviev, he was candid. Trotski was to be seen as 'the basest careerist'.[93]

Lyubimov took no notice. Nor did Rykov and Goldenberg in Russia. A Duma by-election in St. Petersburg led to the setting up of an electoral commission of social-democrats. Rykov joined it. The other members included a Menshevik and a Liquidator.[94]

Lenin then exercised the little power left to him in Paris. Krupskaya belonged to the Bolsheviks' Financial Commission, which was responsible for sending funds to Russia.[95] Rykov, in Lenin's view, was in breach of the anti-Liquidator decisions of June 1909. The Financial Commission was therefore persuaded to cut off monetary support to him.[96] But this was but one small victory, achieved at the price of alienating Rykov still further. It occurred, moreover, at a moment when Lenin's own financial management was coming under scrutiny. The Mensheviks raised a hue and cry about Lenin's insistence that Bolsheviks should retain the Shmidt inheritance for their own exclusive use even though the deceased man had not specified a single faction as the sole beneficiary.[97] Opinion was hardening against Lenin among his Bolshevik colleagues. Why, they wondered, was he persistently calling for a 'war' upon Martov's Mensheviks when nobody doubted that Bolshevik influence in the unified central party apparatus was strong? Was this not evidence of obsessive intransigence? Goldenberg believed so, and went ahead with overtures to Martov in late 1909.[98] Even Zinoviev's loyalty was eroded. In the autumn, Lenin submitted an article to the party's central newspaper *Social-Democrat* calling for a renewed assault upon Recallists and Liquidators.[99] The editorial board discussed this at a two-day meeting starting on 21 October. Zinoviev pointedly abstained from voting, and Lenin's article was turned down for publication.[100] Lenin was furious. He instantly resigned his editorial post with *Social-Democrat*.[101]

It is difficult not to sympathise with those of his colleagues who were losing patience with him. Nobody has been able to show that Recallism had more than very slight support in Russia in late 1909; and the Ultimatumists had in any case never stood very distant from Lenin's own attitude to Duma deputies: he had always urged that the social-democratic fraction comply with Central Committee policies.[102] Outright Liquidationism too was a declining force. Few activists any longer expressed disinterest in the illegal party apparatus. A meeting was held, in the autumn, of leaders involved in the legal labour organisations of St. Petersburg; it was attended by the prominent trade unionist R. V. Malinovski. The necessity of keeping clandestine party cells was endorsed overwhelmingly.[103] Apparently such views were held widely across the Russian empire.[104]

The Bolshevik Centre set itself the task of pulling the entire social-democratic movement together under its leadership. Lenin had sustained an organisational set-back. He also had another of his bicycling accidents, injuring himself sufficiently badly to impel him to start legal proceedings against the driver of the car that hit him.[105] But his colleagues were not unduly brutal to him. Kamenev, Lyubimov and Zinoviev persuaded him to retract his resignation from *Social-Democrat*; and he acceded, probably relieved that nobody had called his bluff, on 23 October 1909.[106] Lyubimov pressed on. Unlike Lenin, he wished to see representatives of all Bolsheviks and all Mensheviks working together in the Central Committee; his other priority was to re-establish the Central Committee's organisational presence in Russia. Bolshevik leaders in Russia supported him.[107] A meeting of the Bolshevik Centre was held in Paris on 1 November. The decision was taken to convoke a plenum of the Central Committee to be attended by all the party's factions. Lenin appended his signature to the decision.[108] It can scarcely have been a joyful occasion for him. Throughout 1909 he had behaved as if only his group inside Bolshevism and Plekhanov's inside Menshevism were legitimate constituent elements of the party. Now his own group opposed such behaviour and wanted to re-combine with Martov, albeit in the hope that this would not lead to a significant diminution of Bolshevik authority in the Central Committee. Bogdanov would be in attendance as a candidate member; and Trotski too would be invited along (in his capacity as editor of *Pravda*).[109]

The plenum lasted from 2 to 23 January 1910. Lenin's tactics were akin to those of a general who, receiving reconnaissance information that conditions are unfavourable for an offensive, nevertheless goes through with it on the grounds that inactivity is bad for the morale of the troops. There was, however, a crucial difference. Lenin had few troops.

He went to the sessions with a motion entitled 'The Situation in the Party'. It apparently repeated the summons to a struggle against the Recallists and the Liquidators.[110] The Central Committee agreed that Recallism and Liquidationism were harmful. Yet Lenin's militance was rejected. The plenum accepted an amendment from Trotski to the effect that the two 'deviations' should be dealt with by means of a 'widening and deepening of social-democratic work'.[111] Comradely persuasion, not administrative sanction, was to be the method used. The plenum recognised that verbal formulations alone would not alter the real state of affairs. Concrete measures were needed. It was even decided that the various factional centres should be abolished. The Bolshevik Centre was to dissolve itself. Factional newspapers such as *Proletari* were to cease publication.[112] Past disputes in the party had been exacerbated by the behaviour of the émigrés. Accordingly the seven-person Russian Board of the Central Committee was given the right to act autonomously in the Central Committee's name.[113] The Mensheviks were determined to spare Lenin no humiliation. His treatment of the Shmidt monies was discussed. And, to his mortification, he was obliged to agree to hand them over. Some were to pass immediately to the Central Committee; the rest were to be held in trusteeship by the German Social-Democratic Party leaders Karl Kautsky, Franz Mehring and Klara Zetkin.[114] His own Bolsheviks were no less keen on the changes than were Martov, Trotski and Bogdanov; the turnabout that had occurred in the Bolshevik Centre in June 1909 was being repeated just a few months later in the Central Committee.

REPUTATION AND STATURE

As we leave Vladimir Ilich Ulyanov-Lenin in his fortieth year, after the January 1910 Central Committee plenum, we note that his impact on the party had never been smaller, his prestige never lower. His isolation was greater even than in the first half of 1904.

And yet we must not dismiss him so casually. If he had died in 1910, the Russian Social-Democratic Labour Party would have remembered him as something more than just a troublemaker. He remained a leader of stature. He occupied a place in the uppermost storey of the party. Others did the same. It was tacitly understood that figures like Plekhanov, Martov, Maslov, Bogdanov, Trotski and Lenin had earned themselves a position above the rest of the leadership. There was an immeasurable but real 'weight' about them. They did not bar acess to newcomers. With its high regard for the articulation of theory and strategy, the émigré fraternity accepted several younger men with fresh ideas such as Nikolai Bukharin and Yuri Pyatakov.[115] But there was little replacement of personnel at the top; the older leaders remained. They knew each other well, having been together in a variety of testing conditions: in clandestine activity in Russia, in the community of emigration, and in the semi-open politics of Russia in 1905–6.[116] Each had proved his mettle in the general estimation of his peers. Of course, all of them were building careers before a very restricted world of observers; no more than a few thousand persons in the Russian empire can have heard of their names and read their works. Inside that world, however, their fame was boundless. They were indeed the party's luminaries.

To be sure, disagreements had dogged their relationships. They were not a happy family. Yet they had valued the ties of kinship. Polemicism, even for them, had its limits. And it was largely because Lenin in 1909 continued to propose the dissolution of the family that his fellow leaders queried whether he deserved their esteem any longer.

The decline in Lenin's reputation by no means plumbed the lowest possible depths. His émigré colleagues continued to acknowledge his gifts as a theorist. Even Bogdanov, who treated his philosophising as ignorant cant, saw him as an economist of importance.[117] Bolshevik Conciliators, moreover, did not disown his writings on political theory. Menshevik leaders were loather to pay him compliments; but they rarely were as contemptuous of his economic expertise as Martynov had been at the Fifth Congress.[118] Undeniably, no Menshevik spared criticism of Lenin's political ideas. His strategical statements were regarded by Martov's group as dangerous nonsense. Charges of 'populism' and 'Jacobinism' had been made in 1905. Lenin, it had been said, was quintessentially a 'voluntarist' who would not recognise environmental constraints.[119] By contrast, left-wing Bolsheviks in 1908–9 accused him of the diametrical opposite: historical fatalism.[120] His entire oeuvre was controversial. But the many critics, in all their variety, conceded that a residue of substance existed in his theoretical output. By 1910, his career's wheel had therefore turned full circle. Until the late 1890s he had impressed primarily as a writer, not as an organiser. He had developed his practical skills gradually. He had shown ruthless flair in founding *Iskra* and co-ordinating communication with groups in Russia.[121] But his organisational divisiveness alienated an ever-increasing number of émigré social-democrats. Moreover, there was no longer a shortage of leaders who could cope with administrative duties. He was not indispensable. His own nearest colleagues implied that his activity led to greater disorganisation than organisation. Ex-collaborators like Martov and Bogdanov denounced his authoritarian style; Gorki came to regard him as a misanthrope.[122]

Thus what was left of Lenin's positive reputation abroad had come to rest upon his ideas and his writings.

His standing in the party in Russia itself is less easy to assess. He had his admirers. V. S. Dovgalevski offered the following description to provincial colleagues: 'This is a magnificent propagandist and agitator, a brilliant diplomat and politician, wholly intelligible to the broad masses, valuable alike in the professorial chair and at the workers' gathering, combining in himself everything necessary for a party chief.'[123]

Such glowing approval was far from universal, even among Bolsheviks. For years there had been hostility to émigré disputatiousness. It was difficult for underground activists to follow the details of the wranglings in Western Europe; but they were acquainted well enough with the basic situation. And, when police files were seized in 1917, the record of arrests of social-democratic groups indicated that Lenin's major works were widely known.[124] This was tribute to his status as a theorist. But it also meant that activists across Russia were aware of his disruptive role. F. I. Goloshchekin, a Bolshevik who opposed Bogdanov's attitude to the Duma, wrote from St. Petersburg in late 1909 imploring the émigrés to terminate disputes about Recallism (which, he suggested, was withering on the vine in Russia without need of artificial poison).[125] Negative evidence reinforces the point. It is altogether remarkable how little material has been produced to demonstrate that elements in the Russian party continued to hold him comprehensively in esteem as a practical leader. His reputation for crankiness grew. Even Stalin, who was operating in the oil-town of Baku and who was not unknown for a penchant for vehement polemics, thought that Lenin had overdone his assault on Bogdanov. *Materialism and Empiriocriticism*, he stated, was 'a storm in a glass of water'.[126]

This fall-off in the appreciation of his qualities irritated Lenin, but did not crush him. There remained much to be pleased about. True, he was accused of dishonourable conduct; he was also notorious for perceiving great issues of principle where others saw only practical minutiae. Yet few indicted him on grounds of complete insincerity.[127]

Consequently, however underhand and ruthless he was in action, he was still widely treated as a serious man with serious ideas. The fact that he obviously relished the possession of authority did not detract from this. His enormous potentiality as a party chief was commonly recognised. Even in 1908–10, when his behaviour had never been more intemperate, he could often charm his adversaries.[128] The contents of his statements and policies were frequently provocative. But he usually refrained from angry public outbursts; Vladimir Medem, a member of the Bund and no friend of the Bolsheviks, was amazed by Lenin's capacity to remain impassive when being harangued or insulted.[129] Lenin's passion was poured into his politics. He was chary of any activity that might deflect his commitment even marginally; he gave up both playing chess and listening to Beethoven on these grounds. He explained that the beauty of the *Appassionata* disturbed him so much as to make him forget that in order to create a better political order it was necessary to 'bang people over the head'.[130] He was, then, not devoid of candour. Little wonder that not only admirers but also critics sensed that he was every inch a Leader. A short sentence from a private letter of Anatoli Lunacharski to his wife gives a neat illustration. Relations between him and Lenin had worsened after 1905. Yet Lunacharski could write, in self-congratulation, about a conversation with Lenin: 'He is terribly satisfied with me.'[131] These are the words of someone who feels another's dominance to be in the natural order of things.

And so the vista of opportunities perceived by Vladimir Ilich Ulyanov-Lenin in early 1910 was not uniformly sombre. At the nadir of his fortunes, this irrepressible optimist intended to re-scale the heights. He aimed to climb higher than before. He would not give up the struggle for his policies, even should the entire party condemn him. There was to be no relenting. He felt that his colleagues' indulgence to other social-democratic factions constituted peril for the entire revolutionary movement; and the keenness of this feeling imparted urgency to his campaign. He had to win back his Bolsheviks. Without them, nothing was achievable. He needed a firm organisational base. The current condition of his reputation and influence did not worry him unduly. It was not an accurate gauge of his significance. Works like *What Is To Be Done?* and *Two Tactics of Russian Social-Democracy* had made a durable imprint upon Bolshevism. He had never, not even in late 1903, held a monopoly of power in the Bolshevik faction,[132] and several of his strategic aims had persistently been rejected by his co-factionalists.[133] It is true, too, that several portions of his writing merely summarised general opinion amongst Bolsheviks and were bereft of originality. Yet he also at times showed both practical brilliance and intellectual profundity. His thought and his methods had left a mark. In 1910 he was still only forty. He was full of zeal and resolve. Time alone would show whether he could re-take his faction, transform it into a powerful party, and prepare that party to win the favour of Russia's working class and peasantry.

Notes

The method of transliteration used in the chapters of this volume is modified in the endnotes. Russian-language book-titles are rendered according to the conventions of the SEER, and authors' names in such instances are rendered likewise. The names of Russian authors of books appearing in a language other than Russian are transliterated as by the authors.

Citations of other endnotes relate to the same chapter unless otherwise indicated.

Not all the documentary material on Lenin is very reliable. The *Biograficheskaya khronika*, so useful in many respects, is often a false guide; I have referred to such works only in instances where the editors seemed to have no political axe to grind.

The review of literature and material in the Prologue and its endnotes is illustrative; it is by no means an exhaustive bibliographical guide.

A number of abbreviations are used in the endnotes for important documentary collections which are cited throughout the volume. They are as follows:

AD   F. Engels, *Anti-Dühring: Herr Eugen Dühring's Revolution in Science*, tr. E. Burns (Moscow, 1947).

BK   *Vladimir Il'ich Lenin. Biograficheskaya khronika*, ed. G. N. Golikov *et al.* (1970–82) vols 1–12.

KA   *Krasnyi arkhiv* (Moscow–Leningrad, 1922–41).

Kapital   K. Marx, *Capital* (London, 1964) vols 1–3.

KMSW   *Karl Marx: Selected Writings*, ed. D. McLellan (Oxford, 1977).

KPSS   *KPSS v rezolyutsiyakh i resheniyakh s''ezdov, konferentsii i plenumov TsK*, vol. 1, *1898–1917*, ed. P. N. Fedoseev and K. U. Chernenko (Moscow, 1970).

LS   *Leninskii sbornik* (Moscow–Leningrad: starting 1924) vol. 1 *et seq.*

MERR   *K. Marks, F. Engel's i Revolyutsionnaya Rossiya*, ed. A. K. Vorob'eva (Moscow, 1967).

NEL   *Narodnicheskaya ekonomicheskaya literatura: izbrannye proizvedeniya*, ed. N. K. Karataev (Moscow, 1958).

OD   *Obshchestvennoe dvizhenie v Rossii v nachale XX-go veka*, ed. L. Martov, P. Maslov and A. Potresov (St. Petersburg, 1909–14) vols 1–4.

PPA   *Perepiska G. V. Plekhanova i P. B. Aksel'roda* (Berlin, 1925) vols 1–2.

PR   *Proletarskaya revolyutsiya* (Moscow, 1921–40).

PSS   V. I. Lenin, *Polnoe sobranie sochinenii*, ed. I. Ya. Gladkov *et al.*
           (Moscow, 1958–65) vols 1–55.
PU   *Perepiska sem'i Ul'yanovykh, 1883–1917*, ed. Yu. Ya. Makhina
           et al. (Moscow, 1969).
SII   *Vtoroi s''ezd RSDRP. Protokoly. Iyul'–avgust 1903 goda* (Mos-
           cow, 1959).
SIII   *Tretii s''ezd RSDRP. Protokoly. Aprel'–mai 1905 goda* (Moscow,
           1959).
SIV   *Chetvertyi (Ob''edinitel'nyi) s''ezd RSDRP. Protokoly. Aprel'*
           (aprel'–mai) 1906 goda (Moscow, 1959).
S(L)   V. I. Lenin, *Sochineniya*, 2nd revised and expanded edition: ed. L.
           B. Kamenev *et al.* (Moscow, 1925–32) vols 1–30.
S(P)   G. V. Plekhanov, *Sochineniya*, ed. D. B. Ryazanov (Moscow–Pet-
           rograd, 1925–8) vols 1–24.
SV   *Pyatyi (Londonskii) s''ezd RSDRP. Protokoly. Aprel'–mai 1907*
           goda (Moscow, 1963).
SWOV   K. Marx and F. Engels, *Selected Works in One Volume* (London,
           1968).
VL   N. K. Krupskaya, *Vospominaniya o Lenine*, 2nd edn (Moscow,
           1968).
VVIL   *Vospominaniya o V. I. Lenine* (Moscow, 1968–9) vols 1–5.

PROLOGUE: THE ENIGMA OF LENIN

1. G. E. Zinov'ev, *Vladimir Il'ich Ul'yanov: ocherki zhizni i deyatel'nosti*
   (Petrograd, 1918).
2. *Sobranie sochinenii* (Moscow, 1920–6) vols 1–20.
3. See *Spravochnik partiinogo rabotnika* (Moscow, 1957) p. 364.
4. *Sochineniya* (Moscow, 1941–50) vols 1–35. This was the fourth edition
   of the collected works.
5. See *LS*, vols 34 (Moscow, 1943) and 35 (1945).
6. *PSS* (Moscow, 1958–65) vols 1–55.
7. See, for example, *LS*, vol. 39 (Moscow, 1980).
8. See, for example, G. Haupt (ed.), *Correspondance entre Lénine et
   Camille Huysmans, 1905–1914* (Paris, 1963); and L. Haas (ed.), *Lenin:
   Unbekannte Briefe, 1912–1914* (Zurich/Cologne, 1967).
9. *BK* (Moscow, 1970–82) vols 1–12.
10. See R. McNeal, *Bride of the Revolution: Krupskaya and Lenin* (London,
    1972) pp. 266–7.
11. The most flagrant example of the many such cases was the suppression of
    the documents known as Lenin's testament. They will be discussed in
    volume three.
12. An early exposé of Stalin's historiographical interventions was made by
    Trotski in his *Stalinskaya shkola fal'sifikatsii* (Berlin, 1932).
13. Proof of this is constituted by the admission that the materials of Lenin's
    remarks on Stalin have been excised from the records of *Devyataya
    konferentsiya RKP(b): stenograficheskii otchet* (Moscow, 1972): see

pp. 79 and 82. As we shall see in this volume too, moreover, materials included in previous collections of Leniniana have been quietly and unreasonably dropped from *PSS*.

14. This sort of study was still being produced in the early thirties: see especially M. Vichniac, *Lénine* (Paris, 1932).

15. The prime product of such activity was Stalin's *Istoriya Vsesoyuznoi Kommunisticheskoi Partii bol'shevikov: Kratkii kurs* (Moscow, 1938).

16. This is not to say that every single Western monograph offered so crude an interpretation. See the outstanding work by B. Souvarine, *Stalin: a Critical Survey of Bolshevism* (London, 1939).

17. P. N. Pospelov *et al.*, *Vladimir Il'ich Lenin: biografiya* (Moscow, 1963).

18. The few who did in fact look seriously at Lenin before the mid-1950s, however, included some who produced work of lasting value. The nearest to a comprehensive study of Lenin's pre-revolutionary career, contained within a larger opus dealing also with Stalin and Trotski, was B. D. Wolfe's *Three Who Made a Revolution* (London, 1948). Other important early studies were E. H. Carr, *The Bolshevik Revolution*, vol. 1 (London, 1950); I. Deutscher, *Trotsky: the Prophet Armed* (London, 1954); L. H. Haimson, *The Russian Marxists and the Origins of Bolshevism* (Harvard, 1955); and L. B. Schapiro, *The Origin of the Communist Autocracy* (London, 1955).

19. See note 17.

20. See S. M. Dubrovskii, *Stolypinskaya zemel'naya reforma: iz istorii sel'skogo khozyaistva i krest'yanstva v nachale XX veka* (Moscow, 1963); E. B. Genkina, *Lenin–predsedatel' Sovnarkoma i STO* (Moscow, 1960); and M. P. Iroshnikov, *Presedatel' Soveta Narodnykh Komissarov, V. I. Ul'yanov-Lenin: ocherki gosudarstvennoi deyatel'nosti v 1917–1918 gg.* (Leningrad, 1974). See also R. I. Nafigov, *Tainy revolyutsionnogo podpol'ya: arkhivnye poiski i nakhodki* (Kazan, 1981).

21. See S. T. Possony, *Lenin: the Compulsive Revolutionary* (Chicago, 1964).

22. See R. Pipes, 'The Origins of Bolshevism: the Intellectual Evolution of Young Lenin' in his *Revolutionary Russia* (Cambridge, 1968) pp. 26–62; R. H. W. Theen, *Lenin: Genesis and Development of a Revolutionary* (London, 1974). Both take a strongly, though not uniformly, Lenin-as-populist approach. On the other hand, V. Strada's edition of *What Is To Be Done?*, while supporting a 'Russianist' interpretation, puts the case for more extensive boundaries for Russian Marxism: see the introduction to *Che Fare?* (Turin, 1971).

23. See N. Harding, *Lenin's Political Thought*, vols 1–2 (London, 1977–81).

24. See R. C. Elwood, *Russian Social-Democracy in the Underground: a Study of the RSDRP in the Ukraine, 1907–1914* (Assen, 1974).

25. See T. H. Rigby, *Lenin's Government: Sovnarkom, 1917–1922* (Cambridge, 1979); and R. Service, *The Bolshevik Party in Revolution: a Study in Organisational Change* (London, 1979).

26. See, for example, Harding, op. cit.

27. See, for example, Possony, op. cit.

CHAPTER 1: CROSS-CURRENTS

1. See M. Shaginyan, 'Predki Lenina', *Novyi Mir*, 1937, no. 11, pp. 269–80; and A. I. Ivanskii (ed.), *Il'ya Nikolaevich Ul'yanov po vospominaniyam sovremennikov i dokumentam* (Moscow, 1963) pp. 8–18.
2. Idem., pp. 24–5.
3. Idem, pp. 44, 46 and 54.
4. Idem, pp. 54–6. Sensible accounts of Lenin's maternal ancestry are given in L. Fischer, *The Life of Lenin* (London, 1966) pp. 2–4; and Theen, op. cit., pp. 120–1.
5. This point is made in Fischer, op. cit., p. 4.
6. An attempt has been made to demonstrate that the Ulyanov children suffered from an acute sense of social inferiority: see S. Page, 'Lenin, Turgenev and the Russian Landed Gentry', *Canadian Slavonic Papers*, 1976, no. 4, pp. 442–56. No direct and conclusive evidence, however, has yet been adduced in favour of this hypothesis.
7. It deserves mention that, although family embarrassment about its own ancestry is not detectable, the plight of the non-Russian nationalities in the empire was certainly a subject of interest to Ilya Ulyanov: see I. Kreindler, 'A Neglected Source of Lenin's Nationality Policy', *Slavic Review*, 1977, no. 1, pp. 86–100.
8. *Il'ya Nikolaevich Ul'yanov*, p. 121.
9. See Dmitri Ulyanov's memoir in *VVIL*, vol. 1, pp. 87–8.
10. See M. Semenov's memoir in A. I. Ivanskii (ed.), *Molodoi Lenin: povest' v dokumentakh i memuarakh* (Moscow, 1964) p. 575.
11. See *Il'ya Nikolaevich Ul'yanov*, p. 121; and *Molodoi Lenin*, p. 114.
12. N. Valentinov, *The Early Years of Lenin* (Ann Arbor, 1969) p. 91.
13. See P. A. Zaionchkovskii, *Krizis samoderzhaviya na rubezhe 1870–1880 gg.* (Moscow, 1964) pp. 116–22.
14. See the memoir by P. A. Garvi, *Zapiski sotsial-demokrata (1906–1921)* (Newtonville, 1982) p. 23.
15. *Il'ya Nikolaevich Ul'yanov*, p. 177.
16. See P. A. Zaionchkovskii, *Provedenie v zhizn' krest'yanskoi reformy 1861 g.* (Moscow, 1958) *passim*; J. Blum, *Lord and Peasant in Russia from the Ninth to the Nineteenth Century* (Princeton, 1961) chs 25–6; P. A. Zaionchkovskii, *Otmena krepostnogo prava v Rossii* (Moscow, 1961) ch. 1; and D. Field, *The End of Serfdom: Nobility and Bureaucracy, 1855–1861* (New York, 1976) *passim*.
17. See G. T. Robinson, *Rural Russia Under the Old Regime* (London, 1932) pp. 94–116. And, for Lenin's account, see below, pp. 67–70.
18. See P. I. Lyashchenko, *Istoriya narodnogo khozyaistva SSSR*, vol. 2, (Moscow, 1956) pp. 90–171; P. G. Ryndzyunskii, *Krest'yanskaya promyshlennost' v Rossii* (Moscow, 1966) *passim*; and O. Crisp, *Studies in the Russian Economy before 1914* (London, 1976) chs 4–7.
19. For Lenin's first proposals to redress the unfairness of the Edict, see below, pp. 61–2.
20. See below, p. 67 for Lenin's interpretation of these statistics.
21. See R. E. Johnson, *Peasant and Proletarian: the Working Class of*

Moscow in the Late Nineteenth Century (Leicester, 1979) pp. 80–97; W. Sablinsky, *The Road to Bloody Sunday* (Princeton, 1976) pp. 5–33; R. E. Zelnik, *Labor and Society in Tsarist Russia* (Stanford, 1971) esp. p. 69 *et seq.*

22. On narodnik activity and ideas in the 1870s see F. Venturi, *The Roots of Revolution* (London, 1960) chs 18 and 19; on the movement's social philosophy in the same period see A. Walicki, *The Controversy Over Capitalism: Studies in the Social Philosophy of Russian Populism* (Oxford, 1969), and V. A. Tvardovskaya, *Sotsialisticheskaya mysl' Rossii: na rubezhe 1870–1880 gg.* (Moscow, 1969).
23. See Venturi, op. cit., chs 20–2.
24. See his oral recollections as recorded by N. Valentinov: *Vstrechi s Leninym* (New York, 1953) pp. 92–4.
25. *Molodoi Lenin*, pp. 26 and 31.
26. The most extreme version of this time-travelling psychoanalysis is E. V. Wolfenstein, *The Revolutionary Personality: Lenin, Trotsky, Gandhi* (Princeton, 1967).
27. See Shaginyan, op. cit., p. 264.
28. See in general *Molodoi Lenin*, pp. 77–89. Vladimir's school reports are reproduced in *BK*, vol. 1, pp. 7–26.
29. Valentinov, *The Early Years*, p. 26.
30. On chess, see D. Ulyanov's memoir in *VVIL*, vol. 1, pp. 98–103.
31. *Molodoi Lenin*, pp. 110, 150 and 152–3.
32. A. I. Ul'yanova-Elizarova, *Vospominaniya ob Aleksandre Il'iche Ul'yanove* (Moscow, 1931) pp. 95–6; *Il'ya Nikolaevich Ul'yanov*, pp. 74–5; and *Molodoi Lenin*, pp. 227–33 and 243–6.
33. Idem, p. 325–6.
34. *Il'ya Nikolaevich Ul'yanov*, pp. 251–5.
35. See the account by Aleksandr's friend O. M. Govorukhin in *PR*, 1925, no. 7, pp. 114–35.
36. A transcript of the trial is available in *Pervoe marta 1887 goda: delo P. Shevyreva, A. Ul'yanova i drugie* (Moscow–Leningrad, 1927).
37. See A. Elizarova-Ul'yanova in *Molodoi Lenin*, p. 250.
38. See note 36.
39. *BK*, vol. 1, pp. 25–6.
40. *Molodoi Lenin*, pp. 301 and 304–5.
41. See, for example, N. K. Krupskaya, *VL*, p. 12.
42. See Valentinov, *Vstrechi s Leninym*, pp. 92–4.
43. *BK*, vol. 1, p. 27.
44. See M. Pushkin, 'Raznochintsy in the University: Government Policy and Social Change in Nineteenth Century Russia', *International Review of Social History*, 1981, part 1, pp. 45–6.
45. See N. A. Troitskii, 'Russkaya advokatura na politicheskikh protsessakh narodnikov (1871–1890 gg.)', *Iz istorii obshchestvennogo dvizheniya i obshchestvennoi mysli v Rossii* (2nd issue: 1968) pp. 89–144.
46. This point is illustrated throughout Venturi, op. cit. See also the discursive considerations in A. Walicki, *History of Russian Thought from the Enlightenment to Marxism* (Oxford, 1980) pp. 152–280.
47. See E. H. Carr, *Michael Bakunin* (London, 1937).

48. See Walicki, *History of Russian Thought*, pp. 92–114 and 162–82.
49. Easily the most useful compendium of narodnik economic writing is *NEL*; see also the discussion in Walicki, *Controversy Over Capitalism*, *passim*.
50. See idem, pp. 132–65; and J. H. Billington, *N. K. Mikhailovski and Russian Populism* (Oxford, 1958) pp. 139–60.
51. See *NEL*, pp. 417–81 and 482–572 for the relevant extracts from, respectively, Vorontsov's *Sud'by kapitalizma v Rossii* (St. Petersburg, 1882) and Danielson's *Ocherki nashego poreformennogo obshchestvennogo khozyaistva* (St. Petersburg, 1893); and *MERR*, pp. 660–7 for Danielson's epistolary discussions on the Russian economy with Frederick Engels.
52. See Billington, op. cit., pp. 95–8 and 162–5.
53. See idem, p. 166.
54. *PSS*, vol. 6, pp. 105–6 and 134–6.
55. Idem, vol. 1, p. 530.
56. Ibid.
57. Idem, vol. 18, pp. 381–4. This does not mean, however, that memoirists like N. Valentinov were correct in implying that Ulyanov's epistemology was hardly different from Chernyshevski's. Chernyshevski, for example, was not enamoured of the mind-matter dichotomy: see A. Walicki's helpful account in *History of Russian Thought*, pp. 194–8. Valentinov's attempt to represent Ulyanov as being a Chernyshevskyite in philosophy is seriously overdone; and it is regrettable that so many Western accounts accept it uncritically.
58. On Tkachev, see D. Hardy *Petr Tkachev: the Critic As Jacobin* (Seattle, 1972).
59. Ibid. See also below, pp. 62–3 and 89.
60. See note 57. On Chernyshevski, see E. Lampert *Sons Against Fathers* (Oxford, 1965) pp. 137–67.
61. *PSS*, vol. 2, pp. 467–9; and vol. 6, pp. 105–6 and 134–6.
62. The most vivid account of the practical pressure on the narodniki to take the workers as seriously as the peasantry is given by F. Venturi, op. cit., *passim*. It is necessary to emphasise in this context, however, that Lenin never attempted to categorise the proletariat and the peasantry together as 'the toiling people'; unlike the narodniki, he kept them conceptually separate. And, in his strategy, he accorded a permanent leading position to the working class. Not even the radically modified populism of V. M. Chernov took such an approach.
63. See below, pp. 98–9. See also Tvardovskaya, op. cit., pp. 172–82; and, for further background, V. A. Malinin, *Filosofiya revolyutsionnogo narodnichestva* (Moscow, 1972).
64. *PSS*, vol. 6, p. 173. An instance of Tkachev's summons to the hanging of 'policemen, prosecutors, ministers, merchants, priests' is found in 'Revolyutsionnaya propaganda', *Nabat*, 1878 (no month mentioned), p. L: as quoted by G. V. Plekhanov in *S(P)*, vol. 2, p. 147. See also Walicki, *History of Russian Thought*, pp. 254–67. D. Hardy's *Petr Tkachev* puts the case that Lenin was uninfluenced by Tkachev. In general, this trilogy's intention in part is to show that populism was

indeed not the only influence upon Lenin. But an influence it nevertheless was. Furthermore, Hardy's rejection of this view is based upon a
confusion of Tkachev and *malenkii Tkachev* in *PSS*, vol. 1, p. 173. The
context makes it plain that the *malenkii Tkachev* in Lenin's mind was not
Tkachev but L. Nadezhdin. For further evidence on how seriously Lenin
took Tkachev see V. D. Bonch-Bruevich, *Izbrannye sochineniya v trekh
tomakh* (Moscow, 1961) vol. 2, pp. 314–6.
65. See below, p. 99.

CHAPTER 2: ROADS TO FREEDOM

1. On student problems in the 1880s see G. I. Shchetinina, *Universitety i
   ustav 1884 goda* (Moscow, 1976) *passim*.
2. *Lenin i Simbirsk: dokumenty, materialy, vospominaniya* (Ulyanovsk,
   1968) p. 68.
3. I owe this point to John Crowfoot. But see also I. Kreindler, op. cit., for
   evidence of other possible early influences in this matter.
4. See M. K. Korbut, 'Kazanskoe revolyutsionnoe podpol'e kontsa 80-kh
   godov i Lenin', *Katorga i ssylka*, 1931, no. 8–9 (81–2), p. 7; and G. E.
   Khait, 'V kazanskom kruzhke', *Novyi Mir*, 1958, no. 4, pp. 189–90.
5. *BK*, vol. 1, p. 30; and see R. I. Nafigov, 'Kazanskaya skhodka 4
   dekabrya 1887 goda', *Voprosy istorii*, 1980, no. 1, pp. 91–103.
6. See idem, p. 95.
7. Police report reproduced in *KA*, 1934, no. 62, pp. 65 and 69–70; and
   the police report cited by M. K. Korbut, op. cit., p. 16. A brief account of
   Ulyanov's affiliation to Bogoraz's group was provided for the first time
   by R. Pipes in his 'The Origins Of Bolshevism', loc. cit., pp. 28–30.
   Official Soviet accounts continue to draw a veil over the episode. On the
   other hand, Pipes's narrative does not make plain that Bogoraz's group
   was not completely hostile to Marxism in political attitude.
8. This was at least the attitude of V. Zelenenko, in Petersburg, who was in
   political contact with Bogoraz: see G. E. Khait, 'V kazanskom kruzhke',
   pp. 190–1. And the contact with Bogoraz's team continued after Kazan:
   see the police report in *KA*, 1934, vol. 62, p. 65.
9. M. K. Korbut, 'Kazanskoe revolyutsionnoe podpol'e', pp. 16–17.
10. See G. E. Khait's archival investigation in op. cit., pp. 191–2.
11. Idem, p. 191.
12. Police report in *KA*, 1934, vol. 62, pp. 55–6.
13. See E. Foss's memoir in *Molodoi Lenin*, p. 406.
14. *PSS*, vol. 1, p. 551.
15. *BK*, vol. 1, pp. 34–5.
16. *VVIL*, vol. 1, pp. 28–9 and 97–8; and Valentinov, *Vstrechi*, p. 103.
17. *BK*, vol. 1, p. 39.
18. The official Soviet contention is that Ulyanov 'entered one of the
    Marxist circles organised by N. E. Fedoseev': see *BK*, vol. 1, p. 40. R.
    Pipes's 'Origins Of Bolshevism', however, points to other evidence: see
    his op. cit., p. 33; his sources are consultable in *Novyi mir*, 1957, no. 4,
    p. 147 and *Moskva*, 1958, no. 4, p. 55. Pipes's demolition of the

Fedoseevian connection seems, in the light of the data presently available, effective. Yet he goes too far in the opposite direction. His own sources do not demonstrate that Ulyanov was an active member of Chetvergova's circle. Occasional attendance at lectures by M. Mandelshtam is not proof that Vladimir was a narodnik terrorist in 1888.

19. See Pipes, idem, p. 33.
20. I base this surmise upon the evidence of Sabunaev's ideas as given in *Molodoi Lenin*, pp. 537–41 (M. Semenov's memoir).
21. See above, p. 31.
22. *BK*, vol. 1, p. 41.
23. *VVIL*, vol. 1, p. 30; N. Valentinov, 'Vstrecha Lenina s marksizmom', *Novyi zhurnal*, 1958, pp. 189–208.
24. *VVIL*, vol. 1, p. 30.
25. *Molodoi Lenin*, pp. 522 and 623–5.
26. The principal source for Ulyanov's involvement with Sklyarenko is M. I. Semenov, 'Pamyati druga' in *Staryi tovarishch Aleksei Pavlovich Sklyarenko (1870–1916 gg.)* (Moscow, 1922) pp. 7–19. See also A. A. Belyakov, *Yunost' vozhdya* (Moscow, 1960).
27. See R. Pipes's review of the evidence in 'The Origins of Bolshevism', p. 37. While agreeing with Pipes's contention that 1888–9 marked the start of Ulyanov's acquaintance with Marx, I have been unable to discover corroboration for his further remark that Ulyanov 'became seriously interested' in Marx 'only in 1892': see ibid.
28. This proposition is based upon the frequency with which particular works are referred to, as annotated in *PSS*, vol. 1, pp. 603–16; and vol. 2, pp. 606–28.
29. For an illustration of how strongly he wanted to maintain a Marxian type of analysis, even when it was not espoused in the party as a whole, see below, pp. 159–64.
30. *Kapital*, vol. 1, pp. 397, 442–50, 454–60 and 543–51. See also *The Communist Manifesto in SWOV*, pp. 41–4. For Lenin, see *PSS*, vol. 1, pp. 101–3, 403 and 434; and vol. 2, pp. 362–5.
31. See the discussion on 'Taylorism' in vol. 2 of this trilogy.
32. See below, pp. 66–7.
33. *Kapital*, vol. 1, *passim*, but especially the summary on pp. 714–15.
34. Idem, pp. 114–15, 199–200 and 714–15. See also *Communist Manifesto*, loc. cit., pp. 40–1.
35. Marx, *Critique of the Gotha Programme* in *SWOV*, p. 327; and *Class Struggles in France* in *KMSW*, pp. 291 and 296.
36. As it happens, several narodniki of the 1880s were not in fact opposed to parliamentarism as a short-term strategy: see *NEL*, pp. 627–8 (a guarded narodnik statement of 1884). Marx's position, however, was clearer and more consistent. *Critique of the Gotha Programme*, for example, accepts parliamentarism as the premise for its discussion of the German social-democratic programme. For Lenin, see below, pp. 160–1. In any case, the general tendency was for populists to seek social rather than political solutions to the problems of the transition to socialism; see G. V. Plekhanov's remarks on this in his *S(P)*, vol. 2, pp. 108–10 and 156–64.

37. *The Communist Manifesto*, loc. cit., p. 63. For Lenin see below, pp. 98–9.
38. *Critique of the Gotha Programme*, loc. cit., pp. 320–1.
39. *Communist Manifesto*, loc. cit., pp. 40–1; *Preface to 'A Contribution to "The Critique of Political Economy"'* in *SWOV*, p. 182. For Ulyanov's views on the passage from feudalism to capitalism, see below, pp. 151–3.
40. See below, pp. 54–5.
41. *Communist Manifesto*, loc. cit., pp. 59–61 and *PSS*, vol. 1, pp. 144–5.
42. Idem, vol. 18, p. 146. See also below, pp. 181–2.
43. See below, p. 80.
44. See below, pp. 78–9.
45. See G. Lichtheim, *Marxism: an Historical and Critical Study* (2nd rev. edn: London, 1964) pp. 234–40 and 245–6; and D. McLellan, *Marxism After Marx* (London, 1979) pp. 9–14. The relation of *Anti-Dühring* to Marx's thought will always be problematical. Whatever divergences are pinpointed, it would probably be wrong to exaggerate them in view of the known fact that Engels read out his manuscript to Marx and, apparently, secured his approval of it. See T. Carver, *Engels* (London, 1981) pp. 63–71 and 75–7.
46. See E. Hobsbawm, 'La fortuna delle edizioni di Marx ed Engels', *Storia del Marxismo*, vol. 1, *Il Marxismo ai tempi di Marx* (Turin, 1978) pp. 358–74.
47. See *Preface to 'A Contribution to "The Critique of Political Economy"'*, loc. cit., p. 182; and M. Sawer, *Marxism and the Question of the Asiatic Mode of Production* (The Hague, 1977) ch. 2.
48. See Marx's letter of 1880 to H. Hyndman, *KMSW*, p. 594; and his speech of 1872 in Amsterdam, idem, pp. 594–5.
49. See, indeed, *AD*, p. 35. Engels also asserts (idem, pp. 109–12) that the natural sciences can nevertheless produce 'eternal truth'. But he attaches qualifications. Firstly, he states that such truths are subject to future discoveries of narrower limits to their validity; and, secondly, he declares that 'eternal truths' are impossible in the social sciences: ibid. See also below, p. 180.
50. *KMSW*, p. 538 (which is an extract from a speech of 1869); and *PSS*, vol. 6, pp. 39–40. See also below, pp. 88–9 and 92–3.
51. See below, p. 135.
52. *MERR*, pp. 78–9.
53. Idem, p. 444.
54. See L. Krader (ed.), *Marx's Ethnological Notebooks* (New York, 1972) for Marx's later research on rural communities.
55. See *MERR*, p. 514 for evidence of Engels's continuing belief in this after Marx's death.
56. See the account by S. H. Baron in *Plekhanov: the Father of Russian Marxism* (London, 1963) pp. 68 and 123.
57. See the account by J. D. White, 'From Karl Marx to Bogdanov', *Co-existence*, vol. 15, pp. 195–6.
58. See the preface to the second Russian edition of *The Communist Manifesto* in *MERR*, p. 89; see also Engels's similar formulation in a letter to Danielson in 1893 in idem, pp. 661–2.
59. See V. Strada's account in *Che Fare?*, pp. xli–xlv.

60. *NEL*, p. 635.
61. Ibid. The programme is given in its entirety in idem, pp. 631–6.
62. Idem, pp. 632 and 635. It is perhaps a sign of the analytical problems posed by the evidence of the contemporary development of capitalism in Russia that the narodnik Aleksandr Ulyanov did not specifically mention capitalism; and that it is only by implication that he aligns himself with traditional narodnik thought on this point. See his brief reference to 'the bourgeoisie' in idem, p. 633.
63. N. E. Fedoseev, *Stat'i i pis'ma* (Moscow, 1958) pp. 97–8. It must be pointed out that Fedoseev still believed that capitalism was 'inevitable' (see idem, p. 99); and that there is no suggestion from him that either small-scale or private agriculture would survive on into the socialist epoch proper.
64. See the account by Y. O. Martov in *Zapiski sotsial-demokrata*, ed. I. Getzler (Cambridge, USA: 1975) pp. 328–30. The original edition appeared in 1922.
65. See S. A. Oppenheim, 'The Making of a Right Communist: A. I. Rykov to 1917', *Slavic Review*, 1977, no. 3, pp. 422–3.
66. See below, pp. 75–6.
67. See Engels's unequivocal remarks in his pamphlet *Socialism in Germany*, translated in *MERR*, p. 110; see also his correspondence with Plekhanov in 1894 in idem, p. 722.
68. *Sotsializm i politicheskaya bor'ba* in *S(P)*, vol. 2, pp. 76–7.
69. *Sovremennye zadachi russkikh rabochikh* in idem, pp. 366 and 370–1.
70. *Nashi raznoglasiya* in *S(P)*, vol. 2, pp. 270–1. See also his *Vserossiiskoe razorenie* in vol. 3, pp. 349–50 and 354.
71. See notes 63 and 64.
72. *Nashi raznoglasiya*, loc. cit., pp. 199–269.
73. Idem, pp. 357–62.
74. See Zasulich's reiteration, with Ulyanov's assent, in 1902: *LS*, vol. 2, p. 132.
75. See the Group's second draft programme, written in 1887 and reprinted in *S(P)*, vol. 2, pp. 400–5. On Akselrod's contribution see N. Harding's helpful analysis, *Lenin's Political Thought*, vol. 1, pp. 45–7.
76. See below, pp. 143–4. It is doubtful whether Plekhanov's philosophical contributions were an initial spur to Ulyanov to align himself with Plekhanov since Plekhanov's work on epistemology as such began only in the late 1890s.
77. *Nashi raznoglasiya*, loc. cit., pp. 108–9. He did not, however, absolutely rule out the desirability of assassinations: see the draft programme, loc. cit., pp. 402–3.
78. Idem, p. 403.
79. See note 77.
80. See R. Geary, 'Karl Kautsky and the Development of Marxism' (unpublished Ph.D.: Cambridge, 1970) pp. 22–3 for an account of Kautsky's early attempt to moderate Marxist political recommendations.
81. *S(P)*, vol. 2, pp. 403–5.
82. Idem, p. 77.

83. See note 80.
84. As we shall see, nevertheless, there quickly developed disagreements on theoretical matters between Plekhanov and Ulyanov even in the mid-1890s; see below pp. 54–5.
85. See S. H. Baron, *Plekhanov*, pp. 125–38.
86. See L. Blit, *The Origins of Polish Socialism: the History of the First Polish Socialist Party, 1878–1886* (Cambridge, 1971), especially p. 24 ff.; and E. Mendelsohn, *Class Struggle in the Pale: the Formative Years of the Jewish Workers' Movement in Tsarist Russia* (Cambridge, 1970) chs 1–4.
87. *Samarskii vestnik* was a notable serious journal, founded in 1883; a monograph on provincial literary politics would considerably clarify the context of the intellectual milieu from which Ulyanov sprang.
88. *Molodoi Lenin*, pp. 537–41: memoir by M. I. Semenov.
89. Idem, pp. 576–7.
90. *PSS*, vol. 43, p. 417.
91. *VVIL*, vol. 2, pp. 31–2.
92. Ibid.
93. The remark is quoted by M. I. Ulyanova from N. K. Krupskaya's recollections: see *O V. I. Lenine i sem'e Ul'yanovykh: vospominaniya, pis'ma, ocherki* (Moscow, 1978) pp. 34–5.
94. *BK*, vol. 1, p. 49.
95. Idem, pp. 51–8; *PSS*, vol. 55, p. 1.
96. *BK*, vol. 1, p. 61.
97. Idem, p. 63; *VVIL*, vol. 1, p 35.
98. Information on the group's reading interests is available in *Molodoi Lenin*, pp. 488, 573, 580, 650, 663 and 665.
99. Idem, pp. 485, 497, 604 and 613; see also *BK*, vol. 1, p. 65.
100. Idem, pp. 63–74.
101. *Molodoi Lenin*, p. 490.
102. Idem, pp. 669–77, 680 and 684. Semenov, a member of the Sklyarenko group, signally failed to corroborate Belyakov's story about Mikhailovski, and it seems unlikely that Semenov would not have known about such a confrontation, and written about it too, if it had occurred: see idem, p. 672.

CHAPTER 3: ARRIVALS

1. *BK*, vol. 1, p. 78.
2. *PSS*, vol. 45, p. 324. For details of Ulyanov's trip see *BK*, vol. 1, p. 77.
3. G. M. Krzhizhanovski has left us his eyewitness account in *O Vladimire Il'iche* (Moscow, 1924) pp. 13–14. Attention was first drawn to the importance of this account by R. Pipes in *Social-Democracy and the St. Petersburg Labour Movement, 1885–1897* (Harvard, 1963) p. 48. Pipes implies that Ulyanov's 'redness' proves that he was an unreconstructed narodnik terrorist. This is to ignore the variety of attitudes to the variegated populist heritage among early Russian Marxists: see above, pp. 39–40.

206 *Notes to pp. 49–53*

4. *BK*, vol. 1, p. 81. See also R. Pipes's investigation in *Social-Democracy*, pp. 48 and 65–6.
5. *BK*, vol. 1, p. 83.
6. M. A. Sil'vin, 'K biografii V. I. Lenina (iz vospominanii)', *PR*, 1924, no. 7, pp. 69–70.
7. *PSS*, vol. 1, pp. 33 and 43–7.
8. *Po povodu tak nazyvaemogo voprosa o rynkakh* in *idem*, pp. 71–122.
9. Some littérateurs such as Plekhanov did little organisational work in their careers. It would be interesting to know how Ulyanov conceived of his future life at this juncture in events; but there is no evidence that he intended to abstain permanently from organisational leadership.
10. See Pipes, *Social-Democracy*, pp. 22–42.
11. See idem, pp. 43 and 51–2.
12. *BK*, vol. 1, p. 91.
13. See A. K. Wildman, *The Making of a Workers' Revolution: Russian Social-Democracy, 1891–1903* (Chicago, 1967) pp. 40–53.
14. See Pipes, *Social-Democracy*, pp. 66–7.
15. *PSS*, vol. 1, pp. 142–8 and 273–5.
16. *BK*, vol. 1, pp. 88–90.
17. The fullest account of these encounters is found in R. Pipes, *Struve*, vol. 1, *Liberal on the Left, 1870–1905* (Harvard, 1970): see especially pp. 137 and 142–3.
18. See Martov's *Iz neopublikovannykh vospominanii* in *LS*, vol. 4, pp. 56–7. See also I. Getzler's discussion in *Martov: a Political Biography of a Russian Social-Democrat* (Cambridge, 1967) pp. 45–6.
19. A lucid exposition of the economics of Struve, Tugan and Bulgakov is made by R. Kindersley in *The First Russian Revisionists* (Oxford, 1962) pp. 146–79. Of the three, Tugan was the most sophisticated economist: see the detailed study by L. Kowal, 'L'analisi dello sviluppo capitalistico in M. I. Tugan-Baranovskij', *Storia del marxismo contemporaneo*, vol. 3, (Milan, 1977) pp. 97–122.
20. See below, pp. 66–9.
21. *Kriticheskie zametki k voprosu ob ekonomicheskom razvitii Rossii* (St. Petersburg, 1894) p. 130. R. Pipes suggests in his biography of Struve (vol. 1, p. 107) that Struve was already in the early 1890s fundamentally hostile to many of Marx and Engels's central philosophical ideas. This appears to be an exaggeration. Close analysis of *Kriticheskie zametki* reveals, for example, Struve's enthusiastic approval of the *Anti-Dühring* (idem, p. 39); his contention that 'existence' determines 'consciousness' (p. 40); his view that Marx and Engels had provided 'a truly *philosophical*' interpretation of historical phenomena (p. 50). The rest of Pipes's points (op. cit., ch. 5) about the contrasts between Marx and Struve are most instructive. I must in this connection express my gratitude to Alexander Wilson for the finding that not even in the 1898 Manifesto written by Struve for the First Party Congress is there a direct call for the 'overthrow' of the autocracy.
22. Idem, pp. 124 and 130.
23. See Kindersley, op. cit., pp. 160–1 and Kowal, op. cit., loc. cit., pp. 107–11.

24. See below, pp. 94 and 138.
25. See *PSS*, vol. 1, p. 444.
26. Idem, pp. 325–31 and 460–1. Since Ulyanov had a political alliance with Struve, his attacks upon Struvian policies were not as strong as they subsequently became. In addition, Struve's position in the mid-1890s was not as far removed from Ulyanov's as it later became. All the same, Ulyanov's *The Economic Contents* suggests that a wide gap already existed between their long-term political strategies. The gap was still wider in private. Ulyanov continued to hold more optimistic views on class differentiation in the countryside and on the peasantry's revolutionary potential: see his December 1893 letter to P. P. Maslov, *PSS*, vol. 46, pp. 1–2.
27. Idem, vol. 1, p. 401.
28. Idem, pp. 330–1.
29. Idem, vol. 46, pp. 1–2.
30. N. Valentinov, 'Iz proshlogo: P. B. Struve o Lenine', *Sotsialisticheskii vestnik*, 1954, no. 8–9, p. 171.
31. *S(P)*, vol. 2, p. 231.
32. See Akselrod's account in *PPA*, vol. 1, pp. 270–6. See also E. Gamzanov, 'Istoricheskie vzglyady G. V. Plekhanova', *Istorik-marksist*, 1928, no. 7, p. 110.
33. See Gamzanov, ibid.; and Plekhanov's own allusions to the 1895 discussion in *LS*, vol. 2, pp. 92 and 95.
34. Martov, *Zapiski*, p. 268.
35. Idem, pp. 268–9.
36. I. V. Babushkin, *Vospominaniya Ivana Vasil'evicha Babushkina* (Moscow, 1955) p. 44.
37. N. K. Krupskaya, *VL*, pp. 17–18.
38. See P. B. Struve, 'My Contacts and Conflicts with Lenin', *Slavonic Review*, 1934, pp. 592–3.
39. See N. Valentinov's examination of the evidence in *Maloznakomyi Lenin* (Paris, 1972) pp. 27–37.
40. This deduction is made from the records of his activity in *BK*, vol. 1, pp. 78–113.
41. Idem, p. 99.
42. Krupskaya, *VL*, p. 12.
43. For an account of their early relationship see R. H. McNeal, *Bride of the Revolution*, pp. 34–66.
44. See idem, pp. 49–50.
45. The most recent example of this condescension is G. D. Obichkin *et al.*, *Nadezhda Konstantinovna Krupskaya: Biografiya* (Moscow, 1978) *passim*.
46. On Krupskaya's pedagogical ideas, see McNeal, op. cit., pp. 194–206.
47. *KA*, 1934, no. 1, pp. 78 and 81.
48. *BK*, vol. 1, pp. 100–1.
49. *PSS*, vol. 4, pp. 340–3. Plainly Lenin was speaking metaphorically here; it is useful to note that he also referred to emotions of 'awe', 'respect' and 'veneration' in connection with Plekhanov: ibid.
50. Martov *Zapiski*, p. 269.

51. See his attacks on 'Mister Struve' in *PSS*, vol. 1, p. 444 *et seq.*
52. Idem, vol. 55, p. 7; *PPA*, vol. 1, pp. 265–75.
53. *KA*, 1934, no. 1, p. 129.
54. *BK*, vol. 1, p. 105.
55. Ibid.
56. Martov, *Zapiski*, pp. 266–88.
57. See Pipes, *Social-Democracy*, pp. 89–95.
58. *PSS*, vol. 46, pp. 10–11.
59. Idem, vol. 2, pp. 75–80; M. A. Sil'vin, *Lenin v period zarozhdeniya partii* (Leningrad, 1958) p. 106.
60. See Martov, *Zapiski*, p. 288.
61. *BK*, vol. 1, p. 113.
62. *PSS*, vol. 4, p. 196.
63. The record of Ulyanov's reading in prison and exile is given with marginal comments in V. I. Lenin, *Podgotovitel'nye materialy k knige "Razvitie kapitalizma v Rossii"* (Moscow, 1970).
64. See D. Ulyanov's recollections in *Novyi mir*, 1963, no. 6, p. 175.
65. See Wildman, *The Making of a Worker's Revolution*, pp. 73–8.
66. See his *Proekt i ob''yasnenie programmy sotsial-demokraticheskoi partii*, first published in 1924 and re-published in *PSS*, vol. 2, pp. 81–110.
67. See Wildman, op. cit., pp. 93–103.
68. See idem, p. 98.
69. B. I. Gorev, *Iz partiinogo proshlogo* (Leningrad, 1924) p. 37. Gorev's memoir is readily credible since it fits the pattern of Lenin's thoughts as expressed in *What Is To Be Done?*: see below, pp. 88–9.
70. *BK*, vol. 1, p. 133.
71. Idem, pp. 131 and 134.
72. Idem, pp. 131 and 134–5.
73. *PSS*, vol. 55, p. 37.
74. See note 39.
75. G. M. Krzhizhanovskii, *VVIL*, vol. 2, pp. 21–2.
76. See note 64.
77. *PR*, 1929, no. 2–3, p. 201.

CHAPTER 4: CAPITALISM IN ONE COUNTRY

1. The only weak link in the concatenation of themes occurs when the author abruptly switches attention from the mining industry to population statistics: see *PSS*, vol. 3, p. 495 *et seq*. The entire book is reprinted in the form of its second edition (1908) in idem, pp. 1–609. Unless otherwise stated, my comments about *Development of Capitalism* refer to the first edition.
2. See the last remarks on the subject made by M. Dobb, 'Considerazioni su "Lo sviluppo del capitalismo in Russia" di Lenin', *Storia del marxismo contemporaneo*, vol. 5 (Milan, 1978) pp. 5–28; and N. Harding, *Lenin's Political Thought*, vol. 2, pp. 310–11 (where the book is described as having been 'in its day, the fullest and most thorough study of Russian

economic development available'). Russian economic thought in the 1890s awaits a full-scale monograph. Lenin's *Development of Capitalism* was a work of enormous importance. But, like other contemporary accounts, it did not cover the entire field of economic development; and, for a general picture of industry and agriculture in that period as seen by experts at the time, Lenin's book should properly be read alongside Tugan-Baranovski's *Russkaya fabrika v proshlom i nastoyashchem* (St. Petersburg, 1898) and Danielson's *Ocherki*.

3. Loc. cit., p. 5.
4. Ibid. and idem, p. 424.
5. See above, pp. 52–4. See also Plekhanov, *S(P)*, vol. 2, pp. 222–7; Struve, *Kriticheskie zametki*, pp. 198–206; and Tugan-Baranovskii, *Russkaya fabrika*, part 2, ch. 4. See also R. I. Nafigov's introductory remarks on P. N. Skvortsov in *Tainy revolyutsionnogo podpol'ya*, pp. 96–100.
6. Op. cit, *passim*.
7. See the summaries in idem, pp. 210–13.
8. Idem, p. 484.
9. N. Harding implies that *The Development of Capitalism* entirely accorded with Plekhanovite attitudes: see op. cit., vol. 1, pp. 79–80. This has not been demonstrated with reference to Plekhanov's direct statements. And it sits uneasily alongside Plekhanov's known disapproval of Ulyanov's postulates that Russia was already a capitalist country, and that the forces producing Russian socio-economic relationships were the same as those in the rest of Europe: see above, pp. 54–5 and below, pp. 152–3. On the other hand, M. Sawer's attempt to place Ulyanov and Plekhanov at entirely opposite ends of the spectrum of opinion on the nature of Russian socio-economic development seems unconvincing. While highlighting 'Asiatic' features in Russian society, Plekhanov nevertheless still referred to the social formation as a whole as 'feudal'. But see Sawer, *Marxism and the Question of the Asiatic Mode of Production*, ch. 5 *et seq.*
10. *KA*, 1930, no. 1, p. 115 (M. Elizarova).
11. See 'Protiv ortodoksii', *Zhizn'* (St. Petersburg), 1899, no. 10, pp. 175–9.
12. See R. I. Nafigov's rehabilitation of Skvortsov in *Tainy*, pp. 99–100.
13. Lengthy extracts are reproduced in *S(L)*, vol. 3, pp. 548–53.
14. *PSS*, vol. 3, pp. 613–36.
15. Idem, p. 60.
16. Op. cit., loc. cit., pp. 552–3.
17. Idem, pp. 550–1.
18. *PSS*, vol. 3, p. 620.
19. See R. Kindersley, op. cit., pp. 147–50.
20. *Zametka k voprosu o teorii rynkov*, *PSS*, vol. 4, pp. 47–8. Ulyanov stressed that these conflicts made capitalism unstable, not impossible: idem, pp. 48–9. He adduced Marx in support. See *Kapital*, vol. 3, section 1. See also Ulyanov's further comments in his controversy with Bulgakov, Struve and Tugan in *Eshche k voprosu o teorii realizatsii*, idem, pp. 73–4 and 78.
21. Op. cit., loc. cit., pp. 552–3.

22. See the account by E. I. Lavrov and N. K. Figurovskaya in *Istoriya russkoi ekonomicheskoi mysli* (ed. A. I. Pashkov: Moscow, 1966) vol. 3, pp. 379–80 and 393–4. Chayanov got into his publishing stride only shortly before the First World War: see for example his *Ocherki po teorii trudovogo khozyaistva*, part 1 (Moscow, 1912); and, so far as I am aware, Chayanov did not engage Ulyanov-Ilin-Lenin in direct debate.

    Chernenkov's remarks, however, appeared early enough for Lenin to want to reply to them. Lenin's ripost comes in the second edition of *Development of Capitalism*: see loc. cit., pp. 139–40. See also N. N. Chernenkov, *K kharakteristike krest'yanskogo khozyaistva* (Moscow, 1905). Chernenkov's book was used by Ulyanov's Russian Marxist critics: see for example A. Martynov's aggressive appendix in *OD*, vol. 2, part 2, especially p. 311. See also the general survey of his own work by P. Maslov, *Teoriya razvitiya narodnogo khozyaistva. Vvedenie v sotsiologiyu i politicheskuyu ekonomiyu* (St. Petersburg, 1910) especially pp. 86–7.
23. See his draft contribution for the Granat Encyclopedia, *PSS*, vol. 17, pp. 103–5 and 116–19. Censorship difficulties prevented publication until 1918.
24. *PSS*, vol. 16, pp. 268–9. See also his general self-defence in a letter to Skvortsov-Stepanov, idem, vol. 47, pp. 226–32. See the further discussion below, pp. 163–4.
25. See especially the important article by I. D. Koval'chenko, 'Sootnoshenie krest'yanskogo i pomeshchich'ego khozyaistva v zemledel'cheskoi Rossii' in *Problemy sotsial'no-ekonomicheskoi istorii Rossii*, eds L. I. Ivanov *et al.* (Moscow, 1971) p. 188.
26. On this continuing debate see A. Gerschenkron, *Economic Backwardness in Historical Perspective* (London, 1966); R. Sutcliffe, *Industry and Underdevelopment* (London, 1971); R. H. Hilton (ed.), *The Transition from Feudalism to Capitalism* (London, 1976). For controversial recent empirical developmental accounts analogous to Lenin's see, for example, P. G. Ryndzyunskii *Krest'yanskaya promyshlennost'*; and P. Kriedtke, *Peasants, Landlords and Merchant Capitalists: Europe and the World Economy* (Leamington Spa, 1983).
27. For an example of the populistic interpretation of Ulyanov's thought in the 1890s see Pipes, 'Origins Of Bolshevism', pp. 38–40.
28. For an example of the economistic interpretation see N. Harding, op.cit., vol. 1, chs 1–3.
29. See G. Procacci's preface to Kautsky's *La Questione Agraria* (3rd edn: Milan, 1968) pp. lxxxv–xcii.
30. See McNeal, op. cit., pp. 52–66.
31. G. D. Obichkin, *Nadezhda Konstantinovna Krupskaya*, p. 32; *BK*, vol. 1, p. 178.
32. Wildman, *The Making of a Workers' Revolution*, pp. 165–74.
33. See *KPSS*, pp. 13–16 for the Congress Manifesto.
34. Idem, p. 16–17.
35. See W. Sablinsky, *The Road to Bloody Sunday*, p. 29.
36. See Wildman, op. cit., pp. 185–7.
37. *PSS*, vol. 4, pp. 216–17. Plekhanov and Akselrod would seem to have

abandoned, around the turn of the century, their call for state support for peasants' and workers' co-operatives: see I. M. Brover, *Ekonomicheskie vzglyady G. V. Plekhanova* (Moscow, 1960) p. 161. Ulyanov too opposed such support: *PSS*, vol. 4, pp. 220–1.

38. Idem, vol. 2, pp. 5, 454–5 and 461.
39. Idem, vol. 4, pp. 218–19.
40. Idem, pp. 224–5.
41. Idem, pp. 225–7.
42. Idem, p. 232.
43. Idem, pp. 227–30 and 233–4.
44. On Rykov, see S. A. Oppenheim, 'The Making of a Right Communist', loc. cit., pp. 422–3; on Nadezhdin, see below, p. 95. For Lenin's arguments see ibid. Lenin's eventual decision to support land nationalisation is discussed below, pp. 132–3.
45. See below, p. 100.
46. *PSS*, vol. 4, pp. 230–1.
47. Idem, vol. 2, p. 468.
48. Idem, vol. 4, pp. 194. This work remained unpublished until 1925.
49. Idem, pp. 194–5.
50. Idem, p. 197.
51. *Nasha blizhaishaya zadacha* in idem, p. 190.
52. See Wildman's penetrating discussion, op. cit., pp. 168–9, 189–98, 212 and 215–16.
53. *PSS*, vol. 4, p. 223.
54. Idem, pp. 272–3 and 315–16.
55. *Zadachi russkikh sotsial-demokratov*, *PSS*, vol. 2, p. 460.
56. See J. H. L. Keep, *The Rise of Social-Democracy in Russia* (Oxford, 1963) pp. 56–60 and 65–6; and D. Geyer, *Lenin in der russischen Sozialdemokratie* (Cologne, 1962) pp. 129–37.
57. See Keep, op. cit., pp. 57–8 and 62–3.
58. See idem, p. 62.
59. See Wildman's detailed analysis of 'Economism' in op. cit., pp. 118–43.
60. *S(P)*, vol. 12, pp. 91 and 100.
61. See Wildman, op. cit., pp. 118–19, 129 and 135–7.
62. See idem, pp. 139–43.
63. See I. Getzler, *Martov*, pp. 38–9.
64. See his later admission in *PSS*, vol. 49, pp. 346 (in a letter to I. Armand).
65. *Protest rossiiskikh sotsial-demokratov* in *PSS*, vol. 4, pp. 165–76. R. Pipes, in his 'Origins of Bolshevism', has characterised the *Protest* as the product of a political *volte face* by Ulyanov in 1899. He argues that between mid-1895 and mid-1899 Ulyanov held views typical of a conventional Russian social-democrat following the ideas of German social-democracy; and these views, according to Pipes, included support for constitutionalist modes of politics and a recognition that Russian capitalism was not fully developed. 'Origins of Bolshevism' also sees a break in the pattern of Ulyanov's organisational attitudes in his sudden declaration of intolerance of Bernstein. Finally, Pipes suggests that Ulyanov's activity as a translator of the Webbs's work indicates a readiness to imbibe aspects of their political strategy.

This case, however, does not withstand close scrutiny. Firstly, Ulyanov did not after 1899 repudiate the usefulness of parliamentary modes of operation; true, he did not believe that such modes alone would bring down the monarchy, but this constituted no change from his pre-1899 views on the subject: see above p. 35 and below, pp. 160–1. Secondly, his standpoint on the condition of Russian capitalism was the hallmark of his pre-1899 as much as of his post-1899 writings: see above, p. 54. Thirdly, Ulyanov and Plekhanov were enraged about Bernstein not so much because they changed their minds about the SPD but rather because they took the SPD's revolutionary rhetoric at its face value. Furthermore, Ulyanov's organisational recommendations had been pretty severe even before 1899: see above, p. 77. And, finally, the Webbs's researches, far from stimulating cosy thoughts about full-blown democratic procedures, contained material that may well have reinforced his penchant for specialisation and centralisation. See below, p. 92.

See N. Harding, *Lenin's Political Thought*, vol. 1, chs 3–4 for the best exposition of Lenin's political strategy over the bridge of 1899.

66. *PSS*, vol. 4, p. 337.
67. Fedoseev, *Stat'i i pis'ma*, p. 120.
68. *PSS*, vol. 1, pp. 141–2; and vol. 4, p. 184.
69. See below, p. 108.
70. Idem, vol. 55, pp. 180–1.
71. Idem, vol. 1, p. 275.
72. See below, pp. 86–7.
73. See Valentinov's vivid account in *Vstrechi s Leninym*, pp. 71–3.
74. *BK*, vol. 1, p. 242.
75. Idem, pp. 240 and 242–3.
76. Idem, pp. 243–5.
77. *PPA*, vol. 1, pp. 104–5 (editorial note).
78. See Pipes, *Struve*, pp. 249–55; and V. I. Novikov, *Lenin i deyatel'nost' iskrovskikh grupp v Rossii* (Moscow, 1978) pp. 21–5.
79. *BK*, vol. 1, pp. 254–9.
80. See Ulyanov's account in *Kak chut' li ne potukhla 'Iskra'* in *PSS*, vol. 4, pp. 334–5.
81. Idem, p. 334.
82. Idem, pp. 335–9.
83. Idem, pp. 343 and 345.
84. Idem, pp. 345–6.
85. Idem, pp. 348–9.
86. Idem, pp. 349–50.
87. *BK*, vol. 1, p. 265.

CHAPTER 5: STRAIGHTENING STICKS

1. *Iskra*, no. 1, December 1900. Krupskaya left an account of the acquisition of the printing facilities in *LS*, vol. 3, pp. 43–9.

2. This is generally true, but Potresov's part in the birth was not trivial either: see R. Pipes, *Struve*, vol. 1, pp. 247–51 and 255–9.
3. See *S chego nachat'?* in *PSS*, vol. 5, pp. 5–31 for a typical article of Lenin's for this period.
4. See A. Wildman, *The Making of a Workers' Revolution*, pp. 128–45.
5. See idem, pp. 186 and 222–4; see also the excerpt from P. P. Maslov's unpublished memoirs in V. I. Novikov, *Lenin i iskrovskikh grupp*, p. 33.
6. For a vehement denunciation of those following 'the tail' of the labour movement see Ulyanov's 'Beseda s zashchitnikami ekonomizma', *Iskra*, no. 12, 6 December 1901.
7. See W. Sablinsky, *The Road to Bloody Sunday*, pp. 28–30.
8. See the studies by D. Kol'tsov (pp. 183–229) and N. Cherevanin (pp. 273–90) in *OD*, vol. 1, part 1.
9. See G. T. Robinson, *Rural Russia*, pp. 145–7.
10. See J. Schneiderman, *The Tsarist Government and the Labor Movement, 1898–1903: Zubatovshchina* (Berkeley, 1967); W. Sablinsky, op. cit., pp. 56–79.
11. See Robinson, op. cit., p. 146.
12. The work is reprinted in *PSS*, vol. 6, pp. 3–190. On the effects on his workload see idem, p. 3.
13. See the book's sub-title: *Painful Questions of Our Movement*; and on the difference from the German political situation see idem, pp. 139–40. An extensive treatment of this point is made by N. Harding in his *Lenin's Political Thought*, vol. 1, ch. 7.
14. *PSS*, vol. 6, pp. 29–31 and 39–40.
15. Idem, pp. 99–102 and 102–4.
16. Idem, pp. 121–2, 124–5 and 140–2.
17. Idem, p. 127.
18. Idem, pp. 106 and 173.
19. Idem, p. 24.
20. Idem, pp. 99–100.
21. Idem, p. 140.
22. Idem, pp. 170–1.
23. Idem, p. 123. See also below, p. 102.
24. *PPA*, vol. 2, pp. 165 and 167.
25. *LS*, vol. 3, p. 286.
26. *Vstrechi s Leninym*, pp. 49–54.
27. For evidence of Bogdanov's reaction see the collection of articles co-authored by him and M. S. Olminski (under the pseudonyms of Ryadovoi and Galerka), *Nashi nedorazumeniya* (Geneva, 1904) *passim*.
28. See below, p. 136.
29. For hints (presumably, hints that were not deliberately dropped) of Bogdanov's future objections to Lenin's organisational ideas see his *Roza Lyuksemburg contra Karla Marksa* in *Nashi nedorazumeniya*, pp. 48–58. See also below, pp. 181–3.
30. See also A. Martynov's account of his self-restraint as regards Lenin's book: 'Vospominaniya revolyutsionera', *PR*, 1925, note 11, pp. 274–5.
31. See J. Frankel's helpful summary of Krichevski's articles for *Rabochee*

delo in the introduction to *Vladimir Akimov on the Dilemmas of Russian Marxism* (Cambridge, 1969) pp. 53–5.

32. This point is advanced by V. Strada in his prefatory remarks in *Fede e Scienza* (Turin, 1982) p. 8.

33. Martynov and Akimov elaborated these judgements at the Second Party Congress: see below, p. 102. Akimov formulated them in lengthier form still in *K voprosu o rabote vtorogo s''ezda Rossiiskoi Sotsial-Demokraticheskoi Rabochei Partii* (Geneva, 1904) and *Ocherk razvitiya sotsialdemokratii v Rossii* (St. Petersburg, 1905). These two works were unavailable to me in Russian, and instead the translation given in J. Frankel's *Vladimir Akimov* is used in this volume.

34. See also Lenin's contribution to the debate on the party programme: below, pp. 97–100.

35. *PSS*, vol. 7, pp. 7, 9 and 15.

36. Idem, pp. 18–9, 21 and 23.

37. Idem, pp. 9–10.

38. Idem, p. 17.

39. See the translation of the *Ocherk sotsialdemokratii* in Frankel, op. cit., p. 199 *et seq.*

40. *PSS*, vol. 6, pp. 39 and 142.

41. Even works like E. P. Thompson's *The Making of the English Working Class* (London, 1963), highlighting the influence of non-workingmen in the formation of socialist ideas, still recognise the working-class contribution too: see idem, *passim*.

42. *SII*, pp. 111–6.

43. Speech in Hanover, 1869: *SWOK*, p. 538.

44. K. Marx and F. Engels, *Collected Works*, vol. 6 (London, 1976) p. 497.

45. For Ulyanov's specific remarks see *PSS*, vol. 6, pp. 48, 52, 99–100, 104 and 176–8. Cf. *Ocherk razvitiya* in Frankel, op. cit., pp. 346–58.

46. *History of Trade Unionism*, chs 2–3.

47. This subject will be picked up again in the next two volumes of this study. Suffice it to say, at this point, the Ulyanov perfunctorily left it to 'comradely pressure' (*PPD*, vol. 7, p. 14) to stop higher party bodies running out of control.

48. This was recognised by the social-democrats' opponents: see V. M. Chernov, *Zapiski sotsialista-revolyutsionera* (Berlin, 1922) pp. 274–5.

49. *PSS*, vol. 4, pp. 386–8. Like *Kak chut' li ne potukhla 'Iskra'*, this piece is a rare autobiographical essay by Lenin.

50. See R. Pipes, *Struve*, vol. 1, pp. 311–37.

51. For Lenin's early reaction see *PSS*, vol. 6, pp. 372–6: *Pochemu sotsial-demokratiya dolzhna ob''yavit' reshitel'nuyu i besposhchadnuyu voinu sotsialistam-revolyutsioneram?* It was first published in 1923.

52. See M. Perrie, *The Agrarian Policy of the Russian Socialist-Revolutionary Party from its Origins through the Revolution of 1905–1907* (Cambridge, 1976) pp. 58–60 and 145–9.

53. Idem, pp. 91–7 and 153–9.

54. *Osnovnoi tezis protiv eserov* in *PSS*, vol. 7, pp. 51–5. It is notable that, for Lenin, Marxism and socialism were co-extensive: see his phrase

'socialism (equals Marxism)', proffered as if self-evident, in idem, vol. 6, p. 378.

55. Chernov, op. cit., ch. 8.
56. *PSS*, vol. 6, pp. 378–9.
57. Idem, vol. 6, pp. 76 and 337–9. See also *Iskra*, no. 5 (May 1901) *et seq.*
58. *LS*, vol. 2, pp. 102–3 and 111; and vol. 3, pp. 46–9.
59. In sheer quantity of material, Lenin outdid even Plekhanov's contributions to *Iskra*.
60. See I. Getzler, *Martov*, pp. 64–5.
61. L. Trotskii, *Moya zhizn': opyt avtobiografii* (Berlin, 1930) vol. 1, p. 168.
62. There has been ceaseless, and largely silly, speculation as to why he called himself Lenin. Some say he called himself after the river Lena just as Plekhanov, who sometimes signed himself as Volgin, linked himself to the river Volga; and it has even been mooted that the Lena, being part of Asia, was chosen to emphasise Lenin's non-European viewpoint (although this latter suggestion is hard to reconcile with what we have seen to be the basis of Lenin's economic thought). Other more frivolous proposals include the guess that he took the name after being jilted by a girl named Elena. It has even been said that the Russian etymological associations of Lenin imply leisure, and that he chose the name to stiffen his resolve not to be lazy. The point, however, is surely that it cannot be shown that Lenin deliberately selected a permanent name in 1901. Revolutionaries used a variety of pseudonyms (and Lenin continued to do so after 1901), and it was usually chance which decided which became the most popular.
63. See I. N. Volper, *Pseudonyme W. I. Lenins* (Berlin, GDR; 1970).
64. See Wildman, op. cit., pp. 240–5.
65. See idem, p. 230.
66. *PSS*, vol. 46, p. 55.
67. G. V. Plekhanov, *Filosofsko-literaturnoe nasledie G. V. Plekhanova* (ed. M. T. Iovchuk *et al.*: Moscow, 1973) vol. 1, p. 116.
68. *LS*, vol. 2, pp. 15–19.
69. Idem, p. 24.
70. Ibid.
71. Idem, p. 27.
72. Idem, p. 65.
73. *LS*, vol. 2, p. 127.
74. Idem, p. 152.
75. Idem, pp. 43–50. See also above, pp. 75–6.
76. Idem, pp. 152–60.
77. Idem, pp. 64 and 84.
78. This matter will be resumed in Volume 2.
79. *LS*, vol. 2, p. 28. I am particularly indebted to Israel Getzler for his detailed bibliographical and substantive advice in formulating this paragraph.
80. Idem, pp. 63–4.
81. Idem, pp. 80–1. See also above, pp. 43–4.
82. *LS*, vol. 2, p. 95.

83. Ibid.
84. *S(P)*, vol. 11, p. 319.
85. *LS*, vol. 2, p. 83.
86. Idem, pp. 79–80.
87. Idem, p. 83.
88. *PSS*, vol. 6, p. 173. See Plekhanov's horrified description of Tkachev's views in *S(P)*, vol. 2, p. 147. On Lenin see above, p. 29 and below, p. 135.
89. This matter will be dealt with in detail in volume two.
90. *SII*, p. 209.
91. See Maslov's project in *S(L)*, vol. 5, pp. 396–7.
92. Lenin's extensive replies to such comments are given in *Agrarnaya programma russkoi sotsial-demokratii* in *PSS*, vol. 6, pp. 305–48.
93. Idem, pp. 337–9.
94. By the Second Party Congress they had put together a weighty critique: see *SII*, pp. 107–22 (Martynov) and 125–7 (Akimov).
95. See Martynov, 'Vospominaniya revolyutsionera', loc. cit., pp. 274–5.
96. See his *K voprosu* in Frankel, op. cit., pp. 133–53.
97. Much, indeed most, historical writing on the prelude to the Congress concentrates all attention on the organisational question. This does not accurately reflect the variety of contemporary social-democratic debate.
98. See Keep, op. cit., pp. 107–8.
99. Accounts of the pre-Congress turbulence are given in Geyer, op. cit., pp. 329–46; and Keep, op. cit., pp. 95–116. A vivid impression of Lenin's determination to keep things on a tight rein is conveyed in *PSS*, vol. 46, pp. 279–82 and 284.
100. *SII*, pp. 443–4.
101. Idem, pp. 136–7.
102. Idem, p. 48.
103. Idem, p. 107.
104. Idem, p. 108.
105. Idem, p. 135.
106. Idem, pp. 181–2.
107. Idem, pp. 205–39 (and, for Trotski in particular, pp. 211–12).
108. Idem, p. 256.
109. Idem, pp. 262 and 717.
110. Idem, p. 425.
111. Idem, p. 279.
112. Idem, pp. 297, 299 and 717–18.
113. Idem, pp. 370–1 and 373.
114. There is a very clear account of the behind-the-scenes turmoil in Getzler, *Martov*, p. 80 (note 92).
115. Ibid.
116. *S(L)*, vol. 6, pp. 223–4.
117. *SII*, p. 371.
118. Idem, pp. 383–4 and 796 (note 217).
119. Idem, p. 402.
120. Idem, p. 403.

CHAPTER 6: FROM THIS ACCURSED DISTANCE

1. *Protokoly II-go ocherednogo s"ezda Zagranichnoi Ligi Russkoi Revolyutsionnoi Sotsial-demokratii* (Geneva, 1904) pp. 63–4.
2. See *PSS*, vol. 8, p. 265; and S. Baron, *Plekhanov*, pp. 245–6.
3. See *PSS*, vol. 8, p. 88.
4. This conclusion is suggested by idem, pp. 88 and 177–8.
5. See J. Keep, *The Rise of Social-Democracy*, pp. 136–7.
6. Ibid.
7. *LS*, vol. 7, pp. 277–88 and vol. 10, pp. 241–6; and G. M. Krzhizhanovskii, *O Vladimire Il'iche*, p. 32.
8. See Keep, op. cit., pp. 139–40.
9. *LS*, vol. 10, pp. 352–3.
10. Idem, p. 117.
11. *LS*, vol. 10, pp. 80–1.
12. *LS*, vol. 15, pp. 32–3.
13. *PSS*, vol. 8, pp. 415–17.
14. See the continuing dispute over this in idem, vol. 9, p. 22.
15. *Perepiska (1903–5)*, vol. 2, pp. 119–23: letters by Lenin and M. M. Essen respectively.
16. *BK*, vol. 1, p. 527.
17. Kautsky's motives are analysed by A. Ascher, *Pavel Axelrod and the Development of Menshevism* (Harvard, 1972) pp. 209–13.
18. See S. Baron, op. cit., pp. 249–51; and Getzler, *Martov*, p. 89.
19. See Ascher, op. cit., p. 198 *et seq.*
20. *Rabochii klass i sotsial-demokraticheskaya intelligentsiya*, reprinted in *S(P)*, vol. 13, pp. 116–40.
21. See her translated article in *Leninism or Marxism?*, ed. B. D. Wolfe (Ann Arbor, 1961) pp. 89–93. The article was first published in *Die Neue Zeit* and then translated into Russian for *Iskra* itself.
22. 'Chego ne delat'?', *Iskra*, no. 52, 7 November 1903.
23. N. Trotskii, *Nashi politicheskie zadachi: takticheskie i organizatsionnye voprosy* (Geneva, 1904) pp. 54–5.
24. P. Aksel'rod, 'Ob"edinenie rossiiskoi sotsialdemokratii i ee zadachi: itogi likvidatsii kustarnichestva', *Iskra*, nos. 55 (15 December 1903) and 57 (15 January 1904).
25. N. Trotskii, *Vtoroi s"ezd Rossiiskoi Sotsial-Demokraticheskoi Rabochei Partii: otchet sibirskoi delegatsii* (Geneva, 1904); this work was unavailable to me in Russian: see, however, *Report of the Siberian Delegation* (tr. B. Pearce: London, n.d.), especially pp. 34–8.
26. Ibid.
27. Op. cit., loc. cit., pp. 84, 89 and 104–8.
28. For an account of the confused reports given to O. A. Ermanski on his arrival in Switzerland, see Ascher, op. cit., pp. 194–5.
29. See Baron, op. cit., pp. 246–53.
30. *Shag vpered, dva shaga nazad: krizis v nashei partii* in *PSS*, vol. 8: see the lengthy commentary on pp. 191–240, 308–15 and 378.
31. See in general Ryadovoi and Galerka, *Nashi nedorazumeniya, passim*; and for their mild reservations about Lenin at this stage see Galerka's

article of the same title in idem, pp. 19–20. These remarks were situated in a context of broad approval of Lenin; and in any case they pale in immediate significance alongside the statement by Bogdanov (Ryadovoi) that Lenin and Plekhanov were 'the two greatest minds and talents of our party': *Nakonets-to!* in idem, p. 39.

32. *PSS*, vol. 8, pp. 379–80.
33. See *Nashi nedorazumeniya, passim* and especially, pp. 13–15, 49–50 and 55–7.
34. See below, p. 183.
35. *PSS*, vol. 8, pp. 253–4 and 378.
36. See above, p. 110.
37. See above, pp. 89–93; see also below, especially, pp. 125–7 and 190–2.
38. Krupskaya, *VL*, p. 86.
39. P. N. Lepeshinskii, *Na povorote* (3rd edn: Moscow, 1935) p. 198.
40. N. Valentinov, *Vstrechi s Leninym*, pp. 150–1.
41. See L. K. D. Kristov's account in *Revolution and Politics in Russia: Essays in Memory of B. I. Nicolaevsky* (eds A. Rabinowitch and L. K. D. Kristov: Indiana, 1972) pp. 28–9. See also above, p. 79.
42. *Vstrechi s Leninym*, pp. 132–41.
43. Idem, pp. 206–10.
44. Official Soviet historians have hardly explored Lenin's finances; but N. Valentinov, while perhaps exaggerating the Bolshevik leader's material comforts, has successfully indicated the importance of maternal assistance: see *Maloznakomyi Lenin*, pp. 58–80.
45. *PSS*, vol. 8, p. 443 and vol. 55, pp. 234–5.
46. Idem, p. 235.
47. Idem, p. 236; and M. M. Essen's memoir in *VVIL*, vol. 2, pp. 117–18.
48. Krupskaya, *VL*, p. 91.
49. See his inspiring letter in *PSS*, vol. 46, pp. 367–8.
50. I base this contrast in Lenin's views upon a comparison of the two drafts given in idem, p. 363 and *Perepiska V. I. Lenina i rukovodimykh im uchrezhdenii RSDRP s partiinymi organizatsiyami, 1903–1905 gg*, eds M. S. Volin *et al.* in 3 vols. (Moscow, 1974–6) vol. 2, p. 362.
51. *LS*, vol. 15, pp. 90–1 and 95–6; *Perepiska (1903–5)*, vol. 2, p. 366.
52. *PSS*, vol. 8, pp. 419–20; *LS*, vol. 15, pp. 95–6.
53. Idem, pp. 123–5.
54. Ibid.; and *Perepiska (1903–5)*, vol. 2, pp. 440–1.
55. *Pss*, vol. 46, p. 364.
56. Idem, vol. 9, pp. 13–21; *Perepiska (1903–5)*, vol. 2, p. 447.
57. Krupskaya, *VL*, pp. 89–92. On Lenin's reservations about his new allies even at this stage, see below, pp. 143–4.
58. *PSS*, vol. 46, p. 386.
59. The editors of *Perepiska (1903–5)*, vol. 3 claim that Lenin too belonged to the Bureau: see p. 12. They cite no source. Certainly it has not been shown that Lenin wanted to be included. He also did not want Bogdanov to be included; in fact his favoured list of candidates was only partially successful: see *PSS*, vol. 46, p. 386.
60. See, for example, *Nashi nedorazumeniya* by Ryadovoi and Galerka.
61. *PSS*, vol. 46, p. 404.

62. Idem, pp. 417–19.
63. For the announcement of *Vpered*'s prospective issue, see idem, vol. 9, pp. 103–9.
64. *LS*, vol. 15, p. 172.
65. See M. Pavlovich, 'Vneshnaya politika i russko-yaponskaya voina', *OD*, vol. 2, part 1, pp. 18–27.
66. See Yu. B. Solov'ev, *Samoderzhavie i dvoryanstvo, 1902–1907 gg.* (Moscow, 1981) pp. 101–16.
67. See idem, pp. 119–37.
68. See S. Galai, *The Liberation Movement in Russia, 1900–1905* (Cambridge, 1973) pp. 214–22.
69. See R. Service, *The Bolshevik Party in Revolution*, pp. 25 and 218 (note 20).
70. See Sablinsky, op. cit., pp. 85–118 and 145–97.
71. See S. Shwarz, *The Russian Revolution of 1905: the Workers' Movement and the Formation of Bolshevism and Menshevism* (Chicago, 1967) pp. 35–9.
72. The letter is reprinted in *S(L)*, vol. 7, pp. 410–16.
73. See Schwarz, op. cit., pp. 38–44.
74. See idem, pp. 45–9.
75. See the pamphlet *Zemskaya kampaniya i plan 'Iskry'* in *PSS*, vol. 9, especially pp. 79–80, 82–3 and 92.
76. 'Pora konchit'', *Vpered*, no. 1, 4 January 1905 (22 December 1904 by the old calendar); and *PSS*, vol. 47, p. 8.
77. See note 75.
78. See Schwarz, *op. cit.*, pp. 43–7.

CHAPTER 7: *STURM UND DRANG*

1. See W. Sablinsky, *The Road to Bloody Sunday*, pp. 172–228.
2. See *idem*, pp. 229–71.
3. See idem, pp. 277–83.
4. See idem, pp. 283–5.
5. See D. Kol'tsov, 'Rabochie v 1905–1907 gg.', *OD*, vol. 1, part 1, p. 198.
6. See A. V. Pyaskovskii, *Revolyutsiya 1905–1907 gg. v. Rossii* (Moscow, 1966) pp. 41–7.
7. See S. Galai, op. cit., pp. 240–3.
8. A case has been made by S. M. Schwarz that the Ivanovo Assembly did not undertake all the tasks usually associated with the soviets proper: see his *The Russian Revolution of 1905*, pp. 335–8. This may well be so. On the other hand, the Assembly's rudimentary involvement in administrative activity gave it a broader scope than a mere strike committee.
9. See Kol'tsov, op. cit., pp. 207–16. See also Schwarz, op. cit., ch. 3.
10. See S. M. Dubrovskii, *Krest'yanskoe dvizhenie v revolyutsii 1905–1907 gg.* (Moscow, 1957) p. 42; and M. Perrie, *Agrarian Programme*, pp. 101–11.
11. See Galai, op. cit., pp. 244–9.
12. Ibid.

13. See Pyaskovskii, op. cit., pp. 94–102; and V. A. Petrov, *Ocherki po istorii revolyutsionnogo dvizheniya v russkoi armii v 1905 godu* (Moscow–Leningrad, 1964) pp. 115–16.
14. *VVIL*, vol. 1, pp. 290–1; P. N. Lepeshinskii, *Na povorote*, pp. 208–9.
15. *LS*, vol. 15, pp. 274–5.
16. *PSS*, vol. 47, p. 8.
17. Idem, vol. 9, pp. 167–9.
18. *Perepiska (1903–5)*, vol. 3, p. 232.
19. Idem, p. 312.
20. *PSS*, vol. 9, p. 35.
21. By 5 January 1905 S. N. Afanasev was admitting to the rise of Menshevik strength in Petersburg itself: *Perepiska (1903–5)*, vol. 3, pp. 442–6.
22. Idem, p. 456. See also S. I. Gusev's acerbic comments on Lenin's lack of consultation with his colleagues in Russia in *Perepiska V. I. Lenina i rukovodimykh im uchrezhdenii RSDRP s partiinymi organizatsiyami, 1905–1907 gg.* (eds D. I. Antonyuk *et al.* in 5 vols. from 1979: Moscow) vol. 1, part 1, p 331.
23. *Perepiska (1903–5)*, vol. 3, p. 481.
24. *Perepiska (1905–7)*, vol. 1, part 1, pp. 113–14, 118 (note 8) and especially p. 135.
25. Idem, p. 221; and *PSS*, vol. 9, p. 246.
26. Ibid.
27. Idem, pp. 247.
28. *Perepiska (1905–7)*, vol. 1, part 1, p. 371; and part 2, p. 34. See also Krasin's memoir in *Leonid Borisovich Krasin ("Nikitich"): gody podpol'ya. Sbornik vospominanii, statei i dokumentov* (Moscow, 1928) p. 43.
29. *SIII*, pp. 17–18 and 684–5.
30. *PSS*, vol. 10, pp. 63–5. See also M. N. Lyadov, 'Nikitich' in *Leonid Borisovich Krasin*, pp. 230–1.
31. See above, p. 81.
32. We shall encounter some striking indications of this in vol. 2.
33. See below, pp. 142 and 154–5.
34. *Two Tactics* is reprinted in *PSS*, vol. 11, pp. 3–131. From *Vpered*'s issue no. 6 (1 February 1905) onwards, Lenin's editorials elaborated his views on the seizure of power from the monarchy.
35. *PSS*, vol. 11, pp. 20–3 and 64. See also vol. 9, pp. 265–7.
36. Idem, pp. 203–4 and 288–9; and vol. 11, pp. 142–3 and 185.
37. Idem, vol. 10, pp. 29–30, 261–2 and 272.
38. See A. Martynov *Dve diktatury* (Geneva, 1905) and L. Martov, 'Na ocheredi', *Iskra*, no. 93, 17 March 1905. Martynov's pamphlet was a major document in the history of Menshevism. Martynov awaits a detailed monograph.
39. See in general Lenin's *Dolzhny li my organizovat' revolyutsiyu?* in *PSS*, vol. 9, pp. 264–73; and *Sotsial-demokratiya i vremennoe revolyutsionnoe pravitel'stvo* in *idem*, vol. 10, pp. 3–31. These articles appeared in February and April respectively.
40. See Lenin's admission in *idem*, vol. 11, p. 64.

41. N. Trotskii, *Do devyatogo yanvarya* (with a preface by A. Parvus: Geneva, 1905). Parvus's career is recounted by Z. A. Zeman and W. B. Scharlau, *The Merchant of Revolution: the Life of Alexander Helphand* (London, 1965).
42. *Do devyatogo yanvarya*, p. 1, *et seq.*
43. Idem, pp. iii–xiv.
44. Trotski refined his thoughts in *Itogi i perspektivy* in a collection entitled *Nasha revolyutsiya* (St. Petersburg, 1906). I have used the English translation in *The Permanent Revolution And Results And Prospects* (New York, 1969): see especially, pp. 116–22.
45. Ibid.
46. Taking Lenin's writings and speeches, published or unpublished at the time, between Bloody Sunday and the publication of *Two Tactics*, we find seventy two references to Martynov and only twelve to Trotski: see *PSS*, vols 9 (pp. 507–55) and 10 (pp. 513–51). Only in *Sotsial-demokratiya i vremennoe revolyutsionnoe pravitel'stvo* does Lenin offer a critique, however short, of Trotski's position: idem, pp. 16–19.
47. Idem, vol. 11, p. 222.
48. Ibid.
49. Idem, vol. 10, pp. 359–62 and vol. 12, pp. 154–7.
50. Idem, vol. 9, pp. 281–2 (for Lenin's first mention of a temporary coalition government of revolutionary parties: *Vpered*, no. 7, 8 February 1905) and pp. 297–8 (for his first mention of 'the revolutionary democratic dictatorship of the proletariat and the peasantry': *Vpered*, no. 9, 23 February 1905).
51. Ibid.
52. *PSS*, vol. 11, pp. 14–16 and 29–30.
53. Ibid.
54. A. Martynov, 'V bor'be s marksistskoi sovest'yu', *Iskra*, nos 102–3, 15 and 21 June 1905.
55. *PSS*, vol. 11, pp. 112–29.
56. It is noteworthy that the Mensheviks, though often branding Lenin as Jacobin or Bakuninist or Blanquist, did not yet question the sincerity of his feelings. See, however, below, p. 191.
57. Martynov, *Dve diktatury*, *passim*.
58. Lenin's first open call for the expropriation of the landed gentry came in 'Proletariat i krest'yanstvo', *Vpered*, no. 11, 10 March 1905 (*PSS*, vol. 9, pp. 345–6); his first use of the land nationalisation slogan occurred in 'O nashei agrarnoi programme', *Vpered*, no. 12, 29/16 March 1905 (idem, pp. 359–60). On his earlier thoughts see above, p. 100.
59. P. Maslov, *Kritika agrarnykh programm i proekt programmy* (Moscow, 1905) contains his essential position; and the debate at the Fourth Party Congress saw him repeat his assault upon Lenin's proposals: see below, pp. 152–3.
60. See below, p. 152. See also, for his actual comments in 1905, *PSS*, vol. 9, pp. 359–61; vol. 10, p. 48; and vol. 11, pp. 282–8.
61. This theme is picked up again in vols 2 and 3.
62. See above, p. 127.

63. *Pervaya obshcherusskaya konferentsiya partiinykh rabotnikov* (Geneva, 1905) pp. 3–4.
64. *SIII*, pp. 29–32, 85–6 and 88.
65. Idem, p. 164.
66. Idem, pp. 118–19. See also N. A. Shevelkin's summary of the variety of opinions in idem, pp. 149–50.
67. Idem, p. 148.
68. Idem, pp. 158 and 450–1.
69. Idem, p. 158.
70. Idem, pp. 167–8.
71. Idem, p. 181.
72. Idem, p. 453; and *PSS*, vol. 10, p. 148. S. Schwarz makes an excellent elucidation of this matter in his op. cit., pp. 154–5.
73. See the project in *SIII*, p. 453.
74. Idem, p. 177.
75. Idem, p. 453.
76. See 'K voprosu o zakhvate vlasti', *Iskra*, no. 96, 5 April 1905.
77. *SIII*, pp. 188–9 and 193–4. See also *The Bourgeoisie and the Counter-revolution*, reprinted in K. Marx and F. Engels, *Collected Works*, vol. 8 (1977) p. 161. See also Marx's *Address to the Communist League* of 1850 in *KMSW*, p. 283 for similar statements.
    I am indebted to Paul Smart for his bibliographical guidance on Marx and the French Terror.
78. *Collected Works*, vol. 4 (1975) pp. 81, 95 and 119–25. See also his later justification of the Paris Commune's execution of a hostage specifically and only as retaliation, not as a positive, first-strike measure: *The Civil War in France* in *SWOK*, pp. 295–7.
79. *SIII*, p. 194.
80. See above, ch. 1 (note 64).
81. We must not, after all, assume that the present-day practices at congresses of the Communist Party of the Soviet Union bear much resemblance to those of Lenin's day.
82. *SIII*, pp. 198–202, 209, 212 and 451–2.
83. Idem, p. 210.
84. Idem, p. 211.
85. Idem, pp. 224–5.
86. Idem, p. 247.
87. Idem, p. 263.
88. Idem, pp. 255, 256 and 261.
89. Idem, pp. 259, 262, 263, 292 and 300.
90. Idem, p. 284.
91. Idem, p. 292.
92. Idem, p. 293.
93. Idem, pp. 270, 272, 279 and 285.
94. Idem, p. 340.
95. Idem, p. 341.
96. Idem, p. 286.
97. Idem, p. 406.
98. Idem, p. 671.

99. Idem, p. 670.
100. Idem, p. 455.
101. Ibid.
102. Idem, p. 337.
103. Idem, p. 466.
104. See Kol'tsov, op. cit., pp. 218–22.
105. See F. Dan, 'Obshchaya politika pravitel'stva i izmeneniya v gosudar-stvennoi organizatsii v period 1905–1907 gg.', *OD*, vol. 4, pt. 1, pp. 321–33.
106. See E. D. Chermenskii, *Burzhuaziya i tsarizm v pervoi russkoi revolyutsii* (2nd edn: Moscow, 1970) pp. 128–35.
107. See Galai, op. cit., pp. 259–63.
108. See L. Trotskii, *Moya zhizn'*, vol. 1, pp. 201–9; and O. Anweiler, *The Soviets: the Russian Workers, Peasants And Soldiers Councils, 1905–1921* (New York, 1974) pp. 5–42.
109. *Ibid*.
110. See Chermenskii, op. cit., pp. 135–46.
111. See idem, pp. 150–1.

CHAPTER 8: PREDICTING THE TIDE

1. See E. D. Chermenskii, *Burzhuaziya i tsarizm*, pp. 146–56.
2. See O. Anweiler, *The Soviets*, pp. 43–64.
3. See S. M. Dubrovskii, *Krest'yanskoe dvizhenie v revolyutsii 1905–1907 gg.*, p. 42.
4. For use of such nomenclature see M. S. Olminski's letter in *Literaturnoe nasledstvo*, vol. 18: *V. I. Lenin i A. V. Lunacharskii: perepiska, doklady, dokumenty* (Moscow, 1971) pp. 601–2.
5. For his attitude to émigré life see his collection, co-authored with Olminski, *Nashi nedorazumeniya*, pp. 18 and 19–20. See also above, pp. 90 and 112.
6. *Moya zhizn'*, vol. 1, pp. 192–203.
7. *PSS*, vol. 47, p. 83; see also idem, vol. 10, pp. 80–1.
8. Idem, vol. 47, p. 83.
9. Idem, p. 71–2.
10. Idem, pp. 55, 70 and 332–3 (note 63).
11. Idem, pp. 82–3.
12. Idem, pp. 83–4.
13. Idem, pp. 92–3 and 99–101.
14. Idem, pp. 39–40 and 76.
15. Idem, pp. 88 and 91–2.
16. A. Bogdanov, 'Opasnyi put'', *Novaya zhizn'*, no. 20, November 1905. See also Krasin's complaints about him in June 1905: *Leonid Borisovich Krasin*, p. 367.
17. *PSS*, vol. 47, p. 80.
18. Idem, pp. 99–101.
19. Idem, pp. 88 and 91–2.

20. See below, pp. 154–5. See also Lenin's conciliatory missives to Y. M. Steklov and G. V. Plekhanov, *PSS*, vol. 47, pp. 33–4 and 103–6.
21. *BK*, vol. 2, p. 195.
22. See *Nashi zadachi i sovet rabochikh deputatov (pis'mo v redaktsiyu)*, which was first published only in 1940 and is reprinted in *PSS*, vol. 12, pp. 61–70.
23. Idem, pp. 61–2 and 64–6.
24. See S. Schwarz's account in *Russian Revolution of 1905*, pp. 18–19.
25. See note 22.
26. For the official record of his doings and whereabouts see *BK*, vol. 2, p. 195 *et seq.*
27. B. Gorev, 'Za kulisami pervoi revolyutsii', *Istoriko-revolyutsionnyi byulleten'*, 1922, no. 1, pp. 14–15. See also Trotski's comments in *Moya zhizn'*, vol. 1, p. 208.
28. See his recollections in a letter to A. M. Gorki: *PSS*, vol. 47, p. 141. Plekhanov discerned the unusualness of Bogdanov's philosophy earlier still, in 1901: see Plekhanov, *Filosofsko-literaturnoe nasledie*, vol. 1, p. 131. And it may well be, if Trotski is correct, that Lenin himself was initially attracted by Bogdanov's philosophy: *Moya zhizn'*, vol. 1, p. 167. But this particular possibility is uncorroborated by documentary evidence.
29. *PSS*, vol. 4, pp. 74–5.
30. F. V. Lengnik, *VVIL*, vol. 2, pp. 65–6. On neo-Kantianism among Marxists in the rest of Europe see L. Kolakowski, *Main Currents of Marxism*, vol. 2, *The Golden Age* (Oxford, 1978) pp. 243–53.
31. On Bogdanov's negative attitude to Kant see his *Poznanie s istoricheskoi tochki zreniya* (St. Petersburg, 1902) p. 199.
32. The ideas of Mach and Avenarius are discussed by L. Kolakowski in *The Alienation of Reason: A History of Positivist Thought* (New York, 1968) pp. 104–25.
33. Bogdanov gathered together his speculations in his trilogy *Empiriomonizm: stat'i po filosofii* (St. Petersburg, 1904–6). For further examination of its contents, see below, pp. 179–80.
34. See below, pp. 179, 181 and 182.
35. See below, pp. 179–80.
36. *PSS*, vol. 47, p. 141.
37. *PSS*, vol. 47, p. 141.
38. Idem, p. 51. See also N. Valentinov, *Vstrechi s Leninym*, pp. 283–305.
39. Ibid.
40. See above, pp. 142–3.
41. *PSS*, vol. 12, p. 317.
42. Idem, pp. 61–70.
43. Idem, p. 317.
44. Idem, vol. 10, p. 338.
45. Idem, vol. 11, p. 103.
46. Idem, vol. 12, p. 86.
47. *SIII*, pp. 262 and 333; and *PSS*, vol. 47, pp. 16 and 66.
48. Ibid.
49. Idem, vol. 11, pp. 336–7 and 342.

50. Idem, p. 340–1.
51. Idem, vol. 12, pp. 85–6.
52. Idem, p. 140.
53. Ibid.
54. For a detailed exposition of Akselrod's scheme see A. Ascher, *Pavel Axelrod*, pp. 235–9.
55. Ibid.
56. *PSS*, vol. 10, p. 242.
57. See for example idem, vol. 12, pp. 138–40.
58. S. Schwarz, *The Russian Revolution*, p. 175.
59. See the account in idem, p. 195.
60. See J. Keep, *The Rise Of Social-Democracy*, pp. 243–7.
61. L. Trotskii, *Moya zhizn'*, vol. 1, pp. 206–7.
62. See Keep, op. cit., p. 247.
63. See idem, p. 250.
64. See idem, pp. 251–7.
65. Police report in *KA*, 1934, no. 1, pp. 185–6; B. Gorev, 'Za kulisami', pp. 15–16.
66. Ibid.
67. Idem, pp. 16–17.
68. F. Dan, 'Obshchaya politika pravitel'stva', loc. cit., pp. 371–5.
69. *KPSS*, p. 138.
70. *Lenin i Lunacharskii*, p. 30.
71. Gorev, op. cit., pp. 16–17.
72. Ibid.
73. Ibid.; and I. V. Stalin, *Pravda*, 24 April 1920.
74. See below, p. 153.
75. *KPSS*, p. 135.
76. Idem, p. 136.
77. Idem, p. 137.
78. *KA*, 1934, no. 1, pp. 186–7.
79. Ibid.
80. I. Teodorovich, 'Eshche ob Ob''edinitel'nom s''ezde RSDRP', *PR*, 1925, no. 4, p. 214.
81. See Dan, op. cit., pp. 385–9.
82. *SIV*, pp. 537–40.
83. Idem, p. 9.
84. *VVIL*, vol. 2, pp. 130–1.
85. *SIV*, p. 40.
86. Idem, p. 55. According to the editors of the 1959 edition of the Congress minutes, the record of Lenin's speech has not yet been discovered: idem, p. 603 (note 27).
87. Idem, pp. 247–57 and 264–8. See also Lenin's concluding speech at the end of the debate: idem, pp. 127–9.
88. Idem, pp. 241–2. See also above, pp. 61–2.
89. Idem, pp. 249–51; see also idem, p. 134.
90. Idem, pp. 55–8.
91. Idem, p. 55.
92. See above, p. 132.

93. *SIV*, pp. 111.
94. Idem, pp. 59.
95. See above, p. 55.
96. *SIV*, p. 75.
97. Ibid.
98. Idem, pp. 76–7 (Suvorov), 78 (Stalin) and 148 (Rumyantsev). An indication of the non-monolithic character of the party's factions is the Menshevik Kostitsyn's support for Suvorov: idem, pp. 106–7.
99. The variants of Lenin's draft are given in idem, pp. 490–1.
100. Idem, p. 132.
101. Idem, p. 160.
102. Idem, p. 59.
103. Idem, p. 192.
104. Idem, pp. 246–77.
105. Idem, pp. 282–5 and 492–3.
106. Idem, p. 295.
107. Ibid.
108. Idem, p. 306.
109. Idem, p. 322.
110. Idem, p. 326.
111. Idem, p. 246.
112. Idem, p. 254.
113. Idem, pp. 361–2: speech by V. Krokhmal.
114. Idem, pp. 401–2.
115. Idem, p. 528.
116. Idem, p. 357.
117. Idem, pp. 639–40 (editorial note).
118. See below, pp. 157–8.
119. See below, p. 157.
120. *SV*, p. 474.

CHAPTER 9: FOR THE GOOD OF THE CAUSE

1. See E. D. Chermenskii, *Burzhuaziya i tsarizm*, p. 265. These figures refer to the situation in the Duma's closing sessions.
2. See idem, pp. 269–75.
3. See below, pp. 158 and 161.
4. See Chermenskii, op. cit., pp. 293–302 and 310.
5. See idem, pp. 311 and 316.
6. *PSS*, vol. 13, p. 337.
7. See F. Dan, 'Obshchaya politika', loc. cit., p. 368.
8. See idem, part 2, pp. 63–7.
9. See S. M. Dubrovskii, *Stolypinskaya zemel'naya reforma*, pp. 130–61.
10. N. K. Krupskaya, *VL*, pp. 132–4.
11. *SV*, pp. 616–17.
12. See his comments in *PSS*, vol. 13, p. 393 on the effects of continued 'partisan' activity.

13. Krupskaya, *VL*, pp. 133–4.
14. *PSS*, vol. 14, pp. 263–4.
15. See the editors' account in idem, pp. 447–8.
16. *SV*, p. 87.
17. This is presumably why the Bolsheviks did a little better than the Mensheviks in getting delegates elected to the Fifth Party Congress and in winning further support from the 'neutrals' in the Bolshevik–Menshevik controversy at the same controversy: see below, p. 167.
18. See A. Levin, *The Second Duma: a Study of the Social-Democratic Party and the Russian Constitutional Experiment* (New Haven, 1940) pp. 67 and 72–3.
19. See idem, pp. 32–3 and 67.
20. See idem, pp. 167–8.
21. See idem, pp. 20–3, 67 and 120.
22. The bulkiest of his commentaries in this period is *Agrarnaya programma sotsial-demokratii v period russkoi revolyutsii 1905–1907 gg., PSS*, vol. 16, pp. 195–411. As the title implies, the work does not survey the entire range of the party's policies.
23. See *Results and Prospects*, loc. cit.
24. See *OD*.
25. *LS*, vol. 38, pp. 23–4 and 25–7.
26. *PSS*, vol. 17, pp. 404–5.
27. Idem, vol. 16, pp. 8–10.
28. Idem, pp. 3–5, 11 and 46–8.
29. Idem, vol. 14, pp. 74–5.
30. Idem, vol. 13, pp. 139–42; vol. 17, p. 400; and vol. 20, p. 11.
31. Treatments of Bogdanov's politics before the First World War sometimes forget about his activity in 1917 when, as a member of the Novaya Zhizn group, he supported the campaign for the convocation of the Constituent Assembly. For further information see J. Biggart, 'Anti-Leninist Bolshevism: the Forward Group of the RSDRP', *Canadian Slavonic Papers*, no. 2, 1981, pp. 146–50.
32. See idem.
33. *PSS*, vol. 15, p 79.
34. This characterisation especially irritated Lenin: he remembered it in 1909 when organising the expulsion of Bogdanov from the Bolshevik Centre: see below, p. 185.
35. *PSS*, vol. 15, pp. 54–6. See also, vol. 14, pp. 263–4 and 302–6 for anti-Menshevik remarks in this vein.
36. See above, p. 55.
37. See M. I. Tugan-Baranovskii, *Russkaya fabrika*, pp. 14–27; and G. V. Plekhanov, *Nashi raznoglasiya* in *S(P)*, vol. 2, pp. 199–205.
38. See *Results and Prospects*, loc. cit., pp. 36–45.
39. *PSS*, vol. 17, pp. 325–8.
40. For his defensiveness towards Martov see idem, pp. 366–7. He rarely referred to Trotski's viewpoint; but, for a rare example, see idem, p. 381.
41. Idem, vol. 16, pp. 169–71; vol. 17, p. 325.
42. Ibid.; and vol. 17, pp. 273–5.
43. Idem, vol. 17, pp. 325–8.

44. Idem, p. 400.
45. See above, pp. 132–3.
46. *PSS*, vol. 15, pp. 226–7; vol. 16, pp. 298–9.
47. Ibid. See also above, pp. 132 and 151.
48. Maslov's major empirical study on the post-1905 period is contained in his *Agrarnyi vopros v Rossii*, vol. 2 (St. Petersburg, 1908); see also his chapter in *OD*, vol. 4, part 1, pp. 1–32.
49. *OD*, vol. 1, pp. 9–10. See also his general theoretical treatment of the demographic factor in *Teoriya razvitiya narodnogo khozyaistva*, pp. 32 and 74–5.
50. *OD*, vol. 1, pp. 4–5 and 14–16. See also *Agrarnyi vopros*, vol. 2, pp. 389–95.
51. Again the absence of a comprehensive monograph on the major economic theorists of Russian Marxism makes assessment difficult; but it is hard to think of a theorist with economic expertise who took Lenin's side in the economic controversies of the Stolypin years. See also Martynov's provocative summary in *SV*, pp. 380–2.
52. See for example *P. Maslov v isterike* in *PSS*, vol. 17, pp. 250–8.
53. Idem, vol. 16, pp. 216–23. It deserves emphasis, however, that this passage by Lenin also stresses his belief that the government's legislation was far from being progressive enough for him.
54. Idem, vol. 22, pp. 16–21.
55. Idem, pp. 390.
56. *PSS*, vol. 16, pp. 268–9. Debate between the Soviet economic historians S. M. Dubrovski and A. M. Anfimov about the implications of Lenin's post-1905 agrarian writings has been picked up and extended in an excellent article by E. Kingston-Mann, 'A Strategy for Marxist Bourgeois Revolution: Lenin and the Peasantry, 1907–1916', *Journal of Peasant Studies*, vol. 7, no. 2 (1980): see especially pp. 134–5. The contrary view is taken by N. Harding (*Lenin's Political Thought*, vol. 1, ch. 9) that Lenin's work on the peasantry after 1905 constituted simply an extension of *The Development of Capitalism in Russia*. He is surely right that a comprehensive *volte face* did not occur. On the other hand it is difficult not to agree with Kingston-Mann that Lenin's own admission (*PSS*, vol. 16, pp. 268–9) shows that a very substantial change nevertheless took place. See also the discussion above, pp. 69–70.
57. *PSS*, vol. 17, pp. 115–18.
58. For his private self-defence see his letter to Skvortsov-Stepanov, idem, vol. 47, pp. 226–32. See also idem, vol. 16, pp. 268–9.
59. See S. M. Dubrovskii, *Sel'skoe khozyaistvo i krest'yanstvo*, pp. 264–5; and I. D. Koval'chenko, 'Sootnoshenie krest'yanskogo i pomesh-chich'ego khozyaistva', loc. cit., pp. 182, 185 and 190. See also below, p. 170.
60. Maslov, *Teoriya razvitiya*, pp. 242–3, 255 and 263–6.
61. Idem, pp. 255 and 285. Tugan, be it noted, was Maslov's chief target in this polemic. This was unsurprising since Tugan had always assumed the most extreme position on the spectrum of opinion on the producer's-and-consumer's goods controversy: see above, p. 69.
62. See above, ibid.

63. See Chapter 4, notes 25 and 26.
64. *SV*, p. 87.
65. Idem, pp. 588–90.
66. Idem, pp. 96 and 184.
67. Idem, p. 666.
68. Idem, p. 696.
69. Idem, pp. 9–10.
70. Idem, pp. 40–1.
71. Idem, pp. 73–88.
72. Idem, p. 72.
73. Idem, p. 178.
74. Idem, p. 166.
75. Idem, p. 175.
76. Idem, pp. 190–208.
77. Idem, pp. 208–14.
78. Idem, p. 273.
79. Idem, pp. 257–66.
80. Idem, pp. 299 and 308.
81. Idem, pp. 293, 342–6 and 352.
82. Idem, pp. 364–6 and 371–3.
83. Idem, pp. 380–1.
84. Idem, p. 382.
85. Idem, pp. 383–7 and 400–2.
86. Idem, pp. 410–11.
87. Idem, pp. 458–60 and 464–5.
88. Idem, pp. 497–8 and 505–6.
89. Idem, pp. 502–3.
90. Idem, pp. 550–1 and 552–3.
91. Idem, p. 561.
92. Idem, pp. 561–2, 570 and 722–3.
93. Idem, p. 567.
94. Idem, p. 573.
95. Idem, pp. 579 and 615–16.
96. Idem, pp. 583–4.
97. Idem, pp. 586–7.
98. Idem, pp. 575 and 586–7.
99. Idem, pp. 597 and 602.
100. Idem, pp. 602 and 827.
101. See Levin, op. cit., pp. 323–5.
102. See G. A. Hosking, *The Russian Constitutional Experiment: Government and Duma, 1907–1914* (Cambridge, 1973) pp. 42–5.
103. See A. Ya. Avrekh, *Stolypin i Tret'ya Duma* (Moscow, 1968) pp. 10–11.
104. See K. A. Bailes, 'Lenin and Bogdanov: the End of an Alliance' in A. W. Cordier (ed.), *Columbia Essays in International Affairs* (New York, 1967) vol. 2, p. 119.
105. *LS*, vol. 38, pp. 23–4; *PSS*, vol. 16, p. 473.
106. Compare the draft in idem, pp. 51–2 with the resolution in *KPSS*, pp. 227–8 (as well as with Bogdanov's draft in idem, pp. 230–1).
107. Idem, p. 231.

108. See Dan, 'Obshchaya politika', loc. cit., vol. 4, part 2, p. 65.
109. See V. S. D'yakin, *Samoderzhavie, burzhuaziya i dvoryanstvo v 1907–1911 gg.* (Leningrad, 1978) pp. 26–8.
110. See R. C. Elwood's account in *Russian Social-Democracy In The Underground*, pp. 36–7.
111. See P. I. Lyashchenko, *Istoriya narodnogo khozyaistva SSSR*, vol. 2, p. 405.
112. See idem, pp. 388–403.
113. See Dubrovskii, *Stolypinskaya zemel'naya reforma*, p. 576.
114. See idem, p. 588.
115. See idem, pp. 67–77, 235–47 and 383–9.
116. See Dubrovskii, *Sel'skoe khozyaistvo*, pp. 219–20.
117. See idem, pp. 264–5.
118. See above, pp. 163–4.
119. See Hosking, op. cit., pp. 77–96.
120. See Avrekh, op. cit., pp. 335–46.
121. See idem, pp. 275–7 and 314–7.
122. For an examination of the killing's retroscena see idem, pp. 367–406.
123. This was true, of course, of all the returning leaders save for Trotski.
124. *BK*, vol. 2, pp. 293–5 and 309–10.
125. *PSS*, vol. 13, p. 164.
126. *BK*, vol. 2, p. 272.
127. Idem, pp. 333–4; and Krupskaya, *VL*, p. 134.
128. *KA*, 1934, no. 1, p. 209; *BK*, vol. 2, pp. 339, 352 and 355.
129. Bogdanov even managed to complete the third volume of *Empiriomonizm* in prison in 1906, and thereupon to write and publish his novel *Red Star*. For Lenin, see above, pp. 159–65.
130. *BK*, vol. 2, p. 346.
131. A. Shlikhter, 'Il'ich, kakim ya ego znal', *PR*, 1924, no. 6, pp. 6–7; Krupskaya, *VL*, p. 128.
132. See S. Possony, *Lenin: the Compulsive Revolutionary*, pp. 122–3; and G. Alexinsky, *Portrait de Lénine* (Paris, 1958) p. 48.
133. *PSS*, vol. 17, p. 306.
134. Idem, vol. 13, p. 211.
135. Idem, vol. 17, p. 258.
136. See G. E. Zinoviev's account in *SV*, pp. 149–52.
137. *PSS*, vol. 47, p. 112.
138. *KA*, 1934, no. 1, pp. 209–10.
139. See above, pp. 136 and 154.
140. See the account by J. Biggart, 'Anti-Leninist Bolshevism', pp. 138–40.
141. See note 25.
142. *KPSS*, pp. 237–8; and *LS*, vol. 38, pp. 25–8.
143. *PSS*, vol. 17, pp. 279 and 282–3.
144. Idem, pp. 278–9.
145. See N. Valentinov, *Maloznakomyi Lenin*, pp. 112–18. It should be noted, however, that Valentinov over-stretches his case in saying that it was these funds that allowed Lenin to publish *Proletari* in 1908; he took no account that Bogdanov was in any case a fellow editor from 1907 through to mid-1908.

146. *BK*, vol. 2, p. 334.
147. Idem, p. 337; *PSS*, vol. 47, pp. 111–12.
148. *BK*, vol. 2, p. 335.
149. Idem, pp. 366 and 368.
150. Idem, pp. 370–3.

CHAPTER 10: DOUBTS AND CERTAINTIES

1. On the post-1905 cultural scene see E. Lampert, *Decadents, Liberals, Revolutionaries: Russia, 1900–1918* (Keele, 1969) pp. 3–18.
2. *Lenin i Lunacharskii*, p. 625.
3. See M. A. Moskalev, *Byuro Tsentral'nogo Komiteta RSDRP v Rossii (avgust 1903–mart 1917)* (Moscow, 1964) pp. 120–1 and 130.
4. See *BK*, vol. 2, p. 362 *et seq.*
5. The second issue of *Social-Democrat* was made only in January 1909: idem, p. 457.
6. See Moskalev, op. cit., p. 130; and R. A. Ermolaeva and A. Ya. Manusevich, *Lenin i pol'skoe rabochee dvizhenie* (Moscow, 1971) pp. 173–4.
7. See Moskalev, op. cit., pp. 130–3.
8. See the police report in idem, p. 139.
9. See idem, pp. 141–3; and I. E. Gorelov, *Bol'sheviki v period reaktsii (1907–1910 gg.)* (Moscow, 1975) p. 109.
10. See the debate on the Central Committee in *Protokoly soveshchaniya rasshirennoi redaktsii 'Proletariya': iyun' 1909* (Moscow, 1934) pp. 82–8.
11. See Gorelov, op. cit., p. 61.
12. Ibid. It is a sign, however, of continuing official Soviet embarrassment about the strength of anti-Duma sentiment among Bolsheviks in 1908 that this book, which covers virtually all the major party committees of European Russia and is based upon primary sources unavailable to non-Soviet scholars, fails to offer a geographical and political summary of Recallism. Recallism awaits its chronicler.
13. *V. I. Lenin i A. M. Gor'kii*, ed. V. A. Byalik (Moscow, 1958) p. 273. The copy of Gorki's original letter has not been published.
14. *PSS*, vol. 47, pp. 150–3.
15. *BK*, vol. 2, p. 411.
16. Idem, pp. 413–14; *PSS*, vol. 19, pp. 86–7 and vol. 47, pp. 283–4.
17. See J. Biggart's analysis in 'Anti-Leninist Bolshevism', pp. 144–5.
18. See Moskalev, op. cit., pp. 134–5; for Aleksinski's article see *Proletarii*, no. 34, 25 August 1908.
19. Ibid.
20. *PSS*, vol. 47, p. 160.
21. Idem, vol. 17, pp. 325–8 (Lenin's speech) and 513–15.
22. See I. A. Teodorovich's memoir, 'Eshche ob Ob''edinitel'nom s''ezde RSDRP, loc. cit., p. 217.
23. The text most frequently cited and discussed is Engels's *Anti-Dühring*;

and Marx's work is generally put less directly under scrutiny (save for a brief discussion of sections of the *Theses On Feuerbach*: see *PSS*, vol. 18, pp. 103–4. See the citational record in idem, pp. 428–9, 431–2, 439–41 and 448–9. A special, lengthy appendix on Chernyshevski is given in idem, p. 381–4.

24. Idem, p. 263.
25. *PU*, pp. 184–5; *PSS*, vol. 55, pp. 261–2 and 264.
26. See *Kritika nashikh kritikov* in *S(P)*, vol. 11, pp. 21, 107 and 138. See also his Letter II in *Materialismus Militans* in idem, vol. 17, especially pp. 23–6.
27. *Empiriomonizm*, vol. 3, pp. xii–xiii. See also his earlier *Poznanie s istoricheskoi tochki zreniya*, pp. 176–80.
28. See the discussion in *Empiriomonizm*, vol. 3, pp. xviii–xx.
29. Idem, pp. iv–vi; and *Vera i nauka* (Moscow, 1910) pp. 185–6.
30. *Empiriomonizm*, vol. 3, p. vii; *Vera i nauka*, pp. 159 and 182–5.
31. *Iz psikhologii obshchestva* (St. Petersburg, 1904) pp. 50–1.
32. *Preface To 'A Contribution To The Critique Of Political Economy* in *SWOV'*, p. 181.
33. *Empiriomonizm*, vol. 3, pp. xxiv. See also *Priklyucheniya odnoi filosofskoi idei* (St. Petersburg, 1908), translated as *Avventure di una idea filosofica* in *Fede e Scienza*, ed. V. Strada; tr. N. Strada (Turin, 1982), pp. 175–7. (It is a reflection of Lenin's political triumph over Bogdanov that the only Russian copy of this work available in Britain is a hideously illegible and incomplete microfilm). A good account of the disagreement between Bogdanov and Lenin on the being-consciousness dichotomy is J. Scherrer's 'Bogdanov e Lenin: il bolscevismo al bivio', *Storia del Marxismo*, vol. 2, pp. 543–4; and on what Marx meant by social being and social consciousness see S. Avineri, *The Social Thought of Karl Marx* (Cambridge, 1971) pp. 75–7.
34. *PSS*, vol. 18, p. 25. For Engels's original statement see *Ludwig Feuerbach and the End of Classical German Philosophy* in *MESW*, p. 594.
35. *PSS*, vol. 18, pp. 125, 275–6 and 345.
36. *Kritika nashikh kritikov*, loc. cit., p. 138.
37. *Empiriomonizm*, vol. 3, pp. xii–xiii.
38. Idem, pp. iv–vi. See also Engels, *AD*, pp. 109–12.
39. *KMSW*, pp. 156–7.
40. See, for example, *Kapital*, vol. 1, pp. 104–5 for propositions about the 'laws' of commodity value.
41. *Vera i nauka*, pp. 182–5.
42. The frequently-encountered East-West division in scholarship is not so easily found in epistemology as might be supposed (despite the continuing academic lip-service paid to Lenin's *Materialism* in the USSR). On the processing effects of our sense organs and of the social context see (for example) F. M. Mikhailov, *Zagadka chelovecheskogo ya* (Moscow, 1976) *passim* but especially chap. 1. For non-Soviet scholars' adherence to the concept of the independent existence of the external world see the resumé of current work in F. Ayer, *The Central Questions of Philosophy* (Pelican: London, 1976) pp. 41–2.

43. *Kritika nashikh kritikov*, loc. cit., p. 71.
44. Idem, p. 138.
45. *PSS*, vol. 18, p. 244.
46. Idem, p. 303.
47. Idem, pp. 290–317.
48. See C. Read, *Religion, Revolution and the Russian Intelligentsia, 1900–1912: the 'Vekhi' Debate and its Intellectual Background* (London, 1979) pp. 77–84.
49. *PSS*, vol. 19, p. 367.
50. Idem, p. 137.
51. *Vera i nauka*, pp. 157–8.
52. Idem, pp. 173–5 and 181.
53. Idem, pp. 160–1.
54. Idem, pp. 197–9 and 202.
55. Idem, pp. 160–1.
56. Idem, p. 159.
57. Idem, p. 156.
58. *PSS*, vol. 18, p. 200.
59. *Vera i nauka*, p. 221.
60. See above, p. 89.
61. This proposal became fully clear in 1910–11: see J. Scherrer, op. cit., pp. 514–19. It was visible in outline in *Empiriomonizm*, vol. 3, *passim*; and even in *Avventure*: see p. 175.
62. *Padenie velikogo fetishizma. Sovremennyi krizis ideologii* (Moscow, 1910) pp. 114–15. See also *Empiriomonizm*, vol. 3, *passim*.
63. *Kul'turnye zadachi nashego vremeni* (Moscow, 1911) pp. 28–31: cited in Scherrer, op. cit., pp. 517–19.
64. This theme will be resumed in vols 2 and 3 of this trilogy.
65. See above, pp. 90–1, 92, 108 and 110–11.
66. See especially L. Akselrod's review, reprinted in *S(L)*, vol. 13, pp. 329–33.
67. Bogdanov justifiably denied that he had this attitude to the trade unions. Many Recallists and Ultimatumists, however, were probably hostile to participation: see below, p. 186. Their attitude is reminiscent of the widespread Bolshevik feelings about the trade unions and soviets in 1905: see above, pp. 134 and 142–3. Bogdanov in any case could not, nor did he wish to, deny that he did not want the emphasis in social-democratic work to fall on legal organisations.
68. For Martov's acute summary see I. Getzler, *Martov*, pp. 125–6.
69. For Plekhanov's post factum explanation see *S(P)*, vol. 19, p. 23.
70. Their instrumental approach to the coalition emerges in ibid.; and in *PSS*, vol. 17, pp. 386–7 and vol. 19, pp. 104–6.
71. *SV*, pp. 583–5; *PSS*, vol. 16, p. 108; *Lenin i Lunacharskii*, loc. cit., pp. 622–3.
72. *PSS*, vol. 16, p. 108.
73. *Lenin i Lunacharskii*, loc. cit., pp. 621–2.
74. *LS*, vol. 38, p. 68; N. Valentinov, *Maloznakomyi Lenin*, pp. 97–129.
75. *BK*, vol. 2, p. 462.

76. *PSS*, vol. 47, p. 178.
77. Idem, vol. 19, p. 13. This volume contains a number of Lenin's remarks and jottings not included in *Protokoly 'Proletariya'*.
78. Idem, p. 171–4.
79. Idem, pp. 62–5.
80. Idem, pp. 76–81. See also *PSS*, vol. 19, pp. 21 and 42.
81. *Protokoly 'Proletariya'*, pp. 82–8.
82. Idem, p. 88. The fact that Lenin suffered this and other defeats at the June 1909 gathering was first described by Geoffrey Swain, and I am most grateful to him for letting me see the preliminary drafts of his edition of the *Protokoly*.
83. Idem, pp. 106–25.
84. Idem, pp. 116–25.
85. See below, pp. 188–9.
86. *Protokoly 'Proletariya'*, pp. 139–44.
87. Krupskaya, *VL*, p. 173.
88. See above, pp. 116–17 and 127.
89. *PU*, pp. 192 and 210.
90. Idem, p. 232.
91. Idem, p. 210; *PSS*, vol. 47, p. 205.
92. Idem, p. 185.
93. Idem, p. 188.
94. See G. Swain, 'Paris or Petersburg: Some Thoughts on the January 1910 Plenum of the Central Committee of the RSDLP', paper delivered to the BNASEES Conference (Cambridge, 1979) p. 5.
95. See idem, pp. 5–6.
96. L. Martov, *Spasiteli ili uprazdniteli?* (Paris, 1911) p. 22.
97. N. Valentinov, *Maloznakomyi Lenin*, pp. 106–7; *LS*, vol. 38, pp. 32–4.
98. See the account by L. Schapiro, *The Communist Party of the Soviet Union* (London, 1960) pp. 115–16.
99. *S(L)*, vol. 14, p. 180.
100. See the editors' account in *PSS*, vol. 47, pp. 356–7. This phase in Lenin's career is only slightly better documented, as yet, than his days as a Volga activist.
101. Ibid.
102. See above, p. 161.
103. See Swain, 'Paris or Petersburg', pp. 7–8.
104. A useful detailed account is given by R. G. Suny in 'Labour and Liquidators: Revolutionaries and the 'Reaction' in Baku, May 1908–April 1912', *Slavic Review*, 1975, no. 2, pp. 319–40.
105. *PSS*, vol. 55, p. 303.
106. Idem, vol. 47, p. 287.
107. See Moskalev, op. cit., pp. 160–1.
108. *PSS*, vol. 47, p. 288.
109. See above, p. 187.
110. *PSS*, vol. 19, pp. 259–60 (for Lenin's account); and *S(L)*, vol. 14, p. 180.
111. The resolutions are reprinted in *S(P)*, vol. 19, pp. 99–121; see especially p. 101.

112. Idem, p. 105.
113. Idem, p. 103.
114. *LS*, vol. 38, pp. 66–7.
115. The importance of these two is discussed in volume two.
116. The exception in this list is Plekhanov, whose ill-health precluded return from emigration in 1905–7. He had nonetheless worked as a clandestine activist in Petersburg before his flight abroad in 1880.
117. *Vera i nauka*, p. 202.
118. Not that Maslov won much sympathy from Lenin. See Chapter 9, note 52.
119. See above, pp. 131, 135 and 153.
120. *Lenin i Gor'kii*, p. 48: letter from Gorki to P. Pyatnitski.
121. See above, pp. 86–7, 96 and 101.
122. See Gorki's letter of 1909 to Natalya Bogdanova, edited by J. Scherrer and partially reproduced in *Fede e Scienza*, p. 266.
123. See Gorelov, *Bolsheviki v period reaktsii*, p. 170.
124. *BK*, vol. 2, pp. 461, 465, 475, 479, 523 and 532 (all for 1909).
125. 'Iz perepiski mestnykh organizatsii s Bol'shevistskim Tsentrom', *PR*, 1928, no. 80, p. 160.
126. See I. M. Dubinskii-Mukhadze, *Ordzhonikidze* (Moscow, 1963) pp. 92–4.
127. A subtle analysis along such lines is contained in Martov's posthumously published work *Mirovoi bol'shevizm* (Berlin, 1923); but see also above, p. 191.
128. *Lenin i Gor'kii*, p. 48.
129. See his autobiography *V. Medem: the Life and Soul of a Legendary Jewish Socialist*, tr. S. Portnoy (New York, 1979) pp. 461–2.
130. See Gorki's recollections in *VVIL*, vol. 2, p. 161. Gorki's warmth of feeling, however, did not survive the roisterings of 1909: see above, note 122.
131. *Lenin i Lunacharskii*, p. 620.
132. See above, pp. 108–9.
133. See above, pp. 126–7, 153 and 155 for examples.

Index

Written works are mentioned below only if and when their titles are given in English in the chapters or the endnotes.